VALENTINO
and the
GREAT
ITALIANS

VALENTINO
and the
GREAT
ITALIANS

—

According to
Anthony Valerio

FREUNDLICH BOOKS

NEW YORK

Copyright © 1986 Anthony Valerio

Library of Congress Cataloging-in-Publication Data

Valerio, Anthony, 1940–
Valentino and the great Italians.

1. Italian Americans.   2. Italians.   I.   Title.
E184.I8V35   1986   973'.0451   86-7564
ISBN 0-88191-041-4

Published by Freundlich Books
(A division of Lawrence Freundlich Publications, Inc.)
212 Fifth Avenue
New York, N.Y. 10010

Distributed to the trade by The Scribner Book Companies, Inc.
115 Fifth Avenue
New York, N.Y. 10003

Manufactured in the United States of America

10   9   8   7   6   5   4   3   2   1

For Billy, Gianna, Francesca

CONTENTS

———

THE

SICILIANS

———

IT would be a nice idea, I think, to provide some space so that everybody could write their own *cantilena*, their own little song. The model would be the very first one, written in the thirteenth century during the reign of Frederick II, Emperor of Germany and King of Sicily. The *cantilena* was a dispute, or dialogue, between a Lover and his Lady, and the four verses consisted of eight lines each. To accommodate today's world, the dialogues could be between any two people so long as there is love between them.

According to Dante, Frederick was a wise and noble gentleman, and he chose as the seat of his throne not Swabia but Palermo. He preferred the southern clime, hot and dry, the cooling shade of the ombu tree, and he was enthralled by the beach at Mondello, which still stands and has sand the texture and glitter of star dust. If you scan the mosaic of bodies you will see in time, standing listlessly at the shoreline, their backs to the sea and gazing blankly up into the salty air, some of the ugliest couples in God's creation: the man dark and short and scrawny, with eyes close together and crossed; his woman tall and obese, with dimpled skin white as dough. On this paradise Frederick gathered to his court the finest players, troubadours and storytellers. They played and sang and told of the joys and sorrow of love—this was their theme, and soon the Court's fame spread up the peninsula, from shore to shore, until all performers of the day became known as "Sicilians."

From Tuscany they came and Apulia and Romagnuolo, Sicilians all. They washed up on the shore in their costumes, carrying lyres, and from his central position on the celestial sand, surrounded by his minstrels and buffoons and his harem, who fanned him with palm leaves, Frederick greeted one and all, including stragglers. He saw some strange things: blond hair and blue eyes, for example, and one Sicilian emerged from the water with a carpet, rolled it out on the sand, stood on it and then flapped his arms, expecting to be ushered up into the sky.

Frederick called to his side his favorite buffoon, Carnivale, who was wise as well as funny. "What do you make of it, Carnivale?"

"It takes all kinds, sire."

"But this—so little."

"I don't really know," said the buffoon. "You hear a lot about the Arabs who overran us, penetrating our land with the fantastic, voluptuous world of the East. Maybe that guy got his idea for a flying carpet from the same place you got your harem. Again, I don't know. Sometimes I think that the trend of history runs straight through our assholes. I mean, I have this Arab friend— at least he says he's Arab, from Palestine—and the other night he told me that he fucked his woman for two solid hours and she had thirty orgasms. Gee, I say to myself, two hours, thirty orgasms. On my best days I can last a half hour, provoking two, maybe three orgasms. You also hear about the daring Norsemen who invaded us: maybe from them you get your blonds with blue eyes. I have a blond, blue-eyed cousin, a handsome devil, but he hasn't worked a day out of his sixty-five years, staying home and reading the papers while his brown-eyed sister goes to work in all kinds of weather. Tales of the Round Table still linger, sire—would you like to hear one?"

"Oh, go ahead," said the King, slightly annoyed yet infinitely patient.

"Sir Lancelot is about to go off to do battle. He gives the key to his wife's chastity belt to Sir Gaylord and says, 'If I'm not back in six months, you may use this key.'

"About an hour later, as his boat is putting out to sea, Sir Lancelot sees his friend running toward the pier.

"'What's the matter?' Sir Lancelot shouts from his boat.

"'You gave me the wrong key!' Sir Gaylord shouts."

Frederick guffawed, which placed him once again in a state of soft repose, and then with his glass he surveyed the shoreline. Far upshore he espied the ancestors of the ugly Sicilian couple: the man short and scrawny and cross-eyed, his woman big and fat.

"Jesus..." muttered Frederick, and he was about to turn his head away in disgust when the couple suddenly came to life: the woman pivoted slowly, raised her meaty arm and with wild eyes brought it down swiftly and square on her man's head of swatches of black wiry hair, knocking him to the sand. Blood spurted from his scalp, and he let out a scream that reverberated around the beach.

"I have to see this," Frederick said, and immediately four of his beauties, naked except for their billowing veils, carried him in his rickshaw to a position directly in front of the battling couple. The furious woman paid the King no mind; she continued to pummel and kick the prostrate man, drawing blood now from his mouth and from the flaring nostrils of his giant mushroom nose. Scowls and curses escaped her ugly mouth. The King watched it closely and saw that hairs black as night sprouted from her upper lip, and there was also hair on her face. The man's chest, back and legs were blanketed with hair but his face was surprisingly clean, boyish in its freshness, and though his brows were thick and arched to the temples, canopying his doleful eyes skeletal in their deepness, there was a mysterious clarity about his eyes. His body shook, racked with pain, and he cried, sobbing to himself.

"The scoundrel's about had it, Carnivale. Shall we intervene?"

"I wouldn't underestimate him, sire. He's what we call in Sicilian

3

dialect and Arabic a *meskeen*, a nice enough guy but he has the Fates against him. A pathetic sort but far from stupid, as we'll soon see. Besides, there's a Sicilian proverb that says, 'Never put a finger between a fighting couple.'"

"True, true," sighed the King.

Never for an instant during his beating had the man taken his eyes from his raging woman. He shielded his head with his arms and from beneath them his narrow slits peered at her feet, sharp ankles, nut-cracking thighs, fatty rounded mons, gargantuan breasts. When she finally exhausted herself and was gathering her breath, he reached out slowly with his trembling hand and touched her hammered toes. She did not draw her foot away. He grasped her legs, using them as an anchor to pull himself to his knees. His beseeching eyes blazed up into her dead ones.

"No! No!" she denied him. But then he spoke to her at some length and she answered. Their dialogue had the effect of softening her face, and she reached down with a hand and gently stroked his bloodied scalp. Then she knelt and caressed him. He guided her body down, mounted her and penetrated her with a cock so huge that it provoked a chorus from the harem, "Woweewow!"

"Perforce she's big—eh, Carnivale? But my curiosity piques at what they said. The tables seemed to turn then. It wasn't Latin— did you pick it up?"

Up until then Latin was the language of the educated classes, doctors and teachers. Latin was also the language of the Court.

"Yes, sire," answered Carnivale.

"Well, then—translate, man!"

"It's the vulgar language of the despicable populace, sire. It's been in existence about a hundred years, ever since the Council of Torsi instructed the priests to deliver homilies in the rustic Roman tongue which was familiar to the Africans, Spaniards and Gauls."

"Rustic Roman, schmustic Roman!" roared the King. "If that's the end result"—and here the King gestured with his head toward the couple who grain by celestial grain of sand were humping their way toward the mainstream of the migration—"if that's what it leads to, then it's good for the land. Translate!"

"He said, 'Baby, I'm your man. Don't be stubborn: you know in the end I win you over with my words. I'll hunt you to the far corners of the world. You can't keep from me. Watch out, baby, or you'll lose me.'

"And she said, 'So? I'd rather die than surrender to you. No good woman'll be shamed because of me. Last night you ran to my place like a young buck. Who are you kiddin'? Get lost—you bore me!'

"And then he said—"

"Enough!" the King commanded. "I get the drift: he implores and implores and she denies and denies, then finally consents. Good. I find his dialogue a bit impersonal for a guy who just took such a beating, but all in all I like it: it's impetuous, fiery, free of rhetoric and artifice.

"Now hear my desire: separate those two, clean them up, give them parchment and quill and have them write their dialogue exactly the way they spoke it. It shall be called a *cantilena*, a little song, a recorded link between lovers. Then I want copies made and distributed to all Sicilians in the land. They should study it, and it would please me if they completed the last two verses of eight lines each in a language that's been in existence at least a hundred years. We all know how the first *cantilena* ends, so it will be good practice for the imagination while we're at rest. Carnivale!"

"Yes, sire?"

"Any *finocchi* in Sicily?"

"A few, sire."

"Then let's head a model parchment, instead of Lover and his Lady, Lover and his Lady or Man. Do it now."

"Consider it done."

MY CANTILENA

Lover: _____
_____
_____
_____
_____
_____
_____
_____

Lady/Man: _____
_____
_____
_____
_____
_____
_____

TONY BENNETT

FRANK Sinatra once said that Tony Bennett is the very best there is. Nothing more needs be said, but I would like to add what everybody probably knows—Tony Bennett is Italian. He was born Anthony Benedetto about sixty years ago, and so it comes as no surprise that he became a crooner. At one point, though, while a student at the Manhattan School of Music and Design, little Anthony was torn between painting and singing. He submitted himself to a test: he sang a song for his music teacher, then he painted a picture for his art teacher. The music teacher told him, "Sing!"

Tony Bennett did not give up painting entirely. Now in his middle years, he is painting more and more and his work is exhibited in fine galleries around the world. He is wise enough to know that his eye will outlast his singing voice and that painting is a way to hold on to the serenity in his heart. Other great singers have held on to it through painting. Amelita Galli-Curci, for example, the great soprano—she secluded herself in her hacienda in California and painted until the day she died. Dame Galli-Curci did not appear at her exhibits, whereas Tony Bennett does, and I believe he is making a mistake. During a program last night called "On the Town with Tony Bennett," he mingled in the crowd at an opening in New York. He was lost, confused, going from one well-wisher to another in search of a familiar face, an Italian or a musician. He was dressed in his singing clothes all right—dark suit, white shirt, dark tie—but he walked around with his jacket unbuttoned when his natural pose is with the jacket buttoned, securing his husky body inside as he swings and sways, raises his arm to the images before his eyes, the sky, the world, the Golden Gate Bridge. Also, Tony Bennett has to talk a little at his exhibits, when he doesn't like to talk at all. He doesn't talk much on talk shows or between songs. "He wants to be remembered solely for his singing," I say to insiders of the music industry who contend that Tony Bennett doesn't talk because he's stupid. "If he's stupid," I go on, "how does he remember the lyrics of so many songs? And he's wise enough to keep on painting. What are *you* going to do in your old age for some peace, some beauty?"

Then last night when the program was about to come on, my girlfriend Elsa said, "I like Tony Bennett's singing, but I can't stand to look at him. He's *brutto come la merda*, ugly as shit."

"Are you referring to his nose?" I asked.

"I guess it's his trademark..."

"That's right—the way Barbra Streisand's nose is her trademark and Jimmy Durante's his. Look what Cyrano made of his nose, and the great Russian writer Nikolai Gogol wrote one of the immortal stories called 'The Nose.'

"I bet you look at Robert Goulet while he sings," I went on, infuriated. "He's a good-looking crooner, I grant you, but his voice comes nowhere near Tony Bennett's. By the way, Robert Goulet is Italian, Canadian-Italian.

"You don't like blue eyes, so why do you look at Frank Sinatra while he sings? Why don't you pick on Ole Blue Eyes' eyes?

"Tony Bennett has a great nose, a great Italian nose, and my hat goes off to him for not having it fixed. You pick on his looks because you have nothing else to go on. You know nothing about Tony Bennett except that he's Italian, which you like, and he can sing."

Elsa played solitaire and listened to the program, which began with Tony Bennett going back to his old neighborhood in Queens, Astoria, Queens. He stood outside his childhood home in his singing clothes. It was a modest house, narrow, made of brick, and tears came to the great singer's eyes as he gazed at the top-floor windows. Nobody hung out the windows, family or new tenants, and no neighbors came out to greet him like long-lost friends. He had taste enough not to go inside his house and take part in a trumped-up family get-together. When Luciano Pavarotti goes home to Modena, Italy, he jokes around with guys he hasn't seen in twenty years. He pulls up to his childhood home in a Mercedes-Benz, but we do not see him trying to squeeze out or waddling to the front door. He charges up the stairs. His massive figure blots out the stairwell. His mother waits for him on the landing. Pavarotti embraces her and she disappears. He goes inside to his father, also a tenor, then father and son ride to church and sing a duet.

Tony Bennett was alone in Queens, alone with his voice, his phrasing, his musicianship. I wasn't fooled one bit by his friendly chat with Jimmy Breslin, a lifelong resident of Queens. There was adulation in the journalist's eyes, and he talked to Tony Bennett like an old crony, but little Anthony and little Jimmy didn't pal around as kids, because in those days the Italians fought the Irish every day. My father had two broken knuckles to prove it. Tony Bennett visited his old public school. He peered through the chain link fence into the yard. Not a single kid was playing. Tony Bennett was quiet, holding his voice in reserve, and he also held it in reserve as he pondered the great leap to Manhattan from beneath a tree at the base of the Queensboro Bridge. He walked down Mott Street, looking around, smiling. The Chinese people paid him no attention. From the shore at Battery Park he sketched the Statue of Liberty, and then the time came for him to sing.

The program was a benefit for the PAL, the Police Athletic League. The League organizes teams for kids of every race, nationality and creed. It provides them with uniforms, gloves and bats, and the kids play on fields with real bases, chalk foul lines, umpires dressed in blue. Tony Bennett sang his heart out for the police and the kids, and I wondered whether they were watching. He belted out one song after another, hardly taking a breath, not saying a word. His voice was soothing and soon lulled me to sleep. But I had stayed awake long enough to discover how Anthony Benedetto came to be known as Tony Bennett. The whole story came out in a talk with Bob Hope.

Hope, Jane Russell, and Les Brown were playing the Paramount Theater. Hope cracked jokes, Jane Russell sang and danced and Les Brown strummed his electric guitar. They performed in between showings of the movie, about six times a day. The gig exhausted them, especially their feet, and in the dressing room they soaked their feet in a basin of warm water. One afternoon their advance man burst in: "You gotta come downtown to hear a guy named Anthony Benedetto! You haven't heard a voice until you hear this kid sing."

That night the trio grabbed a cab downtown and listened to a set in bare feet. Afterwards, Hope said to the young singer, "You're singing tomorrow at the Paramount. No joke. You're going to spell our aching dogs."

"Sure," said Anthony Benedetto.

The Paramount was packed. Laughter rose to the rafters, the men feasted their eyes on Jane Russell, everyone listened tentatively to the metallic sounds of Les Brown's guitar. Anthony Benedetto was nervous in the wings. He buttoned his collar and his jacket, raised his tie. Bob Hope said from the great stage:

"Ladies and gentlemen, I better get this young man out here before he goes in his silk pinstripes. It's his first appearance in a big-time dive like the Paramount. Seriously, ladies and gentlemen, he's the best thing to come along since Italian bread. He'll make you forget all about his gumbahs—Ole Blue Eyes and Frankie 'Mule Train' Laine. You didn't know Frankie Laine is Italian, did ya? Even the music box is Italian. Ladies and gentlemen—a big hand for Tony Bennett!"

Anthony Benedetto froze. "Tony Bennett?" he mouthed, pointing to himself in disbelief.

"Come on out, Tony! He's collapsed, ladies and gentlemen."

He made it onto the stage and whispered to Bob Hope as they passed, "Tony Bennett?" Hope smirked and walked off.

And so Tony Bennett had nothing to do with his name change. Bob Hope had acted alone, and there was nothing Anthony Benedetto could do about it. He did not have the presence of mind to correct the famous comedian. It would come off as just another joke, and besides, he was busy summoning his voice and his feelings. He sang "Because of You" and "I Won't Cry Anymore," and the audience came away with Tony Bennett's voice etched in their hearts.

Tony Bennett had let the name change go, so to speak, but he didn't let it go during his talk with Bob Hope on the program.

"I discovered you, you know," Hope said.

"Yes, and you also changed my name."

"Really!" Bob Hope was taken aback.

"That's right—you changed it on the stage of the Paramount thirty years ago."

Hope said, "I got the story another way. I thought your agent changed it."

"No, no—you changed it!"

Here we discover another reason why Tony Bennett doesn't talk much. He's unable to work from a script. He improvises the truth.

After his repartee with Bob Hope, Tony Bennett sang at the Village Vanguard and Greene Street, well-known night spots not too far from me. During a song I fell asleep, and I wonder now whether the fact came out that Tony Bennett has a brother who was also a singer. I do not know his name, his age, or his singing style, or even whether he's still alive. All I know is that an uncle of mine, Joe Freeze, once managed him and they cut a few records. I would like to say that I heard them and they're not half bad. I have given Tony Bennett's brother a name, Paul, and he sings under his real name, Paul Benedetto. Paul is frail, nervous, has thinning blond hair, and he sings in a colorful sweater with the collar turned out. His voice isn't half that of his brother's, but he sings his heart out and lands gigs in out-of-the-way places, roadside inns and catering halls. Paul's singing style is more jazz-oriented than his brother's—it's closer to Mel Tormé's style or Morgana King's.

The question has plagued me for years: why didn't Tony Bennett help his brother? They could have sung duets to break up Tony Bennett's endless nights of one song after the other. Paul could have broken the ice with some humor, a few jokes. Maybe Paul wanted to make it on his own, or maybe there was friction between the brothers, stemming, say, from the splitting up of their parents' property. This might explain why Tony Bennett didn't sing one song while he was in Queens. There must be a few first-rate clubs there, and little Anthony must have sung in a local glee club or in a talent showcase near his house.

Paul's manager, my Uncle Joe Freeze, was a shylock. He was also a legitimate businessman. Managing Paul was legitimate, and Joe also owned a tavern on the east side of New York. The Green Lantern, it was called. People from all walks of the entertainment business came to borrow or pay off. I met Fred Shwam, author of the mystery thriller, *The Gold Key*. Fred was writing a TV pilot and had high hopes for it. He was a real gentleman, soft-spoken, and he wore a nice suit. I've never met another writer like him. I met Billy Daniels, of "That Ole Black Magic" fame. Billy looked great—golden skin, full crop of wavy white hair, a waist smaller than mine. His entourage included some of the most beautiful women I've ever seen. I kept staring at one, a dark-haired beauty all made up.

Billy told me, "I sang on the Bowery for pennies. If it wasn't for your uncle, I'd still be singing on the street."

"How do you keep so trim, Billy?"

"Liquid diet, kid," and he smiled, then he sang a few bars of "That Ole Black Magic."

Joe Freeze's father and older brother were icemen. They sold enough ice to send Joe to military school. Then the refrigerator was invented and Joe's father retired and his older brother became a milkman. Joe dropped out of school and did what he had to do. He fell in love and married a distant cousin, Connie, and they lived together in a quiet high rise in Brooklyn. Joe's routine consisted of rising at eleven, going to the plastic-covered couch in the living room and making his calls until Connie called him in to breakfast. By two o'clock Joe was driving to his office in midtown Manhattan. He parked in a garage on Forty-sixth Street and didn't have far to walk. The garage was his office.

He was a short, burly man, bald on top, but he had great swatches of white hair on his chest and on his back. He was a lifelong Republican, insisting until the day he died that Nixon was the best President we ever had. He talked out of the side of his mouth, and a Camel cigarette dangled out of the other side. In his seventies he developed emphysema and was in and out of hospitals. The pain was unbearable, but he kept to his style by bullying doctors, saying, "Before I pay you, tell me if you can help me."

One morning Connie called from the kitchen, "Joe, come on!"

When Joe didn't respond, Connie poked her head in the living room. He wasn't on the couch. She went into the living room in her nightgown. She saw that the apartment door was open. Joe had gone up to the roof to throw himself off, but at the last minute he hit on the idea of taking his wife with him. He ran down the stairs, blew into the apartment and on his way through the living room grabbed Connie's arm. "Come with me, Connie. . . ."

She pulled her arm away. "Are you crazy? Joe! . . ."

He kept going and crashed through the bay window, glass and all. His name was like magic. I could go to the Copacabana or Madison Square Garden and say to the manager, "I'm Joe Freeze's nephew," and I got the best seat in the house. They say he died before he hit the ground.

FRANK SINATRA

———

I COME to Frank Sinatra midway through my life when I'm
happy with my woman, when I've learned to dance the tango
and when I discover that Frank Sinatra lost his mother in a
plane crash, depriving him of the opportunity to kiss her forehead
one last time, run his fingers through her hair. Italian boys are
not accustomed to their mothers flying. We see them in the
kitchen shuffling from the sink to the stove, retrieving grocery
bags from the trunk of a car, driving off to the bank. Mrs. Natalie
Sinatra loved her son so much that she was willing to fly to
California just to visit with him. She was also unusual in that she
came from Genoa instead of Naples or Sicily. In Hoboken she
settled for a Sicilian, a good man named Martin who fought fires
and ran a tavern and was so beleaguered by the Irish that he
boxed under the name of Marty O'Brien. Harry James once advised Frank Sinatra to change his name. What's Harry James's real
name, Betty Grable's? Frank Sinatra had a cousin who with his
real name, Ray Sinatra, was doing well behind the scenes of a
radio show. Also, Frank Sinatra never thought he would leave the
neighborhood let alone hit the big time, and so it didn't pay
singing in roadhouses under an assumed name. Up in Canada

after my father finished postgraduate work in dentistry, his prosthetics professor offered him a job.

"My brother has a flourishing practice in New York, on Park Avenue. He's getting on in years and could use a fine young dentist like you, but first you'll have to change your name."

My father belted the professor in the mouth, kept his name and opened a neighborhood practice in Bensonhurst.

Natalie Sinatra was gregarious and full of life, and she went out to work in order to contribute her share. She developed a facility for dialects, not only her husband's but also those of the Irish and Poles and Ukrainians. She was made Democratic ward captain. She was invited to join the Hoboken branch of the Sicilian Cultural League. Some parasites have said that Frank Sinatra's link with organized crime stems from this time, but Waxey Gordon was Hoboken's *capo di tutti capi*—what's a Gordon going to do for a Sinatra? One of Waxey Gordon's descendants became a jeweler and opened a shop in Bensonhurst in the shadows of the New Utrecht Avenue El. He became our jeweler. The watches he sold us didn't work and his gold was bogus. A priest affiliated with a Bay Ridge parish supposedly launched Vic Damone, about whom Frank Sinatra once said, "First there's Vic Damone and then there's everybody else." I'm happy to hear that Vic Damone recently found happiness with Diahann Carroll and that he took the time to help his friend Fugazy launch his fleet of limousines. My parish priest now is Father Bill. He's known as the Priest to the Stars. The stars come back to Father Bill to confess and marry discreetly. If they do not find him in the church, they look for him across the street in Arturo's. Recently, I came upon him sitting at an outdoor table, wearing a Hawaiian shirt and nursing a medicinal libation before evening vespers.

"Father Bill, I'd like to talk to you."

"Sit down, sit down. Waiter, a drink for this fine young man! Now shoot!"

"I'm having a lot of trouble with my girlfriend. She comes from Argentina and has had most everything taken from her by men, beginning with her father and then her husband and then a procession of lovers down there and up here. We live in separate studios, they're very small, and I don't have the money to get us a place. I scrimped and saved and bought her a piano and paid for our round-trip tickets, New York–Buenos Aires–New York. I bought her a king-size Castro convertible so that we could sleep together once in a while. We're two horses, and when we made love our bodies pressed against the cold steel of the frame. I bought her a high rise at Kleinsleep. Then I bought her a regular bed with a futon mattress and she's content and so am I, sleeping with her wonderful body in my arms, but I inherited a chronic disease from my maternal grandfather, excessive flatulence, it's uncontrollable and escapes me while I sleep. Elsa lies awake, waiting, listening, and when I explode she scurries to the bathroom, takes up the aerosol can and returns with it behind her back, then sprays me all over like I'm some kind of insect. No matter what I do she says she's alone, and now she's thinking of going out with other men."

"How old is she, my son?"

"Fifty."

"Be her friend," said Father Bill. "Go to that phone over there and call her and tell her that no matter what she does you love her and want to be her friend."

I got up and hurried blindly to the phone booth on the corner of Houston and Thompson. "No matter what you do," I told Elsa, "including go out with other men, I love you and want to be your friend."

"Me, too," Elsa said, and everything has been fine since then.

At the end of the day when the Sinatras convened for supper, all dialects were left outside on the doorstep. Feelings were communicated with a glance, a meeting of the eyes, a gesture. Words now were simple and clear and true. In his house Frank Sinatra heard most every word he would sing in his songs. The attention he pays to lyrics is in harmony with Enrico Caruso's attitude toward them: "I think to the words of my aria, not to the music, because first is written the libretto and is the reason of the composer to put the music, like the foundation of a house."

For half a century Frank Sinatra has been tough enough to withstand the bloodsucking of a million leeches, mainly male journalists. Ed Sullivan, who I believe married an Italian, was consistently fair with him, as were Sidney Skolsky and Louella Parsons, Sheilah Graham and Dorothy Kilgallen. Some male journalists have said that Frank Sinatra's tumultuous personal life stems from a neglected childhood. Nonsense! His cheeks were hollow early on, it's true, but they've filled out. Latent or full our cheeks are always there, for we need them to eat properly. It was a godsend that Frank Sinatra was at times left to himself. He stood outside his house with his foot up against the door and listened to the roar of the Erie-Lackawanna trains. He was given the time and peace for his feelings to flood his heart, and then they rose to his throat and a song was born. There are prominent Italians in their forties whose mothers were always in the house who still bring home the laundry. Would it have been better for Frank Sinatra to follow in his father's footsteps, like Ray Mancini, who on behalf of his father gets his brains knocked in, losing himself in the process? Natalie Sinatra wanted her son to be an engineer, but at the same time she scrimped and saved and bought him a p.a. system, mike and loudspeaker. They came through to her as she disappeared into the sunset. I see her now saying goodbye. She turns on the top step and smiles and waves to her son on the observation deck. He snaps down the brim of his hat and waves.

On this the forty-sixth celebration of my name day, St. Anthony of Padua, I would like to send Frank Sinatra my condolences. Now I am able to commiserate with him when on entering *his* forty-sixth year he sought to settle down with a good woman, too. His friends were married: there was a Mrs. Martin, a Mrs. Bishop, a Mrs. Davis and a Mrs. Lawford. And so while Frank Sinatra was out driving and happened to pass Juliet Prowse's legs, I fully understand how he hit upon the idea of taking them for a ride, and if Miss Prowse consented, taking them home so that they could do a little dance. Juliet Prowse had been born in India, Bombay, and she stopped dancing only to whip up a few dishes Frank Sinatra was not accustomed to, like curries and yogurt.

Italian boys are usually named after their paternal grandfather or the saint of that day. On the day we're born a family member approaches the religious calendar hanging in the kitchen and with an open mouth, biting the tongue, searches with a forefinger and then stops and reads in small print the name of the saint. "Hey, everybody, here it is: Louie or Tony or Jimmy or Frankie!"

A name day is a day of truth. Just as on their daughters' wedding days all Dons grant any wish whatever, on their name day they are obliged to tell the truth. The truth is that St. Anthony was not born in Padua, he performed his miracles there. He was born in Portugal. As an infant he was sickly and was transported with care to Africa. He gained strength and on the way back to Portugal stopped off in Padua and stayed.

The truth: is it possible for one man, even an Italian one, to romance the likes of the following women, with prime time taken out for a marriage to his first and eternal love, his Italian sweetheart: Lana Turner, Jill St. John, Princess Soraya, Ava Gardner, Lady Beatty, Marilyn Monroe, Kim Novak, Lauren Bacall, Marilyn Maxwell, Gloria Vanderbilt, Linda Christian, Anita Ekberg, Juliet Prowse, Dorothy Provine, Mia Farrow?

A name day is also a festive one, but the truth is I've been alone all day with northerly gales blowing pollen in through my window. Dark clouds are rolling over. My door is kept open a body's width by a dagger. Not a real one, as the blade is made of wood, but the sheath is real, strong Argentine hemp, and so it disguises the nature of the blade enough to keep out prowlers and the neighbors. Elsa gave it to me. Frank Sinatra is singing tunes written by Antônio Carlos Jobim, the great Brazilian composer. Elsa introduced me to his music as well as to the music of all of South America and to musical instruments I had never heard before like the *bandoneón* and the *charango*. Last night she played disc jockey and I was the audience. I asked her, "Would you say it's a reflection of Frank Sinatra's taste that he sings Tom Jobim's music?"

"Oh, definitely and nobody sings it better. Agh!" and she swooned.

"Can you dance to this music, the rumba, merengue?"

"No, no."

"Does Tom Jobim write his own lyrics?"

"No. Vinicius de Moraes wrote these."

"Isn't that the guy who you told me sings with a bottle of Johnnie Walker in front of him and fucks anything that walks?"

"That's him, the old fucker."

"He still alive?"

"Yup."

"Got anything with him singin'?"

"Yes."

She puts on Vinicius de Moraes.

"Please translate."

"You can't really."

"Try."

> *I am going to love you in every goodbye.*
> *I am going to love you desperately.*
> *I know I am going to love you.*
>
> *And every kiss will be to tell you that I know*
> *I am going to love you for all my life.*
>
> *I know I am going to cry.*
> *When you go away, I am going to cry—*

"That's enough. They're very nice, thank you," I said, and then we made love.

Afterwards, Elsa said, "You know, Garibaldi"—sometimes she calls me Garibaldi—"you're a good lay."

"*Gracias*," I said.

The truth is that I fear for those of us named after our fathers, who become known in the neighborhood as "Junior." They spend their childhoods in confusion, forever shouting nervously, "Which one!" They become practitioners of the double take, and by the time they reach puberty they don't know if they have their own dick. Frank Sinatra named his son Franklin after President Roosevelt but it was inevitable that when the boy opened his mouth to sing, he would become known as Frank Sinatra, Jr. He's a loving son and an accomplished musician, plays several instruments, the flute in addition to the piano, and he's composed piano concertos. Frank Sinatra had no way of knowing that many of his contemporaries who went on to become doctors and dentists and lawyers blamed Franklin Roosevelt for letting all the Puerto Ricans into New York. They had not as yet spread to God's country, Bensonhurst, but one day a Chinese couple was seen walking hand in hand to the train. They had moved surreptitiously into the multiple dwelling up near Fifteenth Avenue where the ailanthus trees are older and taller, casting the houses in shadows. Every morning and every evening the couple walked to and from the West End line, on tiptoes, silent, nodding to each and every neighbor they passed. They passed Mr. Rosa's Lincoln Continental parked in his driveway. They had never seen such a car and marveled at how he traded it in every year for a new model. Unfortunately, Mr. Rosa couldn't trade in his wife, and by the time their Junior reached the age of eleven it was too late to give him his own name. When Mr. Rosa married Nellie, he had no way of knowing that after she gave birth to their son, she would refuse to leave the house. She didn't have to leave, everything was brought to her. There was a continuous procession of grocery boys and hairstylists, and then around four o'clock Nellie emerged from the darkness inside her house and stood in the sunlight behind her screen door. She smiled and waved to those of us curious about what she was like. At times she had red hair and at times blond. She always dressed nicely. Occasionally, her adventurous spirit broke through and she opened her door a crack, stuck out her head and spoke to us. She was bright and gay and sounded like our mothers, except that Nellie's voice was many decibels higher. Everything was normal. A crime had not as yet been committed in Bensonhurst and so the doors were always open. Mr. Rosa's door was always open, and I figured if the grocery boy could go in unannounced, so could I. Besides, Junior was my friend, and so at eight o'clock during the summer months I went in holding my ball.

"Junior! Junior!" I called from the parlor. When no one answered, I thought that maybe Junior was still asleep and I sliced through the parlor feeling like an intruder in a room full of phantoms, phantoms who when they materialized would have to sit on plastic, but there was a couch and a coffee table and wing chairs and a big TV console just like in everybody else's parlor. I made a sharp right into Junior's bedroom, stood at the threshold and looked around. Every morning I looked around until my eyes lit upon Junior's bed, and every morning my dream of an all-day ball game was snatched away and was replaced by the vision of Junior lying in his bed in his mother's arms, his head on her breast, and she was stroking his hair.

"Ready to go, Juney?"

Nellie's blond hair rested against the headboard. She turned her head slowly and looked at me. She said nothing, then turned away. Junior raised his head and looked back at me, too. His hair was rumpled, his eyes glassy. He didn't say anything either and then returned to his mother's arms. I wish I could have said what I thought, that though what they were doing was unusual, it was a wonderful way to start the day. I had never been held by my mother in bed; I had never so much as seen her there. And the only time I had glimpsed her naked had been when she thought I was half asleep, when I called her in the middle of the night to bring me a glass of water.

Sooner or later Junior joined us in our play, but he was too gentle to make a first-rate ballplayer. In his frustration of competing with kids with their own names who were also bigger and stronger and whose mothers had kicked them out with the arrival on the block of the sun, Junior often picked a fight rather than play harder. He stammered and cried, and when he was getting the worst of it, he ran away. He ran into his house. If he had picked a fight with me, I ran right after him, mother or no mother, threw open the screen door and flew through the parlor all in a rage, sweating, sniveling. I slowed down a step to make my sharp right into the bedroom. My eyes searched wildly for Junior and found him but to get at him I would first have to fight Nellie. They were in his bed and Junior was once again in his mother's arms, calm, and Nellie was stroking his hair.

Junior didn't join us for our daily pre-dinner orgy. Around four o'clock the girls put away their dolls and jump ropes and chalk, the boys put away their bats and balls, and we all naturally gravitated to the alley between my uncle's office and our garage. There was a wood-slatted door which we could close. By now the sun had traveled all the way to Shore Road. My house was tall, three-stories high, and cast us deep in its shadows. We had to be quiet because my uncle was a cardiologist and he needed silence in order to hear his patients' heartbeats. Maryanne, Nicky, Theresa, Albee, me—whoever was around—we formed a circle, alternating girl-boy-girl-boy. We held hands, felt our warm willing flesh. We let go, and the girls reached right and left, lowered our zippers, then they snaked their fingers under our pants and touched our little dicks. The boys in turn reached right and left, and our fingers crawled under the girls' pants and touched their smooth skin. We touched the crack. Silent, still, we explored with our fingertips, our lips parted, our faces beaming and turned toward the sky. There were two older girls, sisters, who lived around the corner. They were like night and day in that one had blond hair and her sister's hair was black as night. I liked them, they were beautiful and they were kind to me, but I didn't think of touching them because they were always laughing and talking and forever putting the question to me, "Who do you like better: Bing Crosby or Frank Sinatra?"

I thought hard, every day I tried to conjure up the idols' faces, their voices, the heart of the contest. I went alone to the Hollywood Theater under the El and saw *The Kissing Bandit*. Still I could offer no intelligent opinion. I had Maryanne Volpi and Theresa Mineo on my fingertips. I still have them on my fingertips. When Elsa shaved her mons and I ate it anyway, I found that I didn't like it and requested that she let her hair grow. What happened during the intervening years?

The trouble with Frank Sinatra started when my father was ten years old and his mother took him shopping in New York. She lost her pocketbook, so now she had to find a way to get home without money. In her black coat, biting her lip and holding her son's hand, she approached a policeman and said in good English, as she had been raised in a convent in Brooklyn, "Officer, I lost my pocketbook, and my son and I have no way to get home. We live in Brooklyn. Would you please lend us the money? I promise to pay you back."

"Get lost!" snapped the policeman, waving his arm.

Maria and her son took half a day to walk home. They walked across the bridge, and my father would never forget the policeman's accent or his big red lipless face or his uniform. Every day after school he fought the Irish in civilian clothes. He broke two knuckles on his left hand, but he didn't need his knuckles to shoot crap on the New Utrecht High School roof. In the classroom below, the great baritone Robert Merrill prepared to graduate. Robert Merrill sings the National Anthem before the ball games, and Frank Sinatra sings "New York, New York" during the games—why hasn't anyone questioned Robert Merrill's ties with the underworld, *his* political leanings? Across the river in Hoboken, Frank Sinatra also fought the Irish, he has a scar on his neck to prove it, but he was a skinny little kid and got his lumps while my father had a powerful left arm, and so it was inconceivable how his poor opinion of Frank Sinatra was formed for life merely on the hearsay of a patient who had gone to Las Vegas on a junket. Back in the office the patient reported that around a crowded gaming table he saw Frank Sinatra jostle this guy and say some real nasty things. An ordinary-looking guy but one who wasn't about to take any shit from Frank Sinatra or anybody else. He stood his ground, cocked his arm but before he could let one fly was jumped by five goons. At twelve o'clock my father runs up the stairs in his white gown, his hair in front of his wild eyes.

"That punk, Sinatra—he picked on the wrong guy this time!"

"Don't believe it, Pa. If the powers that be didn't know that Frank Sinatra had a mouth, a way with words, American words, if they didn't know he could talk turkey and pay off, he would have been jailed half a dozen times. Pa, Enrico Caruso was put in jail. That's right, the greatest voice the world has ever known was convicted of molesting a woman! At first he didn't even understand the charges. At his trial the interpreter got it all wrong and translated a confession instead of a denial."

It happened in the monkey house at the Central Park zoo. A cold January morning in 1906, one year before my father was born, Caruso takes a leisurely stroll through the zoo, which is near his hotel. He suddenly feels chilled and seeks refuge in the monkey house. It's empty except for a proper-looking woman who is watching two chimpanzees beg for food, stretching their hairy arms through the bars, entreating her with their human eyes. Caruso stands beside the woman and watches, too, as one enjoys company in a zoo.

"Mornin'," Caruso says, doffing his hat.

He had bought some fruit, oranges, grapes and bananas. He loved the bananas of America. They were huge and yellow and meaty. Italian bananas were imported from Africa and were green and small, hardly a mouthful. Caruso tosses the bananas into the cage. Pleased, he looks at the woman. She smiles and moves over to the orangutans, who are playing tag in their tree house. Caruso follows, as it's natural in a zoo to progress from one cage to the next. When the woman moves over to the spider monkeys and Caruso follows her this time, she screams, "Help! Help! He rubbed against me!"

Caruso grasps her arm with concern and says, "*Che c'è, signora?*"

"Help! He touched my side!"

Her partner in crime was a plainclothes policeman named Kulhane. Dressed as a zookeeper, he pounces on Caruso, cuffs him and hauls him off to the Sixty-ninth Precinct station house. Caruso is fingerprinted and arraigned for molesting a woman. He didn't understand the charges, but he understood ignorance and maltreatment. He bellowed to the booking lieutenant, "I'm Enrico Caruso!"

"And I'm Garibaldi!" the lieutenant cried.

"Yeah, and I'm Machiavelli!" said a detective who happened to pass by.

Caruso filled his great lungs and let out a B-flat natural that shook the chandelier.

"All these ginneys think they can sing," said Officer Kulhane.

"Lock him up!"

Caruso tried to put two and two together and in the process suffered the first of a series of fatal headaches. As he was being led away, he offered in his best English the following explanation:

"How I poke from behind when I wore heavy coat and wool suit which I keep bottoned because of cold? I go to monkey house because of cold. I have hands behind back all the time and for nothin' she says I go, 'Whoop! Whoop!'"—and then as a way of simulating the trumped-up charge, Caruso projected his abdomen and took several stutter steps forward.

He was kept in jail overnight, and the next day bail of five hundred dollars was posted. When he arrived at his hotel, he heard the doorman singing "That Funny Feeling." Caruso had him fired. A painting hanging in the lobby was entitled "The Friars of St. Simian." Caruso had it taken down. His next performance was as Rodolfo in *La Bohème*. In the Fourth Act, Musetta hands the dying Mimi a muff. Caruso insisted that it be made of rabbit fur. The great Polish soprano Marcella Sembrich refused to sing with him. Officer Kulhane moonlighted in front of the monkey house, charging admission to hear Caruso sing to the monkeys. Business was brisk. On the other side, the head of the Comédie-Française wrote: "If D'Artagnan were alive today and traveled to New York, he would be locked up, too."

Puccini himself wrote: "It's a tragic misunderstanding. Caruso knows that Italian women love to be rubbed up against by tenors, midgets, too—they bring good luck."

My father says, "Go on, Anthony. Remember that time in the Garden? It was a disgrace!"

Joe Freeze had given the whole neighborhood free tickets to an Italian rally in Madison Square Garden. Frank Sinatra would be presiding and providing the entertainment, including a young singer named Aretha Franklin. We packed the front car, and during the ride my father kept asking, "Who's this Aretha Franklin?"

"Wait till you hear her—she's terrific!"

Ten thousand bleached blondes wrapped in millions of dead

minks accompanied by ten thousand short squat men with bald spots and wearing dark suits descended upon Madison Square Garden. The orchestra, composed mainly of strings, warmed us up with "O Sole Mio" and "Come Back to Sorrento," and then the evening's festivities got underway. There must be a secret tunnel under Madison Square Garden, because the first speaker suddenly appeared at the microphone. His skin was pink and he spoke with a kind of brogue and wore a suit one size too small. He clasped his hands and said, "Good evening, ladies and gentlemen, I'm Ed McMahon."

He paused, looked around, expecting a smattering of applause, but you couldn't hear a pin drop and so he went on with a tremulous voice, "Frank Sinatra couldn't make it tonight, but he's sent along one of the world's finest entertainers, Mr. Sammy Davis, Jr. H-e-e-e-e-r's Sammy!"

The olive of twenty thousand Italian faces grew bright yellow. Insulted faces simultaneously turned right and left in search of corroboration. The men straightened their ties. The women tugged at their skirts, pulling them tight over their knees. The same thought entered twenty thousand dark mysterious minds: "For an ugly little black guy he's got a helluva lot of nerve."

Sammy Davis, Jr., conducted himself royally. He sang and danced and played the drums. He introduced the Italian guest speakers with the required amount of respect, a lot. Scholarships were handed out, and the future of our country ran up and accepted them. Aretha Franklin was being saved for the end, when the momentum of the evening had grown favorable in that everybody was a little tired. But then Sammy Davis, Jr., announced, "Miss Aretha Franklin is ill but her younger sister has agreed to sing in her place. She's never sung before such a large audience, so let's hear it!"

She emerged amid silence from an exit ramp, made her way through an aisle between wooden folding chairs and mounted the stage. The Italians waited until she had sung a few bars, then en masse they got up and made for the exits, creating a racket. The courageous young woman kept singing. She looked around. No one gave her a glance. Sammy Davis, Jr., hopped onto the stage, stopped the song and said with a mixture of outrage and disgust, "Please return to your seats! This is a travesty, the worst display of manners I've ever seen! Never again will I do one of these things!"

Good! thought the Italians still in the Garden.

The *coup de grâce* occurred in 1947 when the papers reported that Frank Sinatra was seen in Havana in the company of Lucky Luciano, Al Capone's brother Ralph, and the Fischetti brothers of Brooklyn, Miami and Chicago. Frank Sinatra had begun his holiday in Mexico. Nothing untoward happened there, but then he flies to Miami to play a benefit and bumps into Joe Fischetti and his brothers. They persuade him to join them on a junket to Havana. Frank Sinatra gets off the plane in Havana carrying a small suitcase. He had never been seen carrying his own suitcase, and neither Joe Fischetti nor his brothers are carrying one, and they do not offer to carry Frank Sinatra's. Packed neatly in the suitcase is six million dollars in small bills destined for the deep, wide pockets of Lucky Luciano, who is vacationing in Havana. The Fischetti brothers, Ralph Capone, Lucky Luciano and Frank Sinatra meet at a bar, then they go to the races together, jai-alai games, dine and spend relaxed evenings of craps and baccarat at the Havana Casino.

I know the truth about all this. I got it from the horse's mouth, from Lucky Luciano himself! A female friend of his was a patient of my father's. She came for bridges, full uppers and lowers, and as such work takes time, my father got to know her. Over dinner he said that she was lovely, had a gay spirit and was respectful, and though he had never heard her sing, he imagined she had a fine soprano voice "because she studies hard and dresses nice." Lucky Luciano drove her to the office, then waited outside. He sat in his car awhile, parked out front in the shade of our tree. He got out, paced and smoked. From our living-room window I watched him walk back and forth in front of our garden of honeysuckle vines and snowballs. He wore the first full-length camel's-hair coat I had ever seen. When he removed his hat to wipe his brow, I saw that his hair was silver and wiry and not a strand was out of place. Sunlight bounced off his full cheeks. He put out his cigarette in the patch of dirt around the tree. Sometimes he stayed under there, and sometimes he kept walking up toward Fifteenth Avenue. I'd lose him in the shadows, but he always came back.

One day while Lucky Luciano's friend was in the chair, I went down to the office through the house. I loved to visit my father while he worked. He was happy in his office, and he greeted me in his white gown with a smile and a genuine salutation. He called me champ and mootzie, short for mozzarella. I surprised him through a door which only he used, the one in the narrow, sunless corridor between his operating room and his darkroom, where he developed his impressions and spent many, many hours in peaceful reverie. In the silent darkness he daydreamed about his one chance at happiness with a woman. Ruby was her name, and he had met her in Canada, Halifax. I got to know her through the photographs Don Antonio showed me. He didn't like my mother, she had a strain of Neapolitan, and so while we were playing *scoppa* on his porch, he fetched some photographs from the bottom drawer of the chest in his dining room. If I was old enough to play Italian cards, I was old enough to know about the woman my father should have married. I remember only that she had blond hair. Maybe Lucky Luciano's friend reminded my father of his Ruby, because when I opened the door a crack, poked in my head and said, "Hi, Pa," I saw that his left arm was around the patient's hair and it was blond and long, extending from the headrest to the motor on the floor which my father kicked to set off his drill. His face was so close to hers that it was practically inside her mouth. He withdrew his exploratory mirror, released her from his grip.

"Hey, champ—what are you doing down here?"

"Thought I'd say hello."

The woman turned and smiled. Her hair was rumpled, and around her neck was a white towel stained with blood. She unclipped it, revealing a peasant's blouse. I stared at the fair hide of her chest. She spoke with cotton in her mouth.

"So this is little Anthony—how are you?"

"Fine."

"You're looking trim and fit."

"Well, you know, I play ball all day."

"I'd like you to go outside and say hello to Mr. Lucania. He's heard a lot about you." She giggled. "He doesn't like to come in here. He says dentist's offices make him nervous."

I go outside through the waiting room. Patients hold their swollen jaws, tears in their eyes. Up the short stairwell deep as a moat then out into the sun and around the hedges to the tree. Lucky Luciano is in his car, behind the wheel, and he's gazing up the avenue. Soft knocks at the window on the passenger side. I mouth very clearly, "I'm the doc's son."

He unlocks the door and I hop in.

"Lock it."

"Oh, sure . . ." When I turn from locking the door, I see a gun glide from his palm into his jacket pocket. "Mr. Lucania," I begin, "I'd like the truth about Frank Sinatra in Havana, but first I want to thank you for helping us win the war." He had aided the Allies in the invasion of Sicily. "You know, I was with my mother when the news came. She was hanging out our clothes to dry and I was beside her, teetering on the sill. Suddenly, people down on the street start screaming. I look at my mother and she's scream-ing. Mrs. Ernesto comes to her window and she screams. I almost fell onto the garage."

Lucky Luciano muses, "We had a good thing going for a while, selling partisan flags."

He had been in partnership with Don Antonio's brother, Santo, who came to America in 1943 with a trunkful of partisan flags. Don Antonio had come with his tool kit in 1915, and his arrival coincided with the widespread use of stainless steel. The huge kitchens in our schools, hospitals, airports—Don Antonio su-pervised building them. He made good money and invested in real estate. He lived in a house around the corner from us, and walking there in the dark beside my father was an adventure. It was the first thing we did together as men. With my father as guardian, holding my hand, I could look up at the black sky filled with stars and appreciate its immensity, its grandeur. Don Antonio's house had a garden in front and a yard with a garage where as a boy my father kept his pigeons. The house had a cellar, a deep cellar, a hundred steps straight down. After dinner I followed Don Antonio down. We knew our way through the darkness to his workbench. He snapped on the naked light bulb, and I sat beside him on my stool. We didn't talk. He lived in the United States sixty years and didn't learn English. He worked naked from the waist up and wore a hat to keep in the heat. He made shovels and wrenches and pots, all out of stainless steel. I still have a few of his knives. He also made locks. He was Frank Uale's private locksmith. Mr. Uale, also known as Frankie Yale, invented the Sicilian handshake and the Sicilian bullet.

"How do you do?" he would say.

You offer your hand, he takes it, pulls you off balance, then blows your brains out with the gun in his left hand. He killed Dion O'Banion this way in his flower shop in Chicago. Frankie Yale didn't trust his eye, he trusted his bullets. "With my bullets," he used to say, "you pump in a case of gangrene. First you boil onions in water, then take out the onions. Toss ordinary bullets into the onion water and while they boil, peel a few cloves of garlic and chop to a paste. Rub the bullets all over with the garlic. You're ready to load."

Don Antonio and Frankie Yale fed the poor of the neighborhood during the Depression. They drove around in Mr. Yale's bulletproof car. He gave Al Capone a short count on some bootleg liquor around the time the Thompson submachine gun was introduced in Chicago. It made its debut in Brooklyn on Frankie Yale alone in his bulletproof car.

Don Antonio also made his own banister: two long solid rods of gleaming stainless steel. His brother Santo found it easily and settled into the house with his flags. He walked around in his shorts. Don Antonio told him, "Please wear your pants."

Santo explained that in Messina he always walked around in his shorts.

"You're in Brooklyn now," said Don Antonio. "Besides, my daughter Anna is pregnant. *Para brutto.*"

The next morning Santo came to the breakfast table in his shorts and Don Antonio kicked him out.

Anna had married a Sicilian named Joseph Garaffa, and it was through Uncle Joseph that Lucky Luciano entered our lives. They had grown up together on the Lower East Side of New York. Joseph liked to gamble and was in a crap game that was raided. His watch was taken. His mother goes to the Lucanias: "I saved my whole life for that watch..." Joseph got his watch back. In turn he bought Lucky Luciano his first pair of silk underwear. Joseph became a cutter for Lily of Saks and cut Lucky Luciano a few suits.

"Tell me, how's your uncle, Joey Gaff?" Lucky Luciano asks me in the car.

"He passed on."

"What a guy, Joey Gaff: flashy dresser, great driver. He was the best driver I ever had. In the old days we were tough, it's true, but, you know, we loved to dance. Joey, me, George Raft, we'd dress to the teeth and go uptown and dance. George, he was the best of us."

"Where did he learn the tango, do you know?"

"The tango was the rage. It was a new import from France. Valentino had danced it in *The Four Horsemen.*"

"Did my father hang around with you guys?"

"Later on. He used to come along with Joey."

"Did my father dance the tango?"

A big smile breaks on his face. "He liked to fox-trot. Let me tell you something about your father: he was so handsome that all the girls flocked around him. We had to dance with ourselves. Once in Havana he was at the bar surrounded by these beautiful hookers, you know, and he puts his arms around them and says with tears in his eyes, 'Now what are nice girls like you doing in a place like this?'"

"My father was in Havana?"

"Your father was anywhere where there was a big crap game: Nassau, San Juan, Mar del Plata, Havana, Monte Carlo—you name it, he was there."

"He did disappear the month of August. Was he in Havana when Frank Sinatra was there?"

"Look, I read the papers. We don't take a roll call. In a foreign country, especially a small one like Cuba, Americans tend to stay together. We meet at the bar—your father, me, Joey Gaff, Ed Sullivan, Frank Sinatra, whoever's down—and, yeah, we eat together and go to the races and jai alai and gamble! Who do you think can afford the best hotels and restaurants and patronize the gambling establishments? The journalists? The Cubans? Puerto Ricans?"

"Ralph Capone?"

"He was in Chicago. I remember for a fact because I called his cousins Charlie and Rocco Fischetti and asked them why they hadn't come down. They said that Ralph needed help in the jukebox end of business. Crooners like the Eberle Brothers, Dick Haymes and Frank Sinatra were breaking away from the big bands. There were a lot of new singles to put in the jukeboxes. It's a cash business, and you should know that when it comes to cash, Italians call on their family."

"So Frank Sinatra wasn't in Florida with the Fischetti brothers."

"Only Joe, and he was legit, in real estate. Frank didn't want to go to Havana with Joe because of his brothers, but what was he supposed to do? Tell Joe he couldn't fly on the same plane? You'll have to talk to the ticket agent."

"This business about a valise with six million in small bills..."

He pulls up his coat, reaches into his back pocket, withdraws his wallet and hands it to me.

"It's heavy."

"There's ten thousand in C-notes in there. Six million in *twenties* would fill your father's office. You'd need ten longshoremen to carry it. Besides, would I have an entertainer in the public eye bring me money?"

We all went out in a boat to welcome Uncle Joseph home from the war. I got lost in a sea of legs, but the thing to watch for was a bridge over the water. As we approached it, I looked up and saw hundreds of sailors in white uniform. Joseph was among them, and they cheered and waved and tossed their white hats. Joseph came home with every inch of his arms covered with tattoos. They set him apart for me. I didn't ask where he had gotten them, what port, what battle, what woman, or what had entered his mind that would make him the only tattooed Sicilian in the family, if they made his skin feel any different or his blood. I preferred that the world of Joseph's tattoos remain a mystery even as the years passed, saying only, "Gee, you gotta lot of tattoos."

I liked to sit next to him at the table because he showed me things he had learned in the Navy, like salt brings out the flavor of watermelon and lemon brings out the flavor of cantaloupe and honeydew. I sat close beside him when he drove and couldn't take my eyes off his tattooed hand working the tall shaft. As I grew older we drifted apart. His role in the family was impermeable to the admiration of a non-blood nephew. He was the husband of the younger sister, the brother-in-law who goes through life unappreciated. He is quiet, respectful, always ready with a smile. He drives you anywhere at any hour of the day and night. He knows how to fix things and does so without complaint. He has a job, a boss, and keeps them for life. He calls home at noon to say hello. His children don't go to the best of schools. They're the apple of his eye. He cares for them when their spouses die and when they divorce. He is an usher in church. Despite illness and inclement weather he shows up on Sunday to pass around the basket. He goes to the barber once a week for a shave and haircut. He numbers the barber among his friends. He suffers one heart attack after another but still smiles and struts like a king, lighting up a Camel.

I say to Lucky Luciano, "Thanks a lot, and I'd like to leave you with a nice little story. When Don Antonio told his brother Santo to wear pants because Anna was pregnant, he was telling the truth. Your old friend Joey Gaff and Anna had a daughter, Alice, and she's had a hard life. Her husband died in an accident at an early age. She raised two children on her own, tried this man and that one. Out of spite she married a cop who on his wedding night turned out to be a virgin. She got cancer and beat it. Then she married a good man named Jake. They're in their sixties now, and recently they went to Atlantic City to see Frank Sinatra. Alice called me:

"'When he was just about to sing, holding the mike, he dropped his shoulder and I couldn't help myself—I got up and screamed, "Frankie! Frankie!"'"

JOE DIMAGGIO

———

ERNIE starts downtown in his Yankee baseball cap and Yankee sweatshirt. He's a professional photographer and has been enthralled with the Yankee logo ever since he saw Joe DiMaggio glide back for a fly ball, go from first to third on a routine single, wait on a curve ball and then line the pitch up the power alley. Bernie claims he's forty-six but a mutual friend who knows his ex-wife says he's fifty-three. I allow Bernie his little lie because I don't like women talking behind a man's back, and also I know that Bernie is a nostalgia buff and lying about his age permits him to stay close to the things he loved in his youth. Bernie was sitting in the upper deck the night Joe Di-Maggio was caught off second base the only time in his career. Out of the corner of his eye Joe thought he saw the relay go awry, into right field, but what he saw wasn't the ball at all—it was a bird flying from left field to right.

To make himself even younger, Bernie stops at the Eagle Tavern for some cocaine. The dealer is a permanent fixture at the bar. His prices have been the same for ten years. His clientele is faithful, and they can pick him out from a thousand ordinary patrons. Bernie worms through the crowd, taps the dealer on the shoulder, then the two men go to a dark corner while I'm up in my kitchen with my apron on, wrapping the flounder in tinfoil so they can bake in their natural juices, steaming the carrots with honey, preparing a modest Italian dish I thought Bernie might like—mushrooms and onions sautéed in olive oil. Playing for the Jolly Giants in San Francisco, Joe DiMaggio was paid two baseballs and a gallon of olive oil. The owner of the team, Tom Nova, also owned an olive oil factory. Joe DiMaggio remembered his playing days in the Pacific Coast League—during his career as a Yankee he rubbed olive oil on his bats to give them smoothness.

After the buy at the Eagle Tavern, Bernie goes to the head shop around the corner for the paraphernalia. Everything must be new for his night with me. Then he thinks about where he's going: "Oh, yeah... the Italian on Charles Street..."

The bell sounds and my heart soars. I greet Bernie on the landing in my apron. I smile and we shake hands. Bernie catches his breath and then begins juggling imaginary props. I smile again, happy that with this friend I can play the straight man.

"What's that?" I say.

"That's what the surgeon is going to do with our prostates if we don't fuck or masturbate every day."

"Gee, Bernie, every day?"

"That's right—every day."

Joe DiMaggio played straight man to his best friend in baseball, Lefty Gomez. Lefty was forever putting rubber snakes in Joe's glove, and if Joe was looking up at the sky, Lefty gave him a hot foot. On feeling the snake in his glove or the pain in his foot, Joe laughed and merely said, "Aw, Lefty..."

Joe once said to Toots Shor, "Toots, I wish I could be like Lefty. Nobody could be like Lefty."

There are times when I wish I could be like Bernie but I don't envy him his relationship with his girl. When it comes to lubricating his prostate, for example, he has to have the patience of a saint. She works in a cancer ward and at the end of the day is spent of all emotion. Bernie tries to revive her with an arsenal of artificial devices. He works over her body like a car mechanic, hopping around it from top to bottom, bottom to top. In each hand he holds a vibrator the size of an outboard motor—all the way from my place I hear the action similar to a jackhammer, and I picture my friend all asweat, red-faced, his penis throbbing, pulsating with anticipation of joining the primed body when it's at the hilt. Bernie came over during a time when he was having trouble with his girl. Not over the priming business, as I might have thought, but over his wanting a permanent relationship, have her move in with him, maybe even marry her. He felt that under the same roof with him twenty-four hours, in time she would relax, relax to the point where he could arouse her by touching her skin with his fingers or merely kissing her lips. He was really fifty-three years old, and he pictured himself living alone with his cat throughout his fifties, his sixties, and he wasn't looking forward to meeting another woman whose body he might have to prime. With the woman he had he knew the routine. He knew the salesman at the Pleasure Palace, a decent gay guy who understood such things and discreetly supplied him with devices hand-tailored for his girl. But she felt that Bernie was too unstable for a permanent relationship and insisted that it go on as it was, a long night here and there making love.

It's a cool night in October, so my window is closed, but Bernie feels stifled, unable to breathe. He throws open the window, making me feel that I can thrive breathing stale air. He drops onto my Castro convertible in his rumpled clothes. Elsa says that Bernie could take care of himself a little better. He has his hair cut only when he visits his mother, who still lives in the Bronx. Bernie remembers his father telling him that Joe DiMaggio was one of the best-dressed men he ever saw:

"I used to go to Vesuvio's on Friday night before the fights. Cary Grant was there and Ray Milland, but they had nothing on Joe D."

In fact, the Fashion Designers of America once voted Joe DiMaggio one of the ten best-dressed men in America. Joe McCarthy, the Yankee manager, had a lot to do with the way Joe dressed. McCarthy insisted that off the field his players dress like bankers, suit and tie. "You don't go into a bank," McCarthy used to say, "and see people with their shirts unbuttoned. You don't see their hairy chests."

Joe DiMaggio's wardrobe consisted almost entirely of dark suits. One reason for this was that he played ball before the advent of the ballpoint pen. Autograph seekers used to shake their pens and the ink splashed all over Joe's clothes. He was wearing a blue pinstripe the night he met Marilyn Monroe. They were supposed to meet at the Villa Penza at seven. Joe arrived at seven-fifteen. Marilyn arrived at nine. Mickey Rooney was in the restaurant, and when he saw Joe DiMaggio, he rushed over to his table and said to Marilyn Monroe, "Do you know who this is?"

"I'm sorry, but I don't know about baseball."

Mickey Rooney said, "This is the greatest ballplayer who ever lived! Lifetime batting average, 325! 131 triples! 389 doubles! 361 homers! 4,529 putouts! 10 pennants! 9 World Championships!"

Later on Joe said to Marilyn, "Don't feel bad—I don't know much about the movies." Then he said, "Would you like to come up to my suite and see my trophies?"

"Are you kiddin'?" said Marilyn.

Joe leaned over and kissed her.

After dinner I switch on the ball game. Bernie takes one look and says, "Joe DiMaggio had the biggest dick around."

"How do you know?"

"Common knowledge."

"Oh. . . ."

As Bernie is leaving I give him a brush made of natural vegetable-fiber bristles. "It takes off all the dead cells," I tell him, "leaving your body alive, refreshed. Brush about five minutes before or after showering. I even brush my dick with it."

Some days later, alone in his bathroom, Bernie takes up the brush and his thoughts turn to me. They especially turn to me when he runs the brush ever so lightly over his dick. He winces, puts the brush aside forever and wonders what kind of a dick his friend has that he can brush it with stiff bristles and enjoy it. He mentioned that he had used the brush, and even brushed his dick with it but it had hurt him, making me feel that my dick wasn't as sensitive as his. Well, I gotta good dick—it ain't the biggest guy in the world but it's sturdy, thick, does the job, so to speak. Each and every spray casts a fresh hue over the world. Each and every spray makes me feel better the next day. My girlfriend, an Argentine lady of great experience, says that my dick is the only one she ever felt inside her, and over the years I've sympathized with men who felt that their penis was too small. "Precious things often come in small packages," I once told a colleague of mine, Ted Price. He had been musing about his life: at the age of fifty-one he was still unmarried, and he had not had a lover for any length of time because, he said, "My penis is too small." We worked in the aftercare unit of the Narcotic Control Commission. We monitored drug use by examining our clients' arms and from time to time taking urine. But Mr. Price took urine every day. He marched his clients to the brightly lit urine room with a look of satisfaction on his face, then he watched and listened as the urine jet-sprayed into the cup, saying to himself, How could scum like this have such a beautiful penis?

Mr. Price's only pleasures were hitting a tennis ball against the gym wall and once a year going on a holiday to Jamaica. He was forever squeezing a rubber ball, strengthening his wrists and forearms and by some miracle his dick. He died at the premature age of fifty-four. I hope he found happiness with an understanding native in a hut by the sea.

JACK CUSIMANO

A FEW years ago, in my fortieth year, I saw a documentary on television about the life of Thomas Edison. He worked in New Jersey, I learned, which impresses me because the light bulb has been ubiquitous during my lifetime and this fact launched Edison to a ubiquitous place, the sky or an undiscovered land reserved for great men. New Jersey is just due west of me, across the river, and from my roof I can see the sun setting on Jersey's horizon. My sister lives in a beautiful ranch-style house in New Jersey, and Edison had his humble beginnings not too far from her, in a wooden outpost with a workbench, a chair, and a kerosene lamp. The idea of Edison in New Jersey also impresses me the way my discovery that Garibaldi lived a short time in New Jersey impresses me. What on earth was the great Italian doing there? Was Edison born in New Jersey? Have family there? The documentary must have mentioned this, and I remember that it showed Edison in the flesh, but the image of his face comes to me now from a postage stamp I bought when I was seven years old. It was a mint stamp, valued at three cents then, unwatermarked, printed on a rotary press. The illustrator had portrayed Edison as an old man, when his face reflected years of toil and doubt and pressure from the business that sprang up from his invention. His hair had turned completely white and was short and unruly. Deep lines framed his mouth. There was puffiness under his eyes, and he peered out at me through narrow slits. This was the way Edison looked, I thought as a boy, and I thought no further—with my tweezer I placed the stamp in a protective sheath called a PM, then I placed the stamp in my book.

Every Saturday afternoon for years I worked on my stamp collection alone in my room. Now and then I heard the roar of a train on the nearby El, comforting me because I had heard the trains day and night for seven years. Occasionally, I looked out my window to the man who flew his pigeons on a roof beyond the El. His pigeon coop was an essential part of the skyline. Earlier in the day, after washing the stairs and simonizing the car, I had taken my pay to Mr. Nielson's stamp store. Mr. Nielson was a big man with yellow hair and red cheeks, and he greeted me with a smile. The suit and tie he always wore assured me that stamp collecting was serious business. Some of the richest men in Brooklyn came to his store, using their surplus money to buy stamps rather than diamonds or gold. A fat, jovial dentist friend of my father's, Dr. Fava—he bought a Ben Franklin for two thousand dollars. Fava's collection, Mr. Nielson told me, was worth millions. With his tweezer Mr. Nielson withdrew those stamps I could afford, and every Saturday afternoon he told me that their value would increase over the years. I can still hear his words: "I'll buy back your collection anytime!"

Thirty years passed, and one day while my father was dying I found myself in desperate need of money. I drove with my stamp book to Mr. Nielson's store, on Fourth Avenue in the Bay Ridge section of Brooklyn. I parked a few blocks away to get my bearings on foot, then I walked up to the store but it was not a stamp store! I entered anyway and asked the new owner if he knew what had become of Mr. Nielson.

"Mr. Nielson? No . . ."

I staggered back onto the sidewalk, into the gutter, shielding my eyes from the sun as I scanned the storefronts. I called the telephone company and inquired about a Mr. Nielson's stamp store in Bay Ridge or any section of Brooklyn. There was no such listing. It was inconceivable that Mr. Nielson had died. He was indestructible like his stamps, and like his stamps he had grown more precious with the passage of time, sweeter, humbler—he would be happy to see his old faithful customer again. It was also inconceivable that Mr. Nielson had run off to Norway with my money. The United States had been good to him and his family, providing them with a decent life, and so Mr. Nielson felt grateful and had conducted his business with a fresh, honest eye. I also reasoned that he could not very well carry on his trade in Oslo, as his specialty was mint United States stamps and his clientele the new money of Bay Ridge.

Broke, my dying father calling, I searched frantically for another stamp store in the same neighborhood. I found one and said to the proprietor, holding out my book, "I bought these stamps thirty years ago from a Mr. Nielson who had a store on Fourth Avenue. I'd like an appraisal. Do you have a current catalogue?"

"I don't need a catalogue," the man said. "Let's have a look."

I handed him my book, and as he leafed through it, lingering over my plate blocks, I felt proud. Each stamp had been set straight in its appropriate place and had been secured with the gummy back of a PM, some the size of a small window. The stamps were all mint commemorations of the great men and events of my country, and they had survived the years with their original color, umblemished, free of dust and other corrosive elements. I estimated conservatively that I had poured five hundred dollars into my book, five hundred dollars of hard-earned money. I had scrubbed our stairs of stubborn scuff marks, beginning at the bottom and working upwards on my knees, careful not to knock over my basin of warm water and soap, conscientious about the balls of lint in the corners. After I finished the top step, I stood on the landing and looked down over my work with a sense of accomplishment, fulfillment, triumph. "Look, Ma!" I called, and my mother came and stood beside me.

"They look good," she said, and withdrew a dollar from her apron.

With a fresh supply of rags produced from some unknown place, I went outside to simonize the car. It was waiting under a tree and I lost myself among the hose, the basin and rags strewn all over the sidewalk, my shoes and pants getting wet, passersby saying things like I was a good boy and do a good job. I anguished over bird droppings on the roof, over rust on the chrome. I worried that the soap would leave a gray film and that the wax would leave an orange film. I worried that if I had missed some pockets of dirt, I would ingrain them deep into the enamel along with the wax, and so I applied several layers of wax and wiped each one furiously. But my father did not see through to my fears. In fact, he did not mention the car at all. I had to bring it up over dinner: "Did you see the car?"

"Oh, yeah! It looks good, champ!" and he reached into his back pocket for his wallet and withdrew a dollar bill.

After dinner, free of charge, I liked to stand beside my mother at the sink and dry the dishes. I used a rag with a high fiber content called a "mopina," "little mop" in translation. There was always a pile of them folded neatly in the drawer next to the silverware, and they lasted as long as the family stayed together. While I dried I looked out the window to the man flying his pigeons, and it felt good to be helping my mother, but I had to wait until my father left the kitchen and went into the living room to count his money. Men, he believed, didn't do things like dry dishes. Men didn't do anything around the house. If something broke down and the woman couldn't fix it, a man who lived somewhere else was called and he came over to fix it. Sometimes my father came back into the kitchen for something sweet, a piece of cake, and he'd say to me with his hands on his hips, blinking his eyes, "What are you doing?"

"Drying the dishes . . ."

"Come inside," he'd say.

The stamp dealer finally made an appraisal: "I can give you fifty dollars."

"Fifty dollars!"

"Yes. There are some nice stamps here but the book isn't complete and we only buy collections, not individual stamps."

"Thank you," I said, and left the store with my book and a clean feeling. I would have to make money another way, through hard work, years of tomorrows of hard work. As I drove back to my dying father, I also realized that Mr. Nielson had envisioned for me a collection of stamps that would occupy not only my boyhood summers but all the seasons of my life. He had held out an optimistic eye for me, but no amount of goodwill ever put a dime in my pocket to buy stamps or anything else. Mr. Nielson was also no prophet—he could not foresee that the string of summers of chores and stamp collecting would be broken when my sister reached the age of five and I was twelve and we were still sleeping in the same bedroom, holding hands in the darkness. My father announced that another room was going to be added to our apartment—in this way we would all have our own bedroom. Another room was going to be added all the way down the house: one to my uncle's apartment downstairs and one to the offices in the basement. The house had been built of brick and so the extension would be built of brick. The overall effect would be that the house was all of a piece, as if it had been built at one and the same time. Only a magician of a builder could do such a thing. My father called him and one day soon after he appeared in our kitchen with a dusty, faded brown hat tilted back on his head, his eyes black and weary, his skin white with lime, a stubble of a beard showing through. He was Jack Cusimano, the master builder of Bensonhurst.

The kitchen was all upset with my mother trying to cook while Cusimano's men scurried in and out, yet the great Italian sat calmly and ate heartily. He smiled at me when nobody was looking. His furtive smiles told me that the confusion in the kitchen meant very little—at the end of the summer I would have my bedroom, my sister would have her bedroom and my father would have a larger office in the basement. Cusimano's smiles also told me that he had come from a world that I would one day discover.

Work went smoothly until the day Cusimano went outside to

lay the new lines of bricks. From his scaffold he talked to passersby, annoying my father so he came out of his office in his
white gown and yelled up from the sidewalk, "What are you
doing there, Cusimano—the line isn't straight!"

From out the kitchen window I saw Cusimano turn and look
down at my father standing in the sunlight, his hands clasped
behind him. Cusimano descended the scaffold with his trowel
and said, "I don't have to take any shit from you or any professional man!"

"What do you mean?" my father said, blinking his eyes.

Cusimano threw down his trowel and walked away. He crossed
Sixteenth Avenue. My father hustled after him, then the two men
talked, my father pointing to his office, which was all upset,
Cusimano turning away—he didn't need the job, there were
enough empty lots left in Bensonhurst to last him the rest of his
life. Mr. Cusimano had built all the houses in Bensonhurst, beginning with the houses around the El. He built our house twelve
years before on top of the lot where my father had played ball.
Life in Bensonhurst began around the El and then spread toward
the ocean. There was everything you needed under the El: a
grocery store, a bread store, and a candy store. The Italians
thrived amid noise and darkness, and enough beautiful women
were born around the El to supply all the professional men who
opened practices in Bensonhurst. The most beautiful woman of
all was the grocer's daughter, Frances Palermo. Her body was
round and full. Her skin was the color of Italian bread. She had
a fine nose, upturned, pointy. Frances was sought after by every
doctor, dentist and lawyer in Bensonhurst, but she fell in love
with the builder Cusimano and they married and had four sons.

And so Cusimano didn't have to take any shit from a professional man, including my father, but the master builder came back
to finish the job. A new tension filled the air, and I was told that
I would be spending the rest of the summer with my grandparents.
That was all right with me because one lived just up the block
and one lived around the corner, so from their houses I could
still hear the trains. My mother's mother had candles in her

bedroom like in a church, and she had hair down to her ankles which I watched her comb in her mirror. My father's mother had a porch flooded with sunlight, and on the porch was a set of books with beautiful pictures. My grandparents lived in real homes, while my home was also a mini-hospital. My uncle was a cardiologist and my father was a dentist. People from all over came to our house for their hearts and their teeth. There was such a cacophony of bells and buzzes that the continual roar of the trains was a soothing symphony. Every bell and buzzer that sounded in the offices also sounded in the upstairs apartments. The office doorbell arrived in the form of a buzz. If my father was eating or taking a nap, I pressed the buzzer in the kitchen, letting in the patient downstairs. Sometimes the pain was so bad that the patient took it upon himself to come upstairs. He walked around our garden of honeysuckle vines and snowballs, then up the brick steps leading to our porch. He rang the upstairs bell. I ran down the stairs, opened the door and discovered a stranger holding his jaw. He mumbled something from a frozen mouth, pointing to the abscess beneath the swelling.

"My father will be right down," I said.

The office telephone also rang in the kitchen. Sometimes the patient was a relative or a friend and wanted to speak to my mother. My father buzzed us three times and my mother picked up the phone in the kitchen. Outside, two busy streets converged at our corner. There was a traffic light but it was hidden in summer by leaves of the tall, old trees. Tires screeched and we cringed, waited for the smashing of steel. Victims didn't have far to go for their bashed-in teeth. Motorcycle gangs had come into vogue. The Good Humor man jangled his bells, and directly above our house, a few miles up, was a traffic lane for jets.

My first peaceful stop was at my maternal grandparents', and within three days I came down with whooping cough. I lay flat on my back, unable to move. A polio specialist came. My mother came and fed me ginger ale through a straw. I survived, I believe, because disease and death had not as yet entered my mind, then I moved on to my paternal grandparents'. A fresh bed was waiting in a cozy alcove off the sun-lit porch. I leafed through the picture books with delight. My grandfather bought a television, a ten-inch black-and-white. He had come to America forty years before yet he spoke no English, but he was enthralled with the prospect of outer space as depicted in the program "Captain Video." He enjoyed movies about cowboys and Indians. He learned to say, "The chief, my father!" and he hooted and hollered in the living room, hopping around on one foot.

The summer ended and I went back home. Ours was a huge, lumbering house now. The broad side of it, the side you can see from the train, occupied practically the entire block. I stood on the sidewalk and looked up at Cusimano's work. The line of demarcation between the old bricks and the new ran from the roof down to the garden, but all the bricks were straight as soldiers. I took out my rubber ball and threw it against the bricks. It flew over the hedges and over the garden, bounced against the bricks and caromed up to the roof then back to me again. A thousand times, a million times I threw my ball against the bricks. The fall passed, then the winter. The years passed. My father died and four years later my mother died. New people moved into the house. Life took me to other neighborhoods, other houses, but when I'm on the West End train and it pulls out of the Seventy-first Street station, I rise from my seat, go to the door and rest my head against the glass. Our house comes into view. I see the back window out which my mother hung our clothes to dry. Then I see our garden and our front door, and I see my father walking around the garden in his white gown on his way up to lunch. "I love you," I whisper, then the train roars on.

CHRISTOPHER
COLUMBUS

———

MY experience at sea is confined to the baths my mother gave me. First she bathed me under the faucet in the kitchen sink. She held me with one arm, and with her other arm she soaped and rinsed me. The forceful spray was my first playmate. My body tingled with delight as the onrushing water blurred my vision and wet me all over. I was confident of my mother's strength, that she wouldn't drop me into the cold sink, and this confidence continued unflagging until my spine grew strong enough to allow me to sit up, first in the kitchen sink, then in the tub where my mother sat and my father planted his feet while taking his shower.

I bathed in the early-morning hours, with sunlight streaming through the kitchen windows. I was never more aware of my nakedness than when sitting in the shallow pool in the kitchen sink, nor was I ever more aware of the casual manner with which my mother treated my nakedness. She soaped and rinsed my penis with the same force she used to scrub my arms and legs and hair. In the bathtub I had difficulty meeting her eyes. I was ashamed of my impatience; I wanted to play with the soap. It was an elusive, funny friend. It was intent on slipping out of my grasp, diving beneath the water, then popping up with a smile at the far end. As I played, my mother rinsed me and I enjoyed the rough treatment. I felt that I was as strong as she but never answered strength with strength, because I trusted her. I enjoyed especially the very last rinse, when she ran her hands up and down my legs, over my penis, up my chest, through my hair and down my back. My body sparkled. I looked at her a lot from the neck down. Water splashed onto her clothes but she paid it no mind. I wondered whether her knees hurt, as she bathed me while kneeling on the cold, hard tiles.

Elsa is afraid of the sea. At the seashore she keeps her clothes on and sits in a chair with her hat on, beneath an umbrella. She has bad legs, varicose veins. I tell her that the salt water is good for them. To get her to go in, I set myself as an example, running across the sand and diving into the crushing surf. I stay in long after my teeth begin to clatter, my lips turn blue. I call to her with a cheerful voice:

"Come on in, honey! The water's great, really warm!"

I toy with her in an attempt to change her humor. Bury her feet in the sand and in the palms of my hands carry water to her and lovingly spread the soothing droplets over her neck, face and arms.

Elsa and I settle onto my Castro for the first installment of "Christopher Columbus," sponsored by IBM. The phone—it's Bernie: "Can you come down, man?"

"'Christopher Columbus' is about to go on."

"I have to talk to you. My life has been threatened."

"Where are ya?"

"The Bagel Nosh."

"Be right there."

Remove the dagger holding open the door, then down one flight and another and another and another. My house is sandwiched between a cab stand and the Fifth Precinct station house. As I hit the air, gas asphyxiates me. I have a coughing fit. The front ends of patrol cars are pulled up onto my sidewalk as if a raid is underway in my house. Hustle up Christopher Street through the proud parade of homosexuals. "Hiya, fellas!" Natalie Sinatra had wanted a girl, and when she had a boy she dressed him in pink anyway. In the whirl of her excitement, in her glorious anticipation she had bought pink dresses, pink booties and a pink coverlet, they were expensive and so she used them, knowing that a Sicilian boy could never become gay. She turned from pink to elegant Little Lord Fauntleroy suits. Her confidence in her son's manliness was unswerving. Cross the island at Sheridan Square where at ten o'clock every evening the papers arrive downtown. A few weeks ago Bernie fulfilled his quota of a daily orgasm by giving me a scurrilous scoop. A Sicilian friend of his named Victor works for Frank Sinatra. They were uptown in a hotel overlooking Central Park, and at three in the morning Frank Sinatra calls Victor and tells him to come up to the suite. Wearing a crimson robe and drunk as a lord, Frank Sinatra greets Victor and ushers him to a long table decorated with flowers. Victor, who had wanted to be a ballplayer, wonders what he's doing there. Bernie would wonder what Victor was doing there. A woman is sitting at the far end of the table. Victor looks at her. He rubs the Italian sand out of his eyes and looks at her again. It's Ava Gardner and she's drunk, too. At this early point I told Bernie I wasn't surprised.

"Frank Sinatra has been a friend and confidant to all his former wives. Furthermore, I don't want to hear another word about it. Frank Sinatra wanted to share the moment, the good feeling all around. This coming December he will be seventy-one years old, Ava Gardner has got to be fifty-eight, and that evening they got together to talk about old times. Frank Sinatra was suddenly struck by Ava Gardner's enduring beauty and he wanted another man, any man, even a failed ballplayer, to witness it. That was all."

There are ten thousand Hunan restaurants in New York City, and beside the one on Christopher Street is the Bagel Nosh. As I open the door I think of that Arab friend of the ancient buffoon, Carnivale, his claim of making love to his woman for two solid hours, eliciting thirty-odd orgasms. Frank Sinatra was married to Ava Gardner for approximately twenty months, that's six hundred days, fourteen thousand four hundred hours—if Ava Gardner had been a damsel in Frederick II's court and had taken up with the passionate Arab for twenty months, she would have enjoyed two hundred and ten thousand orgasms. I see one of them now: Cupid's arrow flies straight and true and pierces Ava Gardner's heart. The pain is fleeting and in its wake she sighs, parts her lips, arches her back. The great expanse of her upper lids, the epicenters of her beauty, close slowly over her vicious narrow slits. She reaches out with her arms and collapses into mine. Bernie is sitting at a round table which has an unimpeded view of the wall phone. He's pale, shaking, has grown thin. He hasn't shaved in weeks. He hasn't been home in weeks. He's unusually incoherent but I make out that he put his finger between a fighting couple and the husband is Sicilian, the very same Sicilian who witnessed Ava Gardner's eternal beauty several weeks ago.

"You have to understand," Bernie says, "that right now Victor is extremely paranoid."

"I understand," I say.

"I'm not used to this."

"You're a Jew, of course you're not used to it. Tell me what happened."

Bernie and the battling couple had been friends for twenty years. When the fighting started, they turned to Bernie for a sympathetic ear. He lent it and invited the Sicilian uptown for a breath of fresh air. At first Victor refused, preferring to stay home and fight it out. Italian boys believe that they have one shot at happiness with a woman. Just as they have one mother, they have one wife and it's forever. The Sicilian belts his wife. She calls Bernie: "He hit me!" The Sicilian takes up Bernie on his invitation. He brings along another woman, a beautiful junkie. They climb up to Bernie's loft bed and fuck, while downstairs in the apartment proper Bernie goes about his merry business while listening rapturously to the illicit lovers' cries of joy.

The wife calls: "My husband there?"

"He just left."

The Sicilian says, "You should have told her I was here." He then asks Bernie to escort the trollop to the airport and put her on a plane to Florida. Bernie does this and when he arrives home, the phone is ringing. The wife again: "Is she in Florida yet?"

"She's on her way. I just got home from the airport."

Confused by all the phone calls, and harboring a secret desire for the beautiful junkie, Bernie writes a letter of explanation and mails it to the Sicilian's house. The wife opens it and relays the contents to her husband.

They make a joint telephone call: "We're going to break your legs!"

Bernie says to me, "They want a sit-down tonight. A guy by the name of Rocco Battaglia is going to be there. I could get killed over this."

"Yes, you could easily get killed."

"Should I go?"

"Let me think. In the meantime call them and say there's no problem and you'll call back in ten minutes to make arrangements."

I think of the wonderful relationship between Frank Sinatra and Sammy Davis, Jr. When Sammy Davis, Jr., fell in love with May Britt and wanted to marry her, he conferred with his friend. Frank Sinatra thought it over: the guy couldn't rent a house in Beverly Hills without my intervention, now what?; an ugly one-eyed black entertainer, together with a fair beauty any man would like to get his hands on; their kids will be dark; Scandinavian women have passing fancies for Sicilians and black guys, too. On the other side: he loves her and she loves him; they're over eighteen; they'll always afford a loaf of bread; Sam has been a gifted entertainer for decades, the rest is nobody's business. Finally, Frank Sinatra said, "Grab yourself some happiness, Sam."

I say to Bernie, "Why did you intervene?"

"I was bored."

"This I can understand. You've broken bread with this couple?"

"Many times."

"Is the wife Italian?"

"She's German."

"Good. Have you ever laid a hand on her or even entertained the idea?"

"Never."

"Did you make love to the beautiful junkie?"

"No."

"What do you feel like doing?"

"If I don't go, I won't sleep tonight."

"Then go. They're not going to hurt a Jew over this. Come, I'll walk you to a cab."

I put him in a cab, then run home. Huffing and puffing, I approach the television and see that Cristoforo Colombo is already in Portugal. I look at my watch: 9:20.

"Where did they begin?" I ask Elsa.

"What do you mean?"

"I missed only twenty minutes and they're already in Portugal. Didn't the program start in Italy, in Genoa, where Colombo was born and spent the first twenty years of his life, where he grew disenchanted with his father's trade of woolen weaver, disgusted over all the sheep being slaughtered, and turned to the natural splendor of the sea?"

"It started here," says Elsa, "in Portugal."

"What are they calling him?"

"Cristoforo Colombo."

"At least that's something."

On September 14, 1451, the child of Domenico Colombo and Susanna Fontanarossa was baptized Cristoforo Colombo in an ancient church located just inside the Porta dell'Olivella, Genoa's eastern gate. Italian cities are surrounded by gates because Italians want visitors to feel at home under the open sky, to feel that when they're in an Italian city it's exactly like being in an Italian home. Colombo's baptismal certificate is in the municipal archive of Genoa, and the ceremony was recorded by the Colombo family's notary, one Vincenzo Failla. He was secretly enamored of Cristoforo's surrogate godmother, Violetta Bianca, a woman of great beauty and property and easy virtue. She loved children, and as she couldn't have any of her own, she volunteered as surrogate for relatives and friends not immediately available. Vincenzo Failla's diary entry of September 14, 1451, reads as follows:

> The priest's scapular was magnificent, creamy white with a giant red cross on the front panel. It appeared to occupy the entire sacristy, infusing it with holiness as it furled and unfurled with

the priest's every movement. Then I saw her—she was holding out the baby called Cristoforo. Over the years her beauty has been maintained, even heightened, by her short-lived passionate affairs. Her eyes sparkled with tears of joy as they consumed the baby, and her full sensuous lips lavished brief sweet kisses all over his body.

And so where do we get the name Christopher Columbus? To rhyme with syllabus? omnibus? bus?

It's the Latinized form of his name, one might say.

Very well, but then why wasn't Amerigo Vespucci Latinized to Amerigo Vespucius? He was a contemporary of Colombo's, a fellow map maker, and he sailed under Colombo during the Third Voyage. We didn't Latinize the Verrazano Narrows Bridge to the Verrazanus Narrows Bridge. Marco Polo had explored the East two hundred years before Colombo—we don't call him Marcus Polus! In French-speaking countries Colombo is called Colomb. The Portuguese call him Colom, and the Spanish and Latin Americans, Cristóbal Colón. But in Italy they don't call Henry Hudson, Enrico Hudsoni! Or Ponce de León, Ponce de Leoni! This question has plagued me since the time of an early marriage. Accompanied by Nicoletta, I had gone up to my alma mater in search of a linguist. We idled on the southwest corner of Broadway and 116th Street, outside Chock Full O'Nuts, where black women wearing white gloves had served me my coffee and crullers. Chock Full has since gone under, putting a lot of black women with clean hands out of work. Out of Chock Full O'Nuts walks my old Italian professor, Dario Flavio. He had been born in Genoa, and his physical type was standard for the boys of Genoa: very short and strong; prematurely balding black hair; bony, square face; not tall with a long face and ruddy complexion and red hair, the way Colombo has been depicted. Professor Flavio had never seen a redhead in Genoa, and he was pale, anemic from all the polenta the Genoans eat, a soupy rice dish smothered with a little tomato sauce. Holding Nicoletta's arm, I went up to Professor Flavio, feeling free to do so because we had talked informally on the street during my college days. It was on the street, for example, that he revealed to me his fascination for Japanese women. We were talking on a corner when an attractive Oriental woman approached then passed us. The professor swooned, rolled his eyes toward the eastern sky. He had once been in love, he told me, with a Japanese sculptress. They had lived together in Kyoto. He dwelled on her memory in silence, leaving me to form my own impressions. He had lived with her for some time. Talk naturally came around to marriage and children. But she was an independent Japanese woman, slightly older, had broken convention for a variety of experience, and on top of everything she didn't fancy having slanty-eyed kids with mushroom noses. In short, she wasn't as taken with Italiana as he was with Japaneseana. It was one thing for an Italian composer like Puccini to write about a love-smitten Japanese wastrel but quite another for a poor Genoan academician to actually settle down with a working Japanese sculptress. Where was he gonna get the dough? Teaching Italian at the Berlitz School? English? The professor looked toward the West, west of Japan and west of Genoa, to New York, where he had a connection at the Casa Italiana of Columbia. He landed a job teaching Italian to undergraduates. His bank account grew. He exercised his sexual preference with the chorus from *The World of Suzie Wong*, which was enjoying a long Broadway run. To keep his intellect in Japan, he pursued a doctorate in Oriental Studies. Often I discovered him in the elevator reading Japanese, then together we walked to class. Sometimes he came upon an Italian word that held a special meaning for him and he wrote it on the blackboard with a flourish of the chalk. Beside it he wrote its equivalent in Japanese, then he pronounced the words with such emphasis, pouncing on certain syllables, his eyes lighting up and his arms gesticulating, that he frightened me, preventing me from learning the word's meaning. It had evoked aspects of his personal life I would never know: nostalgia for his homeland, Italy; his adopted country, Japan; his Japanese woman; his parents, any sisters or brothers. In compensation for my failure to understand, together with my observation of the powerful subjective feelings the word had aroused in him, I ascribed to Professor Flavio total knowledge of the Italian and Japanese cultures, as well as the ways of men.

Nicoletta had been born in Brooklyn, the Brighton Beach section, and she was the first offspring of a talented Barese couple. Now the Baresi of Brooklyn believe that they are markedly different from the Sicilians and Neapolitans of Brooklyn. The Baresi had come to America with skills: they are great stonemasons and carpenters. Instead of settling among the Neapolitans and Sicilians in Bensonhurst and Canarsie, the Baresi settled among the Israelis in Brighton Beach. Their cuisine is different: their sausage, for example, is made of lamb, while the Neapolitan sausage is made of pork. The Neapolitans and Sicilians understand one another in Italian. The Baresi only understand themselves. Ask any Neapolitan or Sicilian, "How do the Baresi talk Italian?"

"Like Chinese," they'll tell you.

The Baresi are also a handsome people: tall, fair, aquiline nose, big beautiful eyes. Nicoletta's big brown eyes opened freely to her temples, and she had high cheekbones. When we strolled through Chinatown, Chinese eyes turned to her. She was often mistaken for Nancy Kwan, the stunning Sino-American actress who co-starred with William Holden in *Love Is a Many-Splendored Thing*. On the corner of Broadway and 116th Street, outside Chock Full O'Nuts, Professor Flavio made the same mistake, because he took an immediate liking to Nicoletta. His body turned slowly until it completely faced hers, leaving me stranded amid the traffic on Broadway.

"I'm an artist," Nicoletta said. "A painter."

"Aha! I'm going to the Yucatán on my sabbatical."

"Oh, how I've always wanted to go to the Yucatán!" Nicoletta had a high-pitched voice that meandered between Brighton Beach, Bari and the Orient. The idea entered the professor's mind to capture it and settle it down in his apartment on Riverside Drive. I believe they went to a museum together. I know Nicoletta saw the inside of his apartment because she described it the way I had once seen it:

"He asks you to take off your shoes. He has a tatami mat on

the floor. The only piece of furniture is a single bed. Nothing on the walls and no books."

I invited Professor Flavio to our home in Brooklyn, and before dinner I asked him about Cristoforo Colombo's name change.

"Ah! The first chronicler of the Voyages was Petrus Martyr, a sophisticated Latinist who held office in the church of Spain. He wrote in Latin. That's about all I know. I would like to ask *you* a question: Do you think Colombo believed to his dying day that America was part of Asia?"

"Well, Italians have been known to be on the stubborn side."

"Do you know what we Genoans say about our native son? That he knew all along he hadn't reached Asia. He wanted to keep the Spanish away and the best way was to tell them they were already there. With their Christian zeal and thirst for gold they weren't prepared to understand the East. The Admiral knew that one day the whole world would be yellow, and so his mission was to hurl a message down through the years which enlightened men could decipher and act upon, look toward the East with tolerance, investigate it, because our survival lies in that direction. Colombo did this by aggravating an error: I reached the East, I reached the East—"

"Dinner's ready!" Nicoletta called from the kitchen.

The professor requested plain white rice. He said he would sleep on the living-room couch. Early the next morning I sauntered into the living room eager to wish him a good day. He was gone. Did anything happen during the night? I investigated this Latinist Petrus Martyr and discovered that he was a fraud and a brigand. He was born in Italy in 1457, on the shores of Lago Maggiore. I couldn't find out his real name. At the age of thirty he migrates to Spain, where he holds office in the Church, like Professor Flavio had said, but he didn't say that Martyr tutored the children of nobles who were in on the latest news and based his chronicles on what they told him. How can we believe the hearsay of a bunch of snot-nose kids? Martyr took holy orders to enjoy ecclesiastical revenues in absentia from a monastery in Jamaica. He lived like a king in Valladolid. But the worst sin of all is that the name "Columbus" does not once appear in Martyr's chronicles. He Latinized the *Spanish* form of Colombo's name!: "A few days afterwards there returned from the western antipodes a certain Christophorus Colonus..." And: "*Colonus ille Novi Orbis repertor*..." I go up to the Casa Italiana with the news.

"Ah, Professor Flavio!" the secretary says. "He's in Japan, teaching Italian decorative arts. Would you like his address?"

I wondered whether he picked up with his sculptress, stopped smoking Kent cigarettes, continued to do fifty push-ups upon awakening. I knew for certain that the women in Japan are Japanese, so there would be no need for the professor to cuckold a Japanese man.

This past year, 1985, ten thousand seafarers representing fifty countries entertained themselves at the International Mariners Club, located on the second floor of the Seamen's Church Institute, which faces Battery Park and New York Harbor. Up until the mid-1800s, our waterfront was dingy and violent. Thieves, crimps and wily innkeepers robbed and shanghaied the vulnerable seamen. Pimps, dance-hall girls and cheap liquor consumed their hard-earned wages. Then in 1888 the Institute was built with funds from the legacy of William H. Vanderbilt, and so now the seafarers were secure inside a bar run by the Episcopal Church and expensive liquor consumed their hard-earned wages. Elsa is the daytime bartender. On her first day a young wise-ass seaman said to her, "Not me, of course, but seamen can be a pretty tough bunch."

"Oh, I'm used to it," Elsa said. "I had seamen in my family." She remembers with special fondness her grandmother's brother, Juan Antonio. He used to bring her dolls and furniture for her dollhouse. Once, he walked off his ship holding a tricycle. He went into a bar and drank all his money. He arrived home drunk and with his feet bleeding. His sister chased him with a broom. Elsa hid under the table. Juan Antonio ran and laughed, and Elsa saw that he had no teeth. He ate steak better than anybody, chewing the bones with his gums. He took her to the bar and sat her up on the counter called *estaño* because it was made of metal. She drank wine and club soda.

A Uruguayan chief mate, Mario Boccancino, lived at the Institute while studying for his captain's license. He and Elsa found that their dialects were similar, and Mario's best friend was Argentinian. As teenagers they had walked over the mountains of Argentina and Chile. They ran out of food, had a lot of fun. Mario was the ugliest man Elsa and I had ever seen. His nose ran and his upper teeth protruded so far that he was unable to close his mouth. Saliva flooded his teeth, his lips. His misshapen body contrasted sharply with his warm and gentle nature and his knowledge of the sea which was a fascinating mystery to us. He became our friend. He had a wife and two sons in Montevideo. She had been unable to conceive for many years. Mario carried her medical records to gynecologists around the world, and they told him it was hopeless. But then she bore a son and then a second son. Mario ascribed it to a miracle. Elsa and I ascribed it to fucking around in her mountaintop village while Mario was at sea. We invited him over for dinner, and he reciprocated by taking us to the Gaucho on MacDougal Street. He was so lost on land that he didn't know enough to leave a tip. Elsa and I returned the next day and tipped the waiters. Her shift ends at eight o'clock and I go to pick her up. I take the IRT to South Ferry. The train pulls in to the station at a sharp angle. Passengers press against the doors. On my first trip I wondered where they were so eager to go. The doors open after a steel grid bridges the large gap between the platform and the train. Passengers push and run and hurtle up the stairs to make the next ferry to Staten Island. Mario couldn't get over the steel grid, he'd hover above it shaking his head as it extended from the platform proper, providing safe passage. This is the man who can tell me about the sea, I said to myself. I asked him if the *Titanic* could have been saved and what the chances are nowadays of surviving in a lifeboat. This is some of what he told me one night at the bar:

"I love the sea, I really love the sea. My home was no more than two hundred feet from the sea, and when I was three years old my father brought me down to the fishing boats. I have always loved the sea. I cannot live in the mountains. I love the mountains, they're beautiful, but I cannot see the sea. Every sunrise, every sunset, every storm is different. You learn to watch the creation around you. You learn that the sea is something you cannot master, cannot dominate. You learn that we are nothing here, we are just dust here. I love ships. For me they are not cold pieces of steel. They have a soul, they have life. Last year I brought a ship to Taiwan, to a port called Kaohsiung. I saw many ships being scrapped, among them the *Patucca* and the *Tunis*, small banana boats about one thousand tons. They were beautiful ships. I enjoyed them. We used to run around the coast of California, San Pedro, down to Panama. They were completely abandoned, dirty, half scrapped. It was like seeing the corpse of a very dear person. I suffered when I was walking on deck and the ship was dead: the engines were stopped for good, the fire boilers were shut off for good, we had no generator. I suffered because any kind of ship—passenger, tanker, old, new, big, small—a ship has a soul, something that lives.

"As long as you stay on the ship, you belong to the crew. You are part of the ship's company. Every man will do his best for you. Not too long ago I was on a ship that sank. I'm alive today because one man gave me his life jacket and pushed me over the side. We weren't good friends—just good morning, good evening. He was a member of the Black Gang, a member of the engine room. He said to me, 'You go, you are a young man. I am old, I have nothing to live for. Just keep going.' I refused and tried to push him. He was a hundred times more powerful than me. He put his life jacket on me and threw me over the side. We lost nine men. I was obliged to write four letters for the members of my watch. I went to the homes of these men to tell directly to their wives and parents that they had lost their men. If you are a loyal seaman, if you are an officer, if you love your profession, you have a moral responsibility for the men in your watch. Never mind who assigned them, never mind who the men are, they are your men, your gang, and you must look after them.

"You ask me about the possibility of surviving in a lifeboat. Forget it, there's none. When a ship is listing more than fifteen degrees, you cannot put a lifeboat down on the water. Ships sink most of the time during the night, in rough weather, in a rough sea, and they sink very fast. You have first-class equipment, well designed, but there's a human factor—shock! You don't survive. You have the will to live, you live until you see another ship or a plane coming to help you. The moment help reaches you, you die. When my ship sank, I floated around holding a board. I was able to swim, I wasn't tired, but when they pulled me out of the water, I passed out. It took twenty days in the hospital to come back. The doctors said they didn't expect me to live. Why? I don't know. We used to say, 'The person is dead on the water even if he's still alive.' When I was in the Navy, I went out for survivors. I had this guy right there, in my hand, and he died.

"If there's a fire aboard a supertanker, that finishes it for the crew. For one reason—the tanker is a bomb. They talk about special rafts, special maneuverings—forget it. You can float in the water twenty-four hours, maybe forty-eight hours, but that's the end of your time. Never mind if you are close to the coast, never mind if you are at a transit point—if you are floating on the sea, nobody can see you. If you are in bright orange—Indian orange, they call it—they say they can see you from a long distance—bullshit! You're a small thing in a big ocean. No ship can see a human head over two hundred and fifty feet. I'm talking about very calm weather and a very calm sea. If somebody tells you you have special flares, special signals—forget it, you're finished. Nowadays there are no sails on lifeboats. You have a small motor and enough food for a few days. You stay around the area where your ship sank, wishing that somebody is coming to look for you. You have a radio but it's no good over five hundred miles, and maybe it's no fucking good at all. I was in a tanker and the whole port side blew up, from tanker number five to tanker number fourteen. We had fires all around. We spent two days fighting for the ship. The whole seamen's community says, 'Never abandon ship. Try to save the ship because it's the only way to reach home again.' And that's a big, big truth, man."

COUNT
PICCOLIMANI

A MAJOR distributor of Italian records, calendars, newspapers, magazines and books is a firm universally known
as Xpress-m-pex. Its base of operations is in Long Island
City, and the chief operating officer is an émigré from Florence,
Francesco Piccolimani, which translated resembles an Indian name,
Frank Small Hands. Long Island City is deceiving in that it is not
on Long Island nor is it a city. I have never been there but I sense
it is near me, a short car or boat ride away. My impression of
Long Island City is that it is a sprawling complex of low-looming
warehouses set upon a marsh of snapping crabs and croaking
toads. In the wintertime the warehousemen freeze. Three sides
jut upon Brooklyn, Queens and Long Island, and the fourth side
juts upon a narrow inlet of the Hudson River, which is only three
blocks away from me. Industrial fog blankets Long Island City
and so it cannot be seen from the opposite shores or from a
moving train. Mr. Piccolimani's telephone voice pierces the fog
and arrives in my ear with a soft resonance, calm, reassuring and
with a genuine Italian accent. I had called him for a copy of
Pavese's diary, The Moon and the Bonfires.

"We have it in Italian," Mr. Piccolimani told me.

"All the better," I said. "Please send it straightaway," and in three days I had my book.

A week later I called Mr. Piccolimani again, this time with the intention of meeting him. Over espressos in a café on the earth's crust we would get to know one another like two truly urban individuals, face to face pool our vast knowledge.

"I do come to the city from time to time," Mr. Piccolimani said.

"I'm happy to hear that," I said, then I said, "Mr. Piccolimani, what's a Florentine of your stature doing in Long Island City?"

"I'm perfectly happy here," he responded.

"Do you know you have royal blood in you?"

"Pardon?"

"You come from Florence, correct?"

"Yes..."

"Your cognomen is Piccolimani?"

"That's right."

"How many Piccolimanis from Florence can there be? You've all got to be one tribe."

"Funny thing," he said, "the last time I looked in a Florentine phone book, there were only two of us."

"There you go. Now listen to this: you're a descendant of a bona fide count, Conte Piccolimani, who as the Florentine representative of the Reverend Fathers of the Holy Land helped Alexandre Dumas sail into Sicily with Garibaldi and the One Thousand! Do you want to hear about it?"

"I'm interested," said Mr. Piccolimani.

Dumas and Garibaldi, I begin, didn't meet in the flesh until 1860, in Torino. They fell into one another's arms, their beards intermingling, one black and one reddish-brown, and Garibaldi said to Dumas, "You are elemental, truly a force of nature."

"And you, my General," Dumas said, "by offering your sword and your blood to the people's struggle against tyranny, are a hero."

But they had been spiritual brothers since the 1840s, sharing, as Dumas said, "the cult of liberty." Both men hated oppression, cruelty, stagnation. In 1847, mounted on his white stallion, brandishing his saber, Garibaldi was fighting in the wilderness of Uruguay against the Argentine despot, Rosas. By 1847, sitting in a quiet garret in Paris, Dumas had written *Les Trois Mousquetaires* and *Monte Cristo*. The books' distributor had stables of the swiftest horses, miles of trains, a fleet of packet ships. Two crossed the ocean to the Americas. In the port of Montevideo, Garibaldi had to borrow his copies. Though he was a General with plenary powers, Garibaldi refused money and land, partly as an example of Republican virtue and partly to leave himself morally free to return at a moment's notice to his homeland. His habit of retiring at sundown and rising with the first light stemmed from his years in South America, twelve in all, when he was so poor he couldn't afford candles. His soldiers brought him candles and it was by candlelight that he read Dumas's romances.

Afterwards, he said to his wife, "I have to meet this guy."

At the same time, dispatches of Garibaldi's real-life exploits reached Dumas and he said to himself, "I have to write about this guy." In a fortnight he wrote *Le Mois*, recording with admiration Garibaldi's deeds in Montevideo and also divining his noble character perfectly.

Garibaldi, however, had no qualms about earning a few pesos by writing. In fact, he would spend his waning years writing novels on his island of Caprera. In Montevideo he borrowed pen, ink and parchment and began writing his memoirs. One night his wife heard him pacing the floor, breathing heavily. She turned over and saw her husband running his fingers through his hair.

"What is it, Peppino?"

"This isn't as easy as I had thought." He held up his hands in front of his eyes. "I know what's in my heart and in my mind but these hands go every which way and either too fast or too slow."

"Why don't you ask Dumas to help you?" Anita Riberas ventured.

"Great idea," and Garibaldi sent his hodgepodge of notes to Dumas, who for the next twelve years occupied himself with writing Garibaldi's *Mémoires*.

In 1860, Garibaldi returned to Italy for the final thrust at unification, the invasion of Sicily. He met with Dumas in Torino and gave him more manuscript. Garibaldi left raw manuscript in various ports with the note attached: "Rally where you hear my guns!" This cry inspired Dumas to action. He joined the student riots in Paris, single-handedly captured the powder magazine at Soissons, a feat D'Artagnan would have been proud of. The captain of the King's guard presents his report.

"Who's responsible!" bellows the King.

"The students of the Sorbonne, sire."

"I can't arrest the whole school! Didn't you single out anybody?"

"There was one Negro—"

"Idiot! There are no Negroes in the Sorbonne! It's that Dumas again—bring him to me!"

Manacled, Dumas is led into the throne room.

"What's wrong with you, Dumas?"

Dumas answers, "As the Abbé Faria said in *Monte Cristo*: 'The young are not traitors,' and so when the students asked for my help, I helped. I guess I belong to that class of imbeciles which does not know how to refuse."

"Imbecile you are!" Suddenly, the King's stern visage melted to a smile and he spread his arms. "But I love you, come here."

Dumas's hands were freed and he stepped up to the throne and surrendered his body to the King's firm, warm grasp. The King guided the weary writer's head onto his massive shoulder, stroked his hair, sighed and said dreamily, "Go away a while and let the clouds roll by."

"Where shall I go?"

"Try Switzerland. The air is brisk and clean, and you're just getting over the cholera."

"No," said Dumas, "Garibaldi is in Genoa preparing to invade Sicily. I'll sail with him and settle *une affaire de famille*."

"*Une affaire de famille?*"

"Sire, I'm going to tell you something nobody knows: I'm known as Dumas Père, my son the dramatist is known as Dumas Fils, but there's also a Dumas Grandpère, my father, who was a valiant General—Dumas le Tigre, we called him—and he died like a dog in a loathsome prison in Naples, poisoned by that Bourbon despot, King Ferdinand."

"I thought your father and Ferdinand were friends? In fact, didn't your father live in the palace?"

"For a while, when he was young, and when he was younger still he and his friend Ferdinand hunted together and raced their steeds and flew their falcons. Then everything changed. Maybe Ferdinand didn't expect his friend to marry an Abyssinian woman who in addition to being black was proud and industrious. She cleaned our rooms and the King's chambers, too, with never a word, as she detested his wife's soft hands. The King grew to despise her and he showed his hatred by remonstrating against my father, turning his back on him, dismissing him with a wave of his royal arm when my father complained about his depleted armies. I was too young to really know what came between them, but I remember clearly the balls we used to have. Every week there was a ball, and the frivolity carried to my bed and awakened me. I could hear the laughter, especially the women's, and I liked to get up and walk right into the middle of the banquet hall. My mother played the harp and everybody was dancing. A resplendent white light emanating from my sleepiness and my desire to be part of the happy throng shone on each and every face. It was like seeing a smile for the first time, a mouth moving in incessant chatter for the first time. I saw pure adult fun: women laughing as they chased their men with open wine bottles, trying to spray them; the men shielding their heads, feigning helplessness—"

The King interrupted, "I'd like to help you sail with Garibaldi. How much do you need?"

"But in the end the revolution will depose you, too."

"There are many kings but only one Dumas and one Garibaldi."

"Forty thousand francs, including *munitions de guerre.*"

"Done! Now fly!"

Dumas knew that Sicily was a land of poetry. The revolution would be carried out amid music, song and laughter, with much dancing, and so as his *munitions de guerre* he bought cases of champagne, Bengal lights and Catherine wheels. He recruited a band of joyous young men and a charming woman attired as a midshipman. All that remained was a ship. Dumas reads in a book of About's that small vessels built in Greece are half the price and more suitable for navigating the Mediterranean than any vessel he could buy in France. He mounts his charger and becomes one with it; like the shadow of a bird of prey moving over the earth, they descend the coast of France, through the port of Nizza, where Garibaldi was born. During Garibaldi's lifetime Nizza was annexed to France and changed to Nice. Fanatic Garibaldians say that God forced the annexation so as to avoid confusion between the Nazarene and the Nizzan. Garibaldi was born during a raging storm at sea, and his birthplace is marked by a stake draped with a red shirt stained with blood. A kepi with an ostrich feather and six cavalry pistols and a naked saber also adorn the stake. The French preserve this landmark as a reminder that no matter how hard one fights for his homeland, he's still capable of losing it. Arriving in Naples, Garibaldi turns east, slicing across the peninsula, and at Bari takes the ferry to Greece, to the island of Milo. The horse stomps on the wet wooden deck, rears and cries, eager to carry his master to his destination. As the ferry maneuvers into the slip, Dumas sees M. Rally, the Bavarian consul, waving and smiling. Standing beside him proud as a peacock is Paghaïda, the finest shipbuilder of Greece. On the beach of stones white as stars the three men embrace.

"When can you have her for me, Paghaïda?"

"Twenty-five days."

"Cholera slows the progress of revolution, but not by that much."

"Fifteen days."

"How much?"

"Seventeen thousand francs."

"Deal. I'll be waiting in Marseilles."

Lent comes and goes, delaying construction. War against Austria breaks out and instead of going to work Paghaïda goes to the parliament house for news. On the thirtieth day, the *Monte Cristo* finally built, Dumas is informed that a ship built in a Greek shipyard cannot become the property of a Frenchman. But he hits on the idea of M. Rally taking the vessel in his name, declaring he received all the rent in advance, then leasing the vessel back to Dumas for ninety-nine years. By 1959 Garibaldi should have unified Italy. M. Rally agrees, and after a voyage of twenty-five days Paghaïda and his crew of Greek sailors weigh anchor in the harbor of Marseilles.

Dumas's doctor, Grégoire, was also a master sailor, and the two men ride in a coach-and-four down to the harbor. "So," Dumas says, "we have ourselves a direct descendant of one of the thousand ships which brought the Greeks to the siege of Troy and took ten years to bring Ulysses from Pergamus to Ithaca. I'm excited about it, Grégoire."

"You have every right to be," says Grégoire.

They climb aboard. As Grégoire inspects the ship, Dumas trails behind, watching every expression, every gesture.

"Watertight deck, good; dining room hung with tapestry, fancy; sitting room painted in the Pompeian style, appropriate; copper bottom, good, good—oops, she's ballasted with stones..."

"Yeah, so—ballasted with stones?"

"With a shifting ballast the first tempest'll make her founder. You need a metal ballast."

"You mean those Greek swine charged me four hundred francs for stones?"

"I'll ballast it for you," said Grégoire. "Other than that you have yourself a charming goélette, graceful in her slim lines—all in all a fine seabird. A pity she has to fly the Greek flag."

"Isn't it?"

"Why don't you nationalize her under the pennon of France?"

"How do I do that?"

"Pay ten percent of the purchase price to the Ministry of Marine."

Dumas decides to cut some red tape by appealing to an influential friend, the witty, erudite Abbé Coquereau. They had attended in Amsterdam the coronation of the King of Holland. At the funeral of the Duc d'Orléans, Dumas had wept in the Abbé's arms. Dumas goes directly to the rectory. The Abbé trundles downstairs red-faced and bloated, banging against the walls. Dumas tells him the object of his visit. The Abbé responds:

"If only you had come eight days sooner, my son. At the

outbreak of the Crimean War, France authorized the naturalization of foreign vessels to facilitate the transport of foreign ships. Eight days ago a law was passed putting an end to the facility."

"*Sacre bleu!*"

"Don't lose heart. Let's have a drink and talk it over."

At the Caffè Momus, over cognac, the Abbé says, "You have the Grand Cross of Jerusalem, adopt its flag."

Dumas raises his head from his arms. "Yes... the flag of Jerusalem... the flag of pilgrims... it bears the red cross, that of the Tancreds and Godefroy de Bouillon... its device is that of our old chevaliers: *Dieu le veult*... the flag is neutral, respected by all nations under the direct protection of France and, in consequence, upheld by French consuls—Abbé, how do I get the authorization to navigate under the flag of Jerusalem?"

"Well, France used to give the authorizations, but during recent years the grants were abused, so the government divested itself of the right and left its exercise entirely to the Reverend Fathers of the Holy Land. They have a representative in Florence."

"I'm sure to find the man I want in Florence?"

"He never leaves the place."

"And his name is—"

"Conte Piccolimani. Let me know how it works out."

Aboard the *Capitole* Dumas sails to Leghorn, known today as Livorno. From Leghorn to Florence is a three-hour ride by coach. Dumas settles into his hotel, and an hour later Conte Piccolimani sweeps into the courtyard, his gait quick and sure, his high shiny boots resounding on the flagstones. His sword jangles at his left side. His perennial tan contrasts sharply with the silver hair framing his forehead. His pleated black cloak unfurls behind him, brushing against the first of two servants carrying ship lamps and a marble table.

Dumas had been waiting on the mezzanine. He approaches the Count with trepidation, holding out the few lines the Abbé had written on his behalf. Dumas opens his dry mouth to speak but the Count stops him, placing a finger across his lips—

"Sh-h-h, I know everything, and I've spoken to Garibaldi and he knows everything, the innumerable unforeseen obstacles. He's waiting for you in Genoa. Give me two hundred and fifty francs and you have a provisional authorization. I'll obtain the ratification of the Reverend Fathers later on. Meanwhile, you're free to sail. I brought you three splendid ship lamps and a marble table. Two lamps for your rigging, one for the main mast. The table goes far better on your yacht than in my house. Oh, and my children gave me this to give to you, a miniature tricolor—they'd like you to tie it to the main mast."

The flag was a toy really. The pole about a foot long and tied to it with golden thread the pennon of thin, transparent silk eight inches wide and five inches deep. The adjacent blocks of red, white and green were faded yet solid, clear.

"How can I repay you?" Dumas said.

Conte Piccolimani said, "You have made my wife cry and you have made me laugh. Laughter and tears come directly from God." Then the Count freed his powerful left arm from deep inside his cloak and tapped Dumas on the cheek. "Say a kind word about me in one of your books so that my children and their children will be proud."

The next morning, at dawn, the patent awaited Dumas at the port of Livorno. He sailed back to Marseilles and went directly to the Abbé. He was asleep but his *valet de chambre* awakened him, having once seen him and Dumas kiss.

"Well, Dumas, are you satisfied with Piccolimani?"

"Enchanted," Dumas replied.

GIUSEPPE GARIBALDI

L AST night a diffused Uragano Roberto, or Hurricane Bob, swept over the city bringing mild winds and intermittent showers. I wasn't pleasantly awakened by thunderclaps and flashes of lightning, and I awoke this morning shaking and sweating from the terrible fear that Joe DiMaggio had the Kennedy brothers killed for fucking around with Marilyn Monroe. I lay in bed a while sick to my stomach, but then I got up and walked under the light rain to visit with Garibaldi in Washington Square Park. A monument to the General stands at the eastern end, where when the sun is shining the disenfranchised do pirouettes on their roller skates. As I approach the park from the west, I see that the statue is hidden behind the lush foliage of trees. The park is empty except for two policemen standing under a tree and they watch me as I gaze up at the statue, then walk around and around. Garibaldi wears the outfit he made famous in South America, the red shirt and white poncho, and so where is his black felt hat with two ostrich feathers? Garibaldi had to clothe his newly formed Italian Legion in Montevideo. A mercantile house offered to sell to the government at reduced prices woolen shirts intended for the workers at the *Saladeros* in Buenos Aires, the great slaughtering and salting markets for cattle. The shirts were heavy, warm, and their red color disguised the blood pumping forth from the cattle. The Buenos Aires port was blockaded, the shirts were useless, and so now they could disguise Garibaldi's blood and his Legion's.

Garibaldi wears a skullcap and clustered beneath it is his full mane of golden brown hair. He stands at about his correct height, 5'6". His broad shoulders together with his square chest lend a sense of power to his body. His heavy mustache and reddish-brown beard cover half his face, turned red by the sun. His nose is straight, with a broad root, and is in line with his forehead high and wide as an expanse of beach. His weight shifts to his right side, as he's about to draw his saber. His right hand clasps the handle, half the blade is free of its sheath. In South America the warfare was amphibious, fought at sea and on horseback. Garibaldi's cavalry composed the larger part of his guerrilla band. The enemy always had superior numbers, and so after surprise attacks at night, Garibaldi and his skilled horsemen of gauchos and half-breeds and freed Negro horsebreakers had to disappear into the space of the prairies and into dense tropical forests. I understand the difficulties of sculpting a ship, but where is Garibaldi's white stallion, his lance, his cavalry pistols, his *boleadoras*? The weapon consists of three round heavy stones, each the size of a large orange, covered with leather and attached to three plaited thongs which diverge and form a center, each thong being five feet long. With erect crest and angry eye the ostrich flew from the chasing band. A gaucho broke from the phalanx whirling his *boleadoras* with grace and dexterity and then he hurled it around the legs of the half-running, half-flying bird. He came down, rolling, fluttering, panting. The company stripped him of his feathers and stuck them in their girdles.

When Garibaldi grew excited his eyes turned black—now they shoot flames as they espy the enemy approaching from the right flank, over toward the arch designed by Stanford White. I linger in the park, thinking...

Garibaldi arrived in New York in July of 1850 aboard the packet ship *Waterloo*. He could have come in the winter of '49 but there hadn't been a vacancy in Liverpool on either a steamer or a sailing vessel, as Europeans were making a mad dash for Sutter's Mill in California in search of gold. The *Waterloo* docked beside the Quarantine Building on Staten Island, and a welcoming ceremony took place on the afterdeck before Garibaldi was carried off on a sofa. He had suffered a severe attack of rheumatism which affected his right arm and legs. He lay sprawled on the red-velvet, tufted sofa and tried to get up, repeatedly lifting his legs and flailing his arms. He winced with pain. His small eyes, always in the shadows of his prominent, arched brows, darted here and there, and beads of sweat covered his brow despite the cool northerly breeze. The great love of his life, Anita Riberas, had recently died and she had been pregnant; their three little children were with his mother in Nizza; and the Roman Republic had fallen to the combined forces of France, Spain and the Neapolitan Kingdom. He hadn't wanted to come to America in the first place. He had sought exile in Tunis but the Bey's government refused him, acting on pressure from France, which had commercial interests in Tunis.

Major Bova settled him. The Major had lost an arm in the fighting in Rome and Garibaldi had brought him along, fearing that a one-armed soldier couldn't find work in Europe. Major Bova said tenderly, "The Italian Committee of New York has come to welcome you. They're waiting on the afterdeck."

"All right. Take me there, but let's make it short."

Slowly, carefully, four sailors carried the sofa to the afterdeck and set it down ten feet from the cluster of men that comprised the Italian Committee, which also included prominent citizens such as Messrs. Hyatt and Stetson. Among the Committee was General Avezzana, who had also fought in Rome and had escaped under the name of Everett; Antonio Meucci, who some Italians claim invented the telephone before Alexander Graham Bell; and Pietro Moresti, who in his fiery youth had been a member of the dreaded revolutionary society the Carbonari. Composed of idealistic students and hardened criminals, the Carbonari's mission had been to overthrow despotic kings and establish egalitarian republics. The method was assassination. The society was called Carbonari because members painted their faces black so that they could assassinate the kings in broad daylight. The Carbonari also grew beards and mustaches and smoked smelly cigars. There was no mistaking them, and in 1814 Pietro Moresti was captured and imprisoned in a dungeon of the Spielberg in Moravia.

Moresti stepped forward and presented the American flag to Major Bova. In turn Garibaldi presented the tricolor to the Committee. They stood at attention as Moresti said with pride, "We Italians are now all brethren, from the Alps to the Rockies."

Messrs. Hyatt and Stetson stepped forward. Hyatt said, extending his arms, "It would be an honor to receive you and the Major in my hotel."

Garibaldi graciously refused.

Stetson, wearing a devilish smile, solicited an endorsement for a new line of hats, knowing that Garibaldi loved hats and wore a wide assortment. "We could do any type you like," said Stetson, "fez, kepi, narrow-brimmed peaked, with the black ostrich feather."

Garibaldi threw back his head and laughed. He then greeted the publisher Walter Francks with a courteous nod and firm handshake. Francks said, "It would be a privilege to publish biographical essays of your comrades-at-arms."

"Oh, I'm not a writer," said Garibaldi.

"You are a poet," Francks said.

Garibaldi looked away, then with tears in his eyes and a tremulous voice said, "If the test of being a poet is to meditate amid bullets on filial tenderness and the memories of childhood or early love, without a thought that your dreams may be rudely shattered by getting your head broken or your arm carried away —then, yes, I am a poet."

He had seen her through his telescope from the deck of the topsail schooner *Itaparica* as it rode the lagoon outside the town of Laguna in the small Brazilian province of Rio Grande do Sul. He paced the deck, grieving not so much over the deaths of his best men one week before, but over the oblivion that soon overtakes the memory of the brave. They had gone down in a tempest despite his efforts to save them, without, in the words of Ugo Foscolo, "a stone to mark their bones from the unnumbered bones which o'er the fields and waves are sown by death." He was a powerful swimmer. As a boy he used to steal out of the house at night and swim among the ships in the harbor. His father, Domenico, a merchant captain, knew the perils of the sea and advised his son to become a doctor, lawyer or priest, especially after observing that the boy often stared dreamily into space and read for hours under an olive tree. When Peppino insisted on talking to the sailors, climbing the shrouds of the ships and gliding along the ropes, trimming the sails and tying knots and coaxing the fishermen into taking him oyster trolling and to the sardine hauls—Domenico's counsel turned to outright irritation and he had the priests scour the shoreline with their dry eyes. On these days Garibaldi roamed truant in the hills behind Nizza, where he learned to love nature and animals. He lay supine in the grass, watching for wounded grasshoppers. During his lifetime he saved sixteen people from drowning. When he was eight years old he saw a woman washing her clothes in a deep, wide ditch. She fell in, pinioning her head beneath the pool. Encumbered by his game pouch, the boy nevertheless lifted her head gently and eased her over onto his lap. During his first days in Rio de Janeiro, where he had exiled himself following an abortive attempt to rouse to revolution the Royal fleet in Genoa, Garibaldi saved a Negro slave from drowning. As the youthful exile walked past the three-story white granite houses, he heard the crackling of whips and cries of pain. In Rio de Janeiro of 1832 slaves were not allowed to wear shoes or ride in the mule-drawn buses, and when they died their bodies were tossed into a pit. While strolling along the waterfront he saw a slave fall into the sea. Garibaldi saved him. The slave was a giant of a man, Santos was his name, and with boiling eyes he said to Garibaldi, "I wish to join you. I can break horses and I know the land."

Garibaldi nodded and then Santos, wearing a blue poncho, accompanied him on a ride across the vast undulating plains, a landscape new to the European, accustomed from childhood to houses and hedges and other labors of man's hands covering every inch of ground. Matching stride for stride, they rode through the woods along the banks of the rivers and the sides of the arroyos, through herds of antelopes and cattle and ostriches.

Santos pulls up, pointing, "There he is, the stallion of the Pampas!"

What a handsome fellow! His lips had never winced at the iron bit. His glossy back, never crossed by a rider, shined like a diamond in the sun. His flowing, uncombed mane floated over his flanks as he assembled with pride the scattered mares, then they outran the wind.

Now Santos was dead. He had been aboard the *Rio Pardo* a week before when it encountered a *pampero*, the violent hurricane that arises so suddenly off the coast of South America that coast dwellers have no time to gather their children, secure their houses, escape inland. One moment the sun is shining and the sky is blue and the next moment the sky, air and sea are a black fizz of gale-force winds, driving rain, thirty-foot waves. They consume the beaches and flatten the houses and trees, which at first resist by bending in the shape of a bow. Garibaldi close-reefed his sails and held his course, but then the ship struck a strip of bayberry-covered sand. The bow held in the sand while the stern swung around broadside to the waves. The ship was laden with food supplies and equipment. The equipment smashed through the bottom. Some of the thirty men aboard were landsmen going to take part in the operations at Laguna. They were in the hold, sick. Santos was among them, and the howling wind drowned out Garibaldi's cry, "Cut away!" as the main and mizzen masts went down. The landsmen made their way to the deck, and Garibaldi commanded, "Each of you seize a plank and swim with a sailor!" A massive wave crashed against the forecastle, and the forecastle came down. "Abandon ship!" One by one the men dove into the raging sea, holding their planks. Garibaldi seized a plank and dove in, and he was making progress against the waves toward the shore when he heard "*Diablo!*" It was Santos and he was trying to free himself from his coat, which had caught on the deck. Garibaldi swam to him, drawing his knife.

"Be calm. I've got you. Hold on to the plank as I swim."

He had the coat almost cut away. The knife broke and just then a wave carried him under. He fought against it with all his strength, but when he came up Santos was gone.

Of his thirty men, fourteen survived, and the survivors were welcomed by the republicans of Laguna. Garibaldi was given the captured fleet of the Brazilian imperialists to command, and now he paced the deck of the *Itaparica* feeling utterly isolated, alone in the world. He needed a human heart to love him, one he could keep near him always. Unless he found one immediately, his life would be intolerable. By chance he cast his eyes toward the houses of the Barra, the hill behind Laguna. It was a beautiful day, the sky and sea the same dark blue. Through his telescope he espied a woman: tall, with long, protruding breasts, thick flowing black hair. He ordered a boat to be got out. He landed and made for the houses he had seen from the deck. He had just given up hope of seeing her again when he met an old man whose acquaintance he had made. He invited Garibaldi for coffee in his house. The first person who met his eyes was the woman he had seen through his telescope. They remained enraptured, silent, gazing at one another like two people who had met before and seek in each other's face something which makes it easier to recall the forgotten past. The old man left, then Garibaldi greeted the woman: *"Tu devi esser mia."*

"What insolence! Why must I be yours when my country is filled with tough hombres! I horsewhipped a man who dared to touch me! What makes you so tough?"

Garibaldi said, "I came to your country with a knowledge of the sea. During the blockade of Montevideo by Brazil, the Uruguayan navy consisted of one cutter, a fishing boat really. I went into a tavern and enlisted twenty sailors. We escaped through the enemy lines and made for a small bay, where I weighed anchor. A big schooner of twelve guns followed us and remained at the entrance of the bay. Night fell and in small boats we boarded the schooner, and after a tough fight we defeated the enemy. The Uruguayan navy had her first fighting vessel. There was nothing to it."

Anita Riberas said, "The man who brought you here is my father, and he has betrothed me to another."

"Who is this other?" Garibaldi inquired. "And where is he now?"

"He's a fisherman and he's out fishing."

Garibaldi raised his brows and smiled. "I'd like that coffee now."

She turned toward the stove and threw back her shoulders all in one fluid motion. Her breasts lifted and extended to their full thickness and length. Their spectacular profile remained in Garibaldi's vision for what appeared like an eternity, and he interpreted her sudden inappropriate action as a way of telling him that for reasons known only to herself she liked him, was proud of the splendor of her breasts and had offered them as a means of bridging idle talk and leisure discoveries. The once-in-a-lifetime invitation lasted a split second, as the woman was on the move, and so Garibaldi decided to act inappropriately and within the time frame of her creation, immediately and over all her objections. By the time Anita Riberas reached the coffee urn she was in his arms, and she did not resist his picking her up and carrying her off.

The ceremony on the afterdeck of the *Waterloo* ended with the Italian Guard playing the American and Italian anthems, then the guard, followed by the Italian Committee, marched off the ship. But then a tall, gangling man, stooped over and with redness under his eyes, approached Garibaldi and tapped him on the shoulder as he was being carried into the Quarantine Building. The man said, "I'm Margaret Fuller Ossoli's brother, Eugene."

Snapping his suspenders, Horace Greeley had told his great correspondent, Margaret Fuller, "Go to Italy, young woman!" not thinking she would marry an Italian count in secret and run a hospital during the siege of Rome.

"Put me down!" Garibaldi roared, then he said to Eugene Fuller, "Your sister spoke highly of you. Tell me, any news from her?"

"She died in a hurricane off Fire Island three weeks ago. Her husband and little Angiolino, too. They were in sight of land but no help came. We haven't found the bodies, nor the journal she kept of the war in Rome. Thoreau searched the beach for it."

"I'm so sorry. Your sister was one of the bravest women I ever met. She took such pleasure in caring for the wounded, their gunshot wounds, their fever. She gave them books and flowers and read to them. When they got better, she walked with them— one on crutches, one in a sling—through the beautiful gardens of the Quirinal. I often sat with her in the Pope's pavilion. Young soldiers sat at her feet, listening to her every word. I remember— the sun was going down over Monte Mario and we could see the white tents of the French light cavalry gleaming among the trees. Now and then we heard the cannonade. My men revered her. They acted brave in her company. They kissed their bones as they were extracted from their arms and hung the bones around their necks as mementos. One of my soldiers, crippled for life, saw her crying. He clasped her hand and said, '*Cara donna*, think only that I can wear my uniform with the holes where the bullets went through as a memory.'

"I saw her as I was leaving Rome for the hills. She had come down to the Corso with some friends, but I picked her out by her fine, soft-spun blond hair and the regal set of her head. She squinted to see sharply my lancers galloping in full career. She followed us to the Porta San Giovanni. I turned and waved to her. She was waving, smiling, her large blue-gray eyes shining."

Three years before, in 1847, Margaret Fuller had sent a dispatch from Rome to her editor at the New York *Herald*, Horace Greeley:

"At night the Corso was illuminated, and many thousands passed through it in a torch-lit procession on their way to the Quirinal to thank the Pope."

Greeley read the dispatch during a general meeting of citizens called for the purpose of giving public expression to Pope Pius IX's recent actions of allying the Papacy with liberal Europe. The meeting took place on the evening of November 29 at the Broadway Tabernacle, the largest building in New York City at that time. For numbers, two thousand, good feeling all around and enthusiasm for a favorable turning point in Italian politics, the gathering had not been surpassed in the short history of New York. Mayor William Brady got up and expressed the hopes and wishes of the American people for the success of His Holiness. "Broad as the ocean which separates us from his sunny land," the Mayor said, "the voice of Americans will reach its remotest shores."

Former President Van Buren sent a letter: "I ardently pray that Italy, twice the master of the world—once in arms and once in arts and literature—will conduct herself in her great struggles as to merit the greatest of all subliminary blessings."

There was a blizzard that November evening, and a few passersby, hearing the cheers and applause, ducked into the great hall for refuge. One was a young man around forty, and his cheeks were flushed and his mushroom nose was red and so much snow was piled on the brim of his hat and the shoulders of his coat that one member of the door committee said to another, "He must have been walking around a long time."

"I have," said the young man, surprising the committee members. "There's more frost and snow out there than since the time of the Pilgrims. Phew!" And he rubbed his hands together and shook the snow from his hat and coat. "What's going on?" he directed to the observant committeeman.

"We're celebrating the liberal measures adopted by the new Pope."

"What did he do?"

"He abolished the secret tribunal for political offenders. Issued a decree of universal amnesty for all political prisoners. Garibaldi is leaving South America and returning to Italy. The Pope also granted freedom of the press—"

"Popes are always doing something..."

"You have to understand, young man, that from the fifth century to the nineteenth Italians had no organized existence as a nation except for a common language. Now, under the leadership of Pius IX, there's hope for a united Italy and freedom from Austrian rule."

"Thirteen hundred years is a long time—what were the Italians doing?"

"They were thrown into confusion by barbarian invasions, warring popes and emperors. Italian consciousness was awakened briefly during the Renaissance through the writings of Dante and Petrarca, but then rival states exhausted themselves in civil wars, making them easy prey to foreign invaders. Austria became master in the north, Spain in the south. But Italians never lost hope in a united nation—it's a heritage that has come down from the days of the Roman Empire."

"Goes to show you the strength of Latin," said the young man. "Mind if I take a seat?"

"Go right ahead."

Six resolutions were passed honoring the brave Pontiff, then before closing the proceedings the Committee Secretary, Charles Deleru, said: "In the audience there's a son of Italy, a gentleman of courage and ability who suffered twenty-two years of imprisonment for the principles now so triumphant through the advocacy of the Pontiff—Mr. Pietro Moresti! Come up and say a few words."

Thunderous applause went up as Moresti made his way to the stage. "I appreciate the unexpected honor," he began, "and I urge my countrymen to prove themselves worthy of their community's interest in Italy. Since coming to New York, I've devoted my energies to teaching in a wonderful private school on the Upper West Side. I find that I can cavort with my students without losing respect. They tell me I rekindle memories of their grandfathers who fought so gallantly in the Revolutionary War. I'm quick to remind them that the first Italian immigrants were political refugees. And I enjoy the environs, the parks, Morningside and Riverside, and like all Italians I'm comforted by the nearness of the sea—"

"Mr. Moresti—I have a question!"

Two thousand heads quickly turned and looked with annoyance at the young man who had come in from the frost and snow. He was standing in the last row.

"Sir, you spent twenty-two years in a damp, rat-infested prison—that's a long time: how did you get out, how did you survive?"

Moresti lowered his head. "I'm ashamed to say . . ."

"C'mon, tell us!" the audience cried.

"Okay. I escaped. I burrowed a hole through the eastern wall with the lip of my copper plate. The walls were made of brick, they were cool and smooth, and for comfort I ran my hands lightly over the bricks. My fingers brushed the spaces between them, which made me think of the space between a woman's legs, the space between her arms, between her lips. Each and every brick I loosened filled me with ecstasy. Each and every orgasm renewed my will to survive. I caught my semen in my copper plate, then spit into it and with the mixture moistened the bricks as I chipped away."

PAOLO

BUONARROTI

T HE Carbonari were the pioneers of modern revolutionary underground organizations such as the resistance
groups in occupied Europe, the IRA, the Sandinistas,
the Contras. There's very good reason for this—of all the peoples
of the world the Italians thrive best in secret. Doesn't everybody
live in secret? we say. Who cares about our individual dreams and
struggles—the Mayor? the King? the President? And so we take
matters into our secretive, sly hands. Also, we know ourselves
extremely well. We know, for example, that we are just as capable
of becoming despot as republican, and so we form secret societies
to guard against our best and our worst inclinations. Reflect that
Fascism took hold in Italy as early as the 1920s, only sixty years
after the Unification, which had taken fourteen hundred years.

The Mafia and the Camorra existed before the Carbonari. The
former were local organizations, confined to the ghettos of Sicily
and Naples. The Mafia opened branches in the United States
only after everybody in the old neighborhoods had been taken
care of. Unlike the Carbonari, the Mafia prefers a king, despotic
or benevolent, preferably despotic, as it thrives on repression and
stability. The Carbonari established branches wherever there was
a king: in Spain, France, Poland, Russia, Holland, Hungary—

but not in England, where the subjects were satisfied with their queen.

One of the Carbonari's first leaders was Paolo Buonarroti, an Italian aristocrat and descendant of Michelangelo's. Paolo, however, couldn't draw a straight line or carry a tune or write a clear sentence. It was his attitude toward dreams that finally opened the way for him to become a revolutionary. He believed that dreams are God's way of providing the inartistic a bit of creativity. He had his voice, didn't he? and he could use it to cry, *"Viva Italia!* Out with the foreigners! Our full expression as a people is not possible until we talk and think in the same language!" And he could ride, and though his ass was soft it would toughen in the saddle. At the head of his black-faced marauders, Paolo Buonarroti rampaged through the tobacco fields of Italy, setting his torch to them.

He had gone to Paris in order to get the "Mona Lisa" and bring it back to the Uffizi in Florence, where it belonged. But Paolo liked it in Paris, befriending Robespierre, who opened for Paolo many a stubborn damsel's chamber door. Paolo walked right through them, saying to himself, "Fuck the 'Mona Lisa'!" and became a naturalized French citizen and settled down to a life of indolence and lasciviousness. As the years passed, he suffered more and more from pangs of conscience, resulting in a sudden inability to make himself understood in French. He began to stutter, and his Parisian trollops looked at him quizzically, then slammed their chamber doors. He got *agita* from eating all those white sauces and finally secluded himself in his quarters. On two successive mornings he awoke with vivid memories of his terrible dreams. In both dreams the images were spare and clear, and the emotions Paolo derived from his dreams and their subsequent message were as clear as the images. In the first dream, from his position on the ground he saw his great ancestor sitting on a closely slatted bench, a two-seater, suspended in the sky. Michelangelo made a sudden awkward movement; turning and reaching up as if to sculpt the sky, he lost his balance and fell through the air and died. The body lay about ten feet from Paolo, and he looked at it with a quiet sadness stemming from centuries of familiarity, love and inaccessibility. Paolo languished in bed replaying his dream, as it felt good to be visited by a cherished lost loved one, especially during difficult times. Even the dream had played itself twice as if its passive eye, Paolo, didn't believe it at first and wanted another chance to express appropriate emotion. Again Michelangelo sat on his bench, turned, slipped, fell and died, and Paolo gazed at the body with stoic reserve.

In the dream of the very next evening Paolo was face to face with Michelangelo. They had made a double suicide pact, and so now they could say a proper farewell, die together in defiance of time and with all their wits and love about them. The pact affected Michelangelo more: he blinked and blinked his tearful eyes in bewilderment, as if an invisible hand were slapping his face.

This time Paolo rose to the occasion—he grasped Michelangelo's powerful forearms and said, "Hey, don't cry—soon we will be together for all eternity."

Michelangelo collected himself. "I'll go first," he said, then turned and resolutely stared into the eye of the sun, his last act. Paolo bolted awake before carrying out his end of the pact.

He cherished the clarity of his dreams, and to keep them with him he attached meaning that held for his waking state. He had been a passive witness while it was Michelangelo who had agonized, and in the daydreams that followed his dreams, invoking Michelangelo's stentorian voice if not always his face, and sometimes seeing him kick the ground in frustration and anger, Paolo heard Michelangelo say:

"While you're fucking your brains out in Paris, the spirit of our people is being extinguished by the despotic powers of Austria, Spain and the Pope. The Italians are going crazy talking German and Spanish and at the same time trying to think in Italian. They're eating paella and sauerbraten. You can't find happiness in a bordello anymore! Soldiers break in under the pretext of searching for arms. An old man of sixty-five was jailed for copying an extract from Tacitus in his memo book. A young man was jailed for sporting a beard. Another young man, Ercoli, was hung from a gibbet for prohibiting his friend from smoking a cigar.

Ercoli was just trying to tell his friend that smoking wasn't good for him. The friend balked, pulled back, but Ercoli snuffed out the cigar anyway. Just then, amid the din of drum, fife and trumpet, a brigade of Austrian troops in blue coats and red trousers paraded by. They arrested Ercoli for advocating the boycott of tobacco, which Austria taxes. Ercoli's executioners puffed smoke in his face before executing him.

"So get up, *figlio mio*—you're not going to accomplish anything staying in bed!"

Paolo bounded from his bed with new life and returned to Italy, not before painting his face black to get past his landlord and tailor, who hadn't been paid for two suits and a winter coat.

CESARE
PAVESE

———

FOR years it galled me that in the introduction to *The Selected Works of Cesare Pavese* it says that he suffered from premature ejaculation. The charge went unsubstantiated and I was outraged that it should find a place beside Pavese's beautiful, important work. I figured it took more than one woman to establish such an awful reputation in a man, especially a man as great as Cesare Pavese, and so I wanted to know the names of these women, their station, specific dates and locales. For their continual outcry, "Hey, Cesare, what about me?" to harden into print, it must have fallen on ears in addition to Pavese's. Who were all these other people?

With the passage of years, keeping in mind my own orgasmic schedule and that of my wife and the other women I knew, I began to ponder this premature ejaculation. If a man's ejaculation is mature, exactly on time—does that make for a perfect life? If the woman comes first, the man holding himself back for later— is his ejaculation precocious now, damaging to him?

Circumstances compelled me to put the book aside, but I carried it with me down through the years, from lifetime to lifetime, domicile to domicile. The cover tore off somewhere and the pages have yellowed and grown brittle: turn one and it falls free of the perfect binding. Today, the first day of autumn, I do not really care whether Pavese was a premature ejaculator or even whether behind it all he had a small dick, as a friend of mine recently suggested. The onset of the fall season has brought with it a reflourishing of my allergies, all fourteen of them. By some miracle of nature a wild tree grew up in my courtyard. Wide-arching branches and thousands of leaves fill the entire expanse of the courtyard, and the top branches reach all the way up to my window four stories high. Each falling leaf holds a beach of pollen. High winds blow the invisible particles through my window and up my nose—I sneeze, my vision is blurred, my digestive tract isn't right. Food lodges in my intestine and putrefies. Toxins enter my blood, making me sick and unhappy. Cesare Pavese was one big pain in the ass. He wanted to be known as a suffering man. He suffered most severely, he claimed, because he was a bachelor: he longed for a wife, children and a home. I have known the joy of a family and a home. I know what it is not only to long for these things but to actually lose them. My sadness is so complete that it is calm. Yet I diet and exercise, I try to be a friend, I try to be a lover, I work.

Let's just read Pavese and forget about his personal life. If we want to know what it was like living under Fascism in Italy, we should read *The House on the Hill*. Drawn to the subject of friendship, its ramifications? Read *The Beach*. Pavese's narrative voice was richest as a woman: *Among Women Only*, which Antonioni used as a basis for a film. Film buffs who like Antonioni's work in general should read Pavese. Antonioni once said that the only difference between him and Pavese was that he, Antonioni, was still alive. Teachers should read Pavese, as he was one of the first writers to treat the teacher in fiction. If we're not in a jocular mood—Pavese! All North Americans owe it to Pavese to read him if for no other reason than he translated great American books: *Moby Dick*, *Of Mice and Men*, *The Hamlet*. It takes some of us a lifetime just to read *Moby Dick*, imagine how long it must take a foreigner to translate it. Pavese spent two decades of his life with his translations, and considering he lived only four decades—that's a lot of time to spend on one thing. Where he learned English well enough to translate it is a mystery. The Lyceum d'Azeglio didn't offer it, and Pavese didn't go out with an English-speaking woman until the end of his life. His last fling at romance was with the American actress Constance Dowling, about whom Pavese knew only that she had starred in a few B movies. One night his lark from America left his bed for the bed of another, an Italian actor. Pavese died shortly afterwards.

He translated English books: *David Copperfield, Portrait of the Artist, The English Revolution of 1688–89*. He distinguished between English and American, something I don't like. He had one friend in London and one in Chicago. He relied on their taste in books, so he had no way of knowing about a bricklayer who lived on Long Island, Pietro Di Donato, whose *Christ in Concrete* is the only important Italian-American novel of the first half of this century. Long Island is a long way from Chicago.

In various parts of his diary Pavese supposedly hinted at suffering from premature ejaculation, but I've gone over with a fine-tooth comb the whole of the diary, in its original Italian and with an open heart, and first of all Pavese wasn't a man to hint, he admitted outright:

> Sometimes I come too soon but what of it? It don't bother me and it don't bother my women. I'm only twenty and if I like what's going on, if I feel the woman's excitement—shit, I come three, four times, and except for my first shot all the others are exactly on time!
>
> I have to shake my head and smile. All this talk about synchronized orgasms when penetration isn't my thing at all. Why, just this morning Deola told me that I'm the best cunt sucker in all of Piedmont. Boy, does that make me feel good! I'll carry the image with me the entire week: my head between her nutcrackers, my hands reaching up for her big balloons, squeezing them, glimpsing the ecstasy on her face, the roll of her eyes—hey, I'm not even *thinking* of coming!

If the woman's juice was too acrid, or if she was bleeding too much, Pavese would go along with ordinary penetration, but first he'd tell her in the Piedmont dialect he loved so much: "Look, I'm gonna come right away but I'm gonna stay inside ya long and hard. Gimme a few minutes and I promise we'll have two, three orgasms together. We'll see the stars."

The women of Pavese's twenties were primarily the prostitutes of a brothel situated near the summit of the Langhe hills. The land around the house was barren, bracken and bare rock, but up higher there were vines and they were lush, really lush, so loaded that grapes trailed on the ground. With his knapsack over his shoulder, a few soldi in his pocket from the translations, Pavese skipped up the path leading to the brothel. Now and then he raised his eyes toward the scorched peak, listened to the whine of the wind getting steadily stronger. Riding down the wind was the bleating of the he-goats as they chased after the she-goats. The he-goats butted their heads against the tree trunks in frustration, and the hill shook. Nearing the house, Pavese spotted the shade of a canebrake where he would stretch out on the way down. Deola, his favorite prostitute, waited at her window. She kept a diary of her own:

> This morning that crazy boy with the balls of an elephant wires ahead that he's coming up. He has enough soldi for a blow job, and then he wants me to kiss him all over like a butterfly—would I please remember to wear the long lashes. With all his desires *in anticipo* he's likely just to rest his head on my bosom, squeeze my arm, tell me to hold him.

Sometimes Pavese stood stock-still and stared at the landscape. At his left might be a wood and at his right a brook with goldfish that mirrored the hills spilling seaward. Suddenly, the boy was seized with a frenzy, a frenzy not to be himself, to become that wood or that brook, to find the word that translated everything, down to the blades of grass, the smells, the emptiness. He no longer existed. The wood, the brook existed. His senses existed— jaws gaping to devour the object. Pavese's fundamental tendency was to assign to his actions a significance that transcends their effective meaning. Let's examine Pavese's fundamental tendency. No, let's examine *my* fundamental tendency. With a man like

Pavese I tend to get *agita*, diarrhea—I've spent the whole fucking year trying to picture his hills and all I come up with is that they were not exactly where he wanted them. They were not in the city he loved, Torino, where he spent his working life and where he found women willing to put up with such a pain in the ass. And they were not in the country he loved, Santo Stefano Belbo, where he was born and spent his childhood summers. In the country he did not see the faces of the cityfolk, and in the city he did not see the faces of the countryfolk. The faces got lost in the hills. His father, Judge Eugenio Pavese, took off the month of August. Every August 1 little Cesare and his sister Mari awoke at dawn and then trailed behind their parents on the walk to the hills, which were a hop and a skip from their house. Once in the hills the boy turned and looked back at the city, at his house, his neighbors' houses. He cried a little, sobbing to himself, but just over the rise, a hop and a skip from the hills on the other side, was the country. After his parents opened the country house, Pavese wallowed around in the grass, in the mud, went alone into the loveliest wildest places, the wood. Emerging from the wood, he entered a rolling meadow strewn with huge, neat dung heaps. The diameter of a heap was bigger than he was. He stood stock-still outside the circumference and stared into it. Soon he became that heap, and he found the word that translated it— *shit!* There were no footprints, and he never saw the creature who made the big shit, and so he imagined that the foul perfect heaps were the waste product of a giant, a giant who could fly, because how could you make such a big shit and get away unless you could fly? At night, when everybody was at the movies or in the café, Cesare stole into the hills. The pounding of the waterfalls and the smell of the flowers, wisteria and chrysanthemums, marked the way to the highest peak. Nearing it, he went down to his knees and crawled. With a strong grip on the crest he pulled himself up until only his eyes surmounted it. The city was lit like a celestial blanket. He saw his house, the neighbors' houses. He saw the streets, the crowds. His eyes felt the hard cruel light cast by the endless streetlights on the tramping feet. The thoughts on the people's faces made him shake with terror. He rolled onto his back and looked up at the stars. He wanted his own private city, he'd set it upon the hills and let it shine and he'd live there always.

I picture insurmountable hills where the Manhattan Bridge is. The Brookhattan Hills, let's call them. On the Brooklyn side the lower slopes are a hop and a skip from the Flatbush extension, and on the Manhattan side the lower slopes are a hop and a skip from my house on Charles Street. In my little world of Charles Street I do not see the people I once knew in Brooklyn, and they do not see me.

After the Second World War, the Pope was under a lot of pressure to close the brothels. The Italian Medical Association refused to send its members into the brothels to examine the prostitutes, a task that during the war had been relegated to American Army colonels. The air was too foul, the Association said. It made them sick just to breathe it. Even the madam left the house in the morning for a walk. The new generation of farmers also complained, saying that the reason the land hadn't been worked was because their fathers were in the brothels all day fucking the prostitutes. And so in 1946 the Pope closed all the brothels in Italy. The women scattered to the *viales* of the great cities—Milan, Rome itself, the ports of Naples and Sicily. Some of the Langhe prostitutes made the short jaunt from the lower slopes to Torino and stayed there. Deola, for example, Pavese's favorite, and her good friend Ella. Deola was dark, hefty, and she had bad legs. An ugly network of varicose veins traversed her legs, which were powerful nonetheless. Once they locked around your head or your waist there was no getting out. Pavese nicknamed her la Morsa, the vise. He nicknamed Ella la Banana Africana, the African Banana, because Ella's breasts were short and skinny and they curled sharply, exactly like the African banana. The only difference between Ella's breasts and the African banana was that the African banana was green and it stayed green even when ripe. Ella was a blonde with fair skin. She had a high-pitched voice, and Pavese liked fucking her long after she came because he loved to hear her siren echo among the hills. After her house closed, .

Ella worked the streets of Torino. Late one wintry night she stopped beneath a streetlight, placed a cigarette in her lips, rummaged in her pocketbook for a match. It was freezing out—she shivered, hugged her body. Pavese saw her from his hotel window. He was a pipe smoker and always had *fiammiferi* handy, those elegant waxy Italian matches that burn yellow and strong. The housemaid at the Hotel Roma in Torino would discover Pavese's body draped over the bed, his shoes off and his brown suit on. She rifled the pockets of his cloak hanging in the *armadio* and found a box of *fiammiferi*, loose change and an open pack of peppermints. Pavese takes up his matches, puts on his cloak, hurries down to Ella on the street. He engulfs her in his cloak. "So good to see you again, Ella." "Good to see you, too, Cesare." He lights a match. The wind snuffs the flame. "Do you have another, Cesare?" "Of course." The wind snuffs this match and Ella laughs softly. "On nights like this," Pavese says, "you can laugh out loud. No one will hear you." They raise their eyes to all the windows above them. Behind the walls eyes are closed in sleep. The couple on the street waits. Ella's teeth clatter. Pavese leads her to the corner, where the wind dies down to nothing. Ella drops the butt, crushes it with her shoe. "I lost the scarf I used to wear to keep me warm at night," she says. "It came from Rio but I don't mind losing it now that I found you again, Cesare." The scarf was a gift from a sailor, and it came across the ocean on a windy night drenched with light by the great liner. "I don't see him now, my sailor, but if you'll come up to my room I'll show you a snapshot. He's tan and curly-haired like you. You're better-looking, Cesare..." She drops a second butt onto the pavement. They look up at the sky. Ella says, "That window at the very top, up there—that's ours." Arm in arm they cross the cobblestones, each warming the other.

Deola worked the music halls. While giving some john the eye or nudging him with her foot, she listens to the orchestra. It makes her feel like a movie star in the love scene with the millionaire. She was forty-seven when her house closed, and she had lost her looks when she was thirty, but she carried away her dream of one day finding a good man and settling down in a modest apartment, one with a kitchen and maybe even a fireplace and a big *armadio* where she could put her linen. Hey, there she is now! Sitting at an outdoor table at the Caffè Lucca on Bleecker Street, smoking, picking at a brioche, shaking her head—

"Mind if I join you, Deola?"

"I can't get over this businessman I had yesterday. He wakes me up at the crack of dawn, kisses me and says, 'I'd stay with you, baby, if I could. Come with me to the train?' So I go to the train, wave goodbye. Think he'll really take me with him?"

"I hope so, if that's what you want. Deola, do you remember a certain youth of Torino, the very best of his generation, Cesare Pavese?"

"How could I forget him? He was the best man I ever had, the only one I ever felt inside me. Not that his dick was that big, mind you . . . you know, a woman of experience can tell a man's dick from his fingers. You, kid, for example—you have thick, sturdy fingers. Wanna come up to my place?"

"Maybe later. First about this Pavese . . ."

"He wasn't your ordinary-looking greaseball. He was tall, gangling, and his torso was lean and angular like a young girl's. I liked the feel of his naked back, it was so smooth. He had legs like an eel, his hairline was low, and he had all this black curly hair—and what a shnozzola! It was a masterpiece, bigger than Tony Bennett's, a gigantic hooked shnozzola, the gelatinous tip descending over the upper lip, casting it in shadow. Here's something nobody knows—he mutilated his hair while he worked, curled it into untieable knots. I'd be running my fingers through his hair and hit a snag. I'd make a face. 'What's this?' I'd ask. 'A knot,' he'd say, blushing."

"Was he a premature ejaculator?"

"The truth?"

"Well, yeah . . ."

"He was. But the important thing to remember is that we understood. Let me explain:

"One day this carton arrives with fifty-one books, one for each of us. On the cover is a white whale and it's angry. Its eyes looked human and they stared straight out at me. Scared the shit out of me. 'Translated by Cesare Pavese,' it said on the cover. We all felt so proud. The book was around a thousand pages, it took me eight years to read it—imagine how long it took the poor guy to translate it.

"'That's nothing,' Pavese told us. 'Wait till you try to read *The Hamlet*.'

"And so we understood that he might have been intent on a difficult passage, it made him nervous, and his nervousness continued long after he put down his pen. He sought solace rowing in a small boat up the Po, and sometimes he sought it in the arms of a woman. The mere sight of our flesh, our first touches, revived his nervousness over his work. The next beautiful passage was located at the tip of his dick, and he came right away as a means of breaking through to it. Afterwards, he sometimes cried a little, sobbing to himself, and though I was hot I'd tell him, 'It's all right, Cesare. There's no reason to cry or even feel remorse.'"

PIETRO
LACLACCA

THE old opera-loving family the DiGeorgios listened to Beniamino Gigli more than Enrico Caruso. Gigli's voice could be light and sweet, appropriate to sing along with on the holidays, while Caruso's voice was dark, dramatic, the kind of voice you listened to when you were alone. But when I was in Italy I mentioned Caruso more than any other tenor, believing that the world at large regarded him as the greatest tenor who ever lived. To my surprise the Italians countered with Francesco Tamagno and Beniamino Gigli. The DiGeorgios had never heard of Francesco Tamagno and so I made a mental note of introducing him, searching out his recordings. At the mention of Gigli the Italians' eyes lit up, making me feel good because a connection had been made between the Italians in Italy and the Italians in Brooklyn. I tried for another connection by saying that the DiGeorgios' favorite wine had been Chianti. Chianti had been the favorite of most Italian families in Brooklyn. I was pleased to discover that Chianti is a place, a region of lush vineyards where the Chianti grape is grown. The Italians told me that nobody in Italy drank Chianti, it was made solely for export. Could it be, I wondered, that Caruso was also only for export?

I was studying medicine in the ancient city of Bologna. The first big exam was *microbiologia*, microbiology. Exams were given orally in Italian, and I studied hard in silence from a big fat Italian paperback. One of the professors who would be sitting at my exam, I learned, was a Professor LaClacca. LaClacca... La-Clacca—the name rang a bell! We had a neighbor only two doors away named LaClacca, a friendly old man with steely white hair and a ruddy face. He spoke with a thick accent that turned out to be Italian. Maybe he still had some relatives in the homeland, a brother, a sister, a few cousins—how many LaClaccas could there be in the world? And our Mr. LaClacca had liked me. On my counterclockwise drives around the block in the Blue Streak, his house was along the very last stretch of road. He would be outside working in his garden, and when he saw me driving up he came out onto the sidewalk, approached my car and gave me a hearty smile. He called me little Anthony boy. "Hi there, little Anthony boy!" his tremendous voice boomed.

I wrote home and in no time the news arrived that indeed Mr. LaClacca and Professor LaClacca were related. The professor was a nephew, a beloved one, son of a brother who had stayed behind. There wasn't anything he wouldn't do for his uncle. He owed him a debt of gratitude for putting him up in Brooklyn, a stopover on his way to Seattle, where he was going on a research grant. Small world, wasn't it? I should call him right away, he was expecting it.

How could I fail microbiology now? To make matters even more foolproof, my parents came over for a visit the summer before the exam. I went down to Rome to pick them up. From the observation deck I saw a man in a beige raincoat and brown fedora, my father, approach his turn on the customs line with a brown paper bag tucked tight under his arm. He grew so nervous that he dropped the bag and forty packs of Chesterfield regulars went flying all over. The customs officer and I shook our heads, laughed. First thing back in Bologna my father calls Professor LaClacca and in Brooklyn Neapolitan invites him and his wife to dinner at the best restaurant in town, Il Pappagallo, The Parrot.

"So this is little Anthony boy," the professor says on meeting me.

"Hi," I say.

I do not recall saying anything over dinner. I was intent on studying the professor's physical appearance so as not to miss him at the exam. He was a big bruiser with a face round and red as an apple. Nor do I recall saying anything in the professor's swanky apartment, where we all went for coffee. I listened:

"I liked Seattle," the professor said. "It's clean, modern, and I'm looking forward to going there again."

I made a mental note of one day visiting Seattle myself. At some point the professor also said, "I'm a big fan of Louie Armstrong's."

"Ah, Louie Armstrong," my father said.

"Yes," said the professor, "but not all his records are available in Italy."

"No problem," my father said. "There's a record store on Eighty-sixth Street and I'm sure it has every record Louie Armstrong ever made. I'll send them to you as soon as I get back."

The records arrived around the time of the microbiology exam. I took them with me, held them on my lap as I awaited my turn in a cold room. My mind fought for a clear picture of Professor LaClacca. He breezes in smiling, wearing a white lab jacket. "Little Anthony boy..."

"Hi." I hand him the records, then follow him to the exam room.

He was really an associate professor. The professor who asked the questions was somebody else. Professor LaClacca sits next to him and I take a seat across the table. The first question flies across, something about a virus.

"Uhhhh—"

Professor LaClacca must have told the big professor about his uncle, me, my family—all neighbors back in Brooklyn—because he darts Professor LaClacca a glance that clearly says, "This is your uncle's neighbor? He's an idiot!"

"May I answer in English?" I say.

"Okay," the big professor says.

"Uhhhh—"

The big professor gets up and goes, leaving Professor LaClacca to toil with his conscience. He smiles, answers the question himself, now and then asking me if I concur, which I do. He browses through the records. "You like Louie Armstrong?"

"Uhhhh—"

"Louie Armstrong! Satchmo! You know who he is?"

"Of course I know who he is," I break through, "but see, for us in the United States it's not a question of liking or disliking Louie Armstrong. He's one of our pioneers, like Davy Crockett, and we need our pioneers. Satchmo was instrumental in bringing New Orleans jazz up North, to Chicago, making it accessible to the top half of our country, including Seattle. Even at that Harry James was more popular. You heard of Harry James?"

"Yes."

"If you ask me, Satchmo was a bit lucky. There were musicians in New Orleans as good if not better. Earl 'Fatha' Hines, for example—ever hear of him?"

"No."

"There you go—it's a question of accessibility, the temper of the times, taste. My taste runs toward Earl Hines, Bix Beiderbecke, Charlie Parker."

"Sounds like Louie Armstrong is just for export."

"Don't say that. The important thing is that you like him."

He wrote my grade in a little black book called a *libretto*, then I staggered outside and dropped against the fence. I peeked into my *libretto*—hey, an 8! Considering a scale from 1 to 10, with 5 passing, 8 was pretty good! I had my old neighbor Mr. LaClacca to thank. He had remembered his little Anthony boy with fondness. The boy was only four when he began driving around the block, yet every morning when the sun was out he found the strength to pick up the Blue Streak from its parking spot on the porch and carry it down to the corner. The corner was an ideal place to start and finish because there were no trees to block the sun rising over the El. The whole block to the corner of Seventy-fourth Street was lit up, determining a counterclockwise route, and the first stretch of sidewalk was smooth as it was directly outside his uncle's office. His uncle was a cardiologist and didn't want his patients tripping and falling on the sidewalk. Little Anthony boy drove beneath his kitchen window. It shot open, his mother stuck out her head and yelled down, "Be careful, little Anthony boy!"

He pedaled hard to get past the window, then he took his feet off the pedals in order to glide by his uncle's operating room. He was always complaining that he couldn't hear his patients' heartbeats. Up ahead was the garage, and the sidewalk outside was also smooth so that the big cars going in and out wouldn't get flats. The garage signaled the end of his house and as he drove past he looked up at the clothesline out his mother's bedroom window. He saw their clothes. His mother also had an ironing board in her bedroom.

Next to his garage was Dr. Pico's garage. It was always white because Dr. Pico painted it a lot. He spent a lot of time outside sweeping his leaves, straightening his garbage pails and painting his garage white and his wrought-iron fence black. If a patient came to the block in pain and his father wasn't home, little Anthony boy would say, "Go to Dr. Pico's," as he was a friend as well as another dentist. His voice was high yet tender, and behind his rimless glasses his eyes looked hurt. There was big trouble between him and his wife, Sarah. They lived above the office with their daughters, Maryanne and Angela, and every night after dinner Sarah came over, sat in the kitchen and cried. Little Anthony boy liked to watch her cry and listen to his mother's soft, kind voice.

"Go inside, little Anthony boy!"

From the parlor he stole glances into the kitchen. Sarah was big and fat and when she cried she bounced up and down like a bowl of jelly. Dr. Pico came over after office hours in his white gown. His eyes already looked hurt, so there was nothing extra-special for him to do. He said hello to everybody with his fine voice, then joined the men in the parlor. He was permanently stooped over from decades of hovering over his patients. He worked hard to pay for Sarah's trips around the world, then her condo in Florida. Maryanne marries a Cuban doctor. Their first kid is black. They move to Westchester. Angela becomes a spinster schoolteacher. Sarah dies first, of a heart attack. Angela moves near her sister's. Dr. Pico is still working, and if he was outside when little Anthony boy passed, he tapped him gently on the head.

The corner of Seventy-fourth Street was dangerous because drivers who suddenly decided to go in the opposite direction used this corner for a U-turn. Big cars came straight at him and so he hugged Dr. Pico's fence, made a sharp left and accelerated up Seventy-fourth Street. It was an enchanting block. His grandparents lived halfway down, and often at night he walked there with his father. During the walk back home he was conscious of being beside his father and felt free to look up at the black sky filled with stars. At the top of the block lived the three poor brothers, Tommy, Jimmy and Frank. Tommy was the youngest and was also short for his age, but he more than compensated for his position in the family and his height by being the toughest kid of his generation. He got into all kinds of trouble off the block, coming home filthy and bloody. Later on, little Anthony boy palled around with him and grew to sense what it was to be short, tough and poor. Jimmy, the middle brother, was left-handed. Not only did he use his left hand for everything, but his face also slanted toward the left. He was special because of this, and little Anthony boy watched him closely during punchball games. With his strong left fist Jimmy could punch a ball five sewers. Little Anthony boy couldn't punch the ball half as far with his right fist. He settled for line drives through the infield. Frank, the oldest brother, was little Anthony boy's idol. He was one of the big kids yet he talked to him, smiled at him. Frank was tall, strong, and cut a figure like Robert Taylor's. He could hit a spalding out of sight, over the El where it crossed Seventy-third Street. Then one day he came to a game late with a newspaper tucked under his arm. He had what was called a job and had to take a train to get to it. He took an exhibition swing anyway, but little Anthony boy knew that his idol's stickball days were over.

The three brothers lived in a big shingle house with a red roof. It had to be big because of all the people who lived inside, and it was easy to see because at the top of the block the trees weren't high. Still, little Anthony boy never saw the father, and the mother looked more like a maid than a mother. She was smaller than her son Tommy, her hair was messy and she wore a house-dress to the stores. She was crazy because she only spoke another language.

The trees got higher in the heart of Seventy-fourth Street, from the three brothers' house to his grandparents'. He didn't know anybody in these houses, so he concentrated on the road. It was slightly uphill, but the important thing was that each house he passed got him closer to his grandmother's, to the mozzarella and Pepsi she would have waiting. He knew he was almost there when he passed the dark, dark house with the front door prac-tically on the sidewalk. The old man who lived inside knew no fear. His blinds were always drawn, and the house was also sad because the old man lived inside alone. He was a friend of his grandfather's, a fellow member of the lodge. Little Anthony boy went inside the house with his grandfather, sat still in the backyard and listened to the two friends talk about old times in another language.

There was a black fence outside his grandparents' house with flowers beyond it. He parked along the fence, got out and looked at the flowers. He climbed the white glistening steps leading to the front door, holding on to the stainless-steel banister his grand-father had made in the cellar, a deep, dark cellar where they went after dinner. He rang the bell. In no time his grandmother was coming down the stairs. He heard her and he could also smell her. She smelled a little like her kitchen, but the smell was strong-est when the door opened and she was upon him, kissing him. The slip under her housedress was tight under her armpits. He stared at it, and as he grew he decided that the smell came directly from her. She was a short, stocky princess of a woman, all one piece, with black hair done up in a bun except when she went to sleep. She had doughy skin and a mustache. Little black hairs grew out of a pimple above her lip, which she chewed. He raised his head to meet her kiss, turning it to the side slightly, then he sat on the top step with his mozzarella and Pepsi.

Sometimes the two sisters who lived next door came out and sat around him. They laughed and talked to him. He couldn't take his eyes off Lily's long blond hair, and he was captivated by Matilda's dark, sharp beauty. He heard people say that they were poor and fooled around a lot with boys. As he grew he thought about a connection between being poor and beautiful and becoming a *putana*. Once, the sisters brought out cards and taught him a game he could play alone. But solitaire was never so thrilling as when he played it on the top step with Lily on one side, Matilda on the other. If they didn't come out, he walked quietly into their alley and looked up at their windows.

Replenished by the mozzarella and Pepsi, and after being showered by the beauty and kindness of the sisters, he climbed back into the Blue Streak and set out for the corner of Fifteenth Avenue. A short yet uneasy ride because the trees disappeared again, exposing him, and he felt alone with the multiple dwelling near the corner. The poor people lived inside. They lived in multiples because they couldn't afford to live in houses all by themselves. Their bricks were dirty, and they had no power to clean them. The whole house smelled like his grandmother. He never saw anybody go in or out. They stayed in their kitchens. The foyer beyond the front door was dark and empty. On the outside of the house was a zigzag of iron stairs so the people could come and go without passing one another's door. His first ballplaying days little Anthony boy led his team around the block to this very house. They could throw their ball against it because nobody complained, nobody was there.

He made a wide turn onto Fifteenth Avenue, hugging the gutter, braving the big cars rather than the stores and the people who lived above them. There was a plumbing supply store and a florist. He didn't like them, because his mother didn't use them. All the customers were strangers, and he never saw the same stranger twice. He couldn't understand the things that were sold in the stores. The loose pipes in the window of the plumbing supply store—who knew how to use them? People who knew how to use them would grow more frightening than the pipes themselves. As for a florist—wasn't it enough that a black fence had encircled his grandparents' flowers? What kind of people went into a faraway field and uprooted the flowers, trucked them back to a store, then put them in a big glass refrigerator against the back wall?

The greatest danger of Fifteenth Avenue lay in the people who lived above the stores, the Italians from Italy. They had been banished from Italy to America to live among the stores, and they were unhappy, vicious and dirty. Their kids had dirty faces and legs and shiny black hair. They hung out in front of the stores, carving guns out of wood. They wanted to live where little Anthony boy lived, around the corner where there were big shingle and brick houses with a garage and a tall old tree out front. Little Anthony boy took his drive early so as to be home by lunch, twelve o'clock, because immediately after lunch the Italians from Italy invaded the block. The enemy was the Italian kids born in Brooklyn, on Seventy-fifth Street, and these kids also carved guns from wood. The opposing armies used the same ammunition, carpet, and so the guns became known as carpet guns.

Around 1947, the Italians of Bensonhurst began enjoying a little prosperity. One way this could be seen was by the huge rolls of linoleum carpet that suddenly appeared around the garbage pails. Old, faded linoleum was being replaced by new, colorful rug. The rolls of linoleum attracted the kids:

"Hey, we gotta use this stuff! Bullets, we'll use it for bullets!"

They carved pistols and rifles from wood, cut up the linoleum into millions of tiny squares. A short nail was hammered into the tip of the gun, a rubber band was stretched taut along its length and fastened over the barrel, then a piece of carpet was inserted in the rubber band. A flick of the thumb and the carpet went flying, soaring out of sight, over the roofs, or nose-diving only a few feet away, crashing to the pavement, or boomeranging, coming back to kill you. During little Anthony boy's stretch in the military, he was unable to make his own gun, a fellow soldier had to make his, but he was nevertheless a good and brave soldier. He rose to the rank of second lieutenant during a time when battalion morale was extremely low. To a man they were disheartened by the unpredictable trajectory of the bullets. Little Anthony boy rose to the occasion, rallying them:

"Men, the enemy is led by a big dirty greaseball named Pasquale. He lives above the plumbing supply store, and I've seen his mother. To neutralize his size and dirt, we'll set an ambush: Vinnie, you hide behind the hedges, Nicky, behind the garbage pails, I'll hide on my porch. Pasquale attacks like a wild Indian, hootin' and hollerin' and under no cover. When he's upon us, we'll open fire. It's the nature of our ammo that it flies in every which direction and so Pasquale'll think he's outnumbered."

Little Anthony boy and his men knew the terrain. They knew that at the end of each alley was a garage, and behind the garages a wooden fence traversed all the yards.

"And so, men," little Anthony boy went on, "our ambush is mere decoy for a second line of soldiers who will scale the fence and gain access to the alleys up near Fifteenth Avenue. They, of course, lead into the street, so we'll be able to come up behind Pasquale, attack his rear guard and at the same time cut off his only avenue of retreat."

Time and again Pasquale's army was slaughtered. Then at five o'clock all the kids went home to eat.

He headed straight for the barber's pole on the corner. The red and white stripes were swirling and so Joe was inside and maybe Sam the Bookie. Joe had given him his first haircut, and he gave him a haircut whenever his mother gave him a dollar and told him to go up the block to Joe's. While cutting his hair, Joe told him that he was so handsome that one day he would be a movie star. Little Anthony boy liked this and stopped off at Joe's on his drive around the block.

He parked at the pole of endlessly swirling red and white stripes. Where did they all come from, and where did they go? He opened the door and was comforted by the action of the scissors and the race results coming over the radio. Joe wore a white gown like his father, a slippery gown so the hair could slide down. He tugged at it: "Hi, Joe."

"Little Anthony boy . . . wanna haircut?"

"No, just sayin' hi." He looked into the corner for Sam the Bookie. If he wasn't in jail, he would be sitting at the table in the corner reading the scratch sheet, his glasses on the tip of his nose, his gray hat tilted back on his head. His father said a lot that the police were always after Sam and that he had spent most of his life in jail. So if he wasn't in jail, why did he come to the barbershop? Wouldn't the police know where to catch him? A dog's life, little Anthony boy grew to realize. Sam came to the barbershop because he had no place else to go, that was the truth of it. Every morning his mother or sister kicked him out.

When Sam was in jail, his good friend Joe took the bets. Men came in, handed Joe a slip of paper, then left without getting a haircut. The police didn't suspect Joe. He was the barber, clean-shaven, velvety voice, always ready with a smile.

Little Anthony boy suspected that his father bet with Sam. "He's a patient of mine," his father would say, but if Sam was in the corner and little Anthony boy said, "Hi, Sam," Sam turned and smiled and you could see he had no teeth. He had never had any teeth, and no work was being done on his mouth, because he didn't come to the house. Another thing—when his father said, "The cops are always after him, he's spent half his life in jail," his voice was sad and tears came to his eyes. Sam had confided in him over years of transacting bets.

Joe's barbershop and his pole signaled the last leg of the journey. They would always signal this, even when he drove a big car. They stood on the corner of Fifteenth Avenue, the block before Sixteenth Avenue, where he lived. The last block was a long, shady, downhill ride, but he telescoped it and through the shade saw the sun shining all the way down on the corner. He drove close to the hedges in order to stay away from the big fat trees. They had been planted around the same time as the sidewalk, but the engineers had not foreseen their strength and persistence. The trees grew up out of the sidewalk, creating high peaks and deep valleys. With one eye on the corner he glanced at the exposed roots—they looked like snakes. He passed Grace and Moonie's house in the middle of the block. He looked at it. Grace was a friend of his mother's, and she was nice. She smiled and said hello on her way to the stores. His father and Moonie had been friends when they were small. Moonie was nice *now*, smiling and saying hello on his way to and from the train. So why didn't he come up to the house? To get an idea, little Anthony boy would say, "He's such a nice man, Moonie."

"Moonie's nice," his father would say.

A funny name for a man, Moonie, little Anthony boy decided. And his skin is a little dark and he takes a train to work while a doctor walks downstairs.

Home began with the appearance of the lions outside Mr. Rapelli's house. Two life-size lions made of stone, and they had long-flowing manes and open jaws that bared needle-sharp teeth. When he put his hand in their mouth, they didn't bite. Mr. Rapelli was friendly, too. He shouted, "Hello there!" even if you were a block away. And he was a good neighbor—after a hurricane he helped bail out the cellars, and he swept the leaves off the sewer. Once, he passed his father's office right by and went to Dr. Pico's. That night his father said, "Rapelli? He's a nothing. He tried to play ball with us but he couldn't hit his way out of a paper bag. We made him the mascot."

Mrs. Rapelli was beautiful. Clara, her name was, and on the way to her job, crossing the street, she turned and gave him a sweet smile. Maybe his father was jealous. Not that his wife hadn't been beautiful, but she worked on Wall Street while Clara hung around the ballfield. His father was a long-ball hitter, and so how could Clara pick a mascot over a long-ball hitter?

He was in the sunlight, the corner was only two houses away, but he suddenly put on the brakes, stood up and looked around for the old man. He would be working in his garden, stooped low among his flowers and ivy, and he emerged from it like a beast from the forest, slowly, with measured steps. He was big, bigger than Dr. Pico, Frank and Mr. Rapelli. The old man blocked the whole sidewalk and a vision of the corner. He had hair white as snow and a square, red face. As he approached the car, he smiled, and from his smiling lips and white teeth the boy had heard it for the first time when he was four and he heard it every day when the sun was out until he was six:

"Hi there, little Anthony boy!"

It was a great booming voice. It shook the trees and froze the boy. He dropped his hands from the wheel, tensed his arms and surrendered his neck. The old man pinched a section of skin and pulled up. The boy rose to his tiptoes and raised his head as high as it would go. He looked at the tops of the trees. Gritting his teeth, he said, "Hi, Mr. LaClacca."

The old man didn't let go. He squeezed harder and said it again: "Hi there, little Anthony boy!"

The boy's mind fought for the magical words that would release the grip. He could ask after the old man's daughter with the Mona Lisa smile, Amelia. Maybe that's how he always knew when he was driving up—he missed having a son, and every morning when the sun was out he hid in his garden and watched him set the Blue Streak on the corner, then he timed his work with the tour around the block. Mr. LaClacca didn't mean to hurt him, you could tell from his smile. He blocked the sidewalk really and truly just to talk to a little boy, the little boy who lived on the corner who hadn't as yet heard that many big people talk, so he wouldn't mind the strange accent. He might also understand that his old neighbor with the white hair and eager face was lonely, his heart was in the country of his native language, and that in America he had used his hands instead of his mouth. He said only, "Hi there, little Anthony boy!" because he didn't know anything else to say. The viselike grip of the neck, the pain, was a way of saying that he *understood* English and was waiting to hear something meaningful, something other than hello and goodbye. Something about the work he had done with his hands maybe. Yes, that was it—he was waiting for a compliment on his cement work. Fixed in the cement that bordered his garden and the iron fence that separated his house from his neighbors were thousands of semiprecious stones. Dark blues, bright reds, golden yellows— all caressed by the cement and shining in the sun. He looked down at them first thing on coming out his front door. They attracted his attention as something wonderful outside, as wonderful as the trees and the traffic. They would last as long as the cement and the houses and the people. While he marveled at them, he also thought about the old man and his genius.

His lips fumbled for the words. He strained his head to look into the old man's eyes. He tried a smile, then he felt the tears come up. The old man let go, and with his head ringing he drove to the corner, picked up his car and carried it up the brick steps to its parking spot on the porch.

RUDOLPH
VALENTINO

I BEGAN reading about Rudolph Valentino while my father was dying. I carried my book to his home and placed it among the Valium, the codeine and the syringes. One day I showed him a photograph of the Great Lover to distract him from the imminent loss of his earthly life. Perhaps the beauty of Valentino's face would call to mind a former lover he wished to visit one last time. As a boy he went to the Metropolitan with his mother and father to hear Caruso sing. Perhaps they also went to the cinema under the El to see *The Four Horsemen.* He accompanied his mother to the chicken market and helped the butcher track down a chicken. Valentino was alive then, too. Or perhaps my father would recall his own physical beauty, of which he was so proud. Women in their seventies stop me on the street and say, "Are you Edward's son? You look just like him."

"Yes," I answer with pride.

"Your father was so handsome."

Fifty years earlier these same women waited in the rain to get a three-second glimpse of Valentino's body, if it was really his resting there in the bronze coffin. Some said it was a wax image: Valentino had been disfigured by a jealous husband and rather than be seen that way sought refuge in an asylum.

My father was grotesque now. Only I could look at him. His grotesqueness compounded my love. I adored him. Exactly half of his head was bald and half had some prickles of gray hair. He resembled an Indian. One of Valentino's guides was an American Indian named Black Feather. The other was an old Egyptian named Meselope who lived in the time before Christ. Valentino did not make a move without consulting them, especially during the reign of his second wife, Natacha Rambova, a stage designer. My father lived under one ruler. On the bald half of his head was an enormous crater carved out by a foreign, well-dressed neurosurgeon named Catibe. My father had difficulty with the name because if he got it right he would know he was dying. He felt the crater with his beautiful gentian-violet fingers. The muscles in his neck had also been carved out. He had no shoulder. Clothes did not stay on him and he died with a pajama top thrown over his chest. He had lost the vision out of his left eye and was unable to walk. He had been proud of his legs. "I had legs of steel," he said. He was also proud of his chest expansion. Valentino was not let into the Royal Naval Academy because his chest expansion lacked one inch. He grew conscious of his chest expansion and worked on it until it reached the prescribed width and surpassed it.

My father looked at the photograph of Valentino and said nothing. He said nothing when I played Caruso or wheeled him to a window to look onto the light of day. He was alone with his vision of eternity, but at the same time repressed levels of his earthly being rose in him. He greeted everyone by name, then immediately flew into a rage, hallucinated, depersonalized, swore and punched, without warning fled to some part of his past. He was disrupting the routine on the desert to the point where the other Arabs conspired to send him to the hospital. There's no room on the desert for a crazy dying man. He asked me to stay at his side. A dying man knows everything and he knew that I loved him. I became his eyes and his legs. It was January, and a blanket of snow covered the sand. He insisted it was August, the month he had taken for his vacation. It was August. Just to witness another day was worth all the trouble. He had to keep peeing, otherwise a catheter had to be inserted, and Dr. Habibe did not have one in his office. They have catheters in hospitals, but my father did not want to die in a hospital. He wanted to die in the open air, he wanted to see death approaching on a horse in the sky.

My task harnessed me to his body. For example, I became intimate with his penis. It was a beautiful uncircumcised penis hidden deep in waves of pubic hair that had already begun to straighten. He insisted on standing up to pee and held on to his walker while I guided his penis into the urinal with my forefinger and thumb. His body trembled. Pain spread over his face, focusing in his kind hazel eyes.

"Now pee!" I commanded. "I'm so happy when you pee!"

He pressed down with all his strength, his soft belly inflating. "Come on!" he prodded himself. "Turn on the faucet! Flush the toilet!"

Listening to the running water helped him along. The tips of my fingers felt far-off urine begin its trek from his bladder. A wave of exhilaration spread through me the way it spreads through the Indian who with his ear to the ground hears the stampeding buffaloes.

"Let her flow!" I screamed. Soon wonderful urine would pass through that self-same penis that had contributed to my creation. For this alone my father earned my respect. As his child I am living proof that he made love to a woman at least on one occasion. He may have used his penis on other occasions, as from my bed I often heard him moan and groan. His partner, however, was silent as mine often is, but when I want to hear the words when she is entering an ecstatic throe and I look up at her beautiful face communing with the cosmos, I sometimes implore her to say something nice. "Let me hear it!" I exhort her and then do my best to intensify her throe to assure her that her proclamations will not be in vain. She sounds off, telling me she loves me, repeats it over and over, I love you, I love you, unleashing me now to fulfill myself on a perfectly acquiesced woman.

Valentino's penis was likely uncircumcised, but there is no evidence he ever used it. Sworn testimony during his divorce trials indicates that neither of his marriages was consummated, and no woman came forward to say that she had felt him. Yet millions of women adored him, while my father and I made love to women in the ordinary way time after time, year after year, and we had to appeal for adoration.

My father was unable to pee and dropped into his armchair. He asked to be taken down to the porch to put some distance between ourselves and his deathbed. We had not used the porch much. In foul weather we raised the awning. When the sun was bright we lowered it. The family next door had the exact same awning, and we raised and lowered ours in keeping with theirs so as not to lose the continuity of the corner. Going down there now was a pilgrimage to a distant land of health and beauty. A sparrow streaked in front of us and the sun was red. A lovely garden of honeysuckle and snowballs separated us from the passing caravans.

Valentino was just a boy when he died, thirty-one years old, and if time stops for the dead I am older than he, I feel like his father and my impulse is to protect him. I want to protect the way he was as a man. I want to protect the way I am as a man. If I feel genuine love for another man, I don't want some gossip columnist calling me a sissy boy. Such accusations contributed to Valentino's early death by a busted gut and I don't want to die the same way. I want to die the way they say John Garfield died, in the arms of a woman. I want to live the way Errol Flynn lived. I want to be understated like Richard Barthelmess and agile like Douglas Fairbanks.

Today is March 26, 1977. My father has been dead two months. It has been a brutal winter, more frost and snow than since the time of the Pilgrims. A mountain of snow covered his grave as recently as a week ago. The ground above him and the lake nearby are still frozen, but he rests between two trees and they are about to bloom. Birds are singing and as time passes he emerges more clearly in my mind's eye. He is walking toward me with that characteristic gait of his, placing one foot directly in front of the other and musically swinging his arms. He is smiling, he is happy to see me. I hear his gentle voice. There's no particular message. The date is also noted in anticipation of a film scheduled for release this summer on the life of Valentino starring Rudolf Nureyev, the great ballet dancer. A photo album with extensive legends is also scheduled. I learned all this from a librarian at the public library who has a large private collection of Valentino photos, a rare book of his poems and an out-of-print copy of Natacha Rambova's memoirs. This librarian is also a devotee of the dance and lover of women, going out with a different one every night and making love to her, and he assured me that although Nureyev is an avowed homosexual his portrayal of Valentino will be forthright, fair and accurate. This is so because Nureyev himself is forthright, fair and accurate. He has received numerous offers to star in films, including one from Federico Fellini. Nureyev is a good choice because little if anything is known about his private life, just as little is known about the private life of Valentino. We can dismiss all the junk written about Valentino because he was not taken seriously. His acting, for example, was not taken seriously. As an actor he was way ahead of his time, especially as Monsieur Beaucaire, which he played opposite the great Nazimova. Nazimova will not survive her time, Valentino will.

"Let's hope so," I said, "but why start out with a Russian homo-sexual ballet dancer when Valentino's sexuality is almost impossible to determine? It's best to leave it up in the air rather than say it's this way or that. Furthermore, Valentino was not a great dancer, he was a good ballroom dancer whose tango was a little above average. George Raft's tango was just as good. Nureyev is closer to being a Nijinsky than a Valentino and Valentino taught the tango to Nijinsky. Most important of all, Valentino was a swarthy, willowy Italian and a bit of a lowlife, having been arrested for white slavery and bigamy—he spent three days in the Tombs. No, I think an unknown Italian would be better. You need an element of mystery when treating the life of Valentino."

"I have to go," the librarian said.

"Wait a minute, wait a minute! There may be an element of mystery here neither you nor I nor Nureyev are aware of."

Shortly after Valentino died, I told the librarian, there was a party in Greenwich Village attended by the sultry actress Nita Naldi, my Uncle Artie and other suspected gigolos, actors, singers and dancers. Artie has not worked a single day out of his fifty-nine years. He followed to the letter the Italian custom that if the father leaves the home the eldest son replaces him; he is now the man of the house and lords over everything in it, especially any abandoned women. Every day throughout his thirties, forties and fifties, Artie's mother made him go down to his knees and kiss her hand as a way of promising that he would never leave, and so he sits home and reads the papers while his abandoned sister Rosie goes to work in all kinds of weather just so her valiant brother can buy the finest clothes, play high-stakes poker on Friday night and bet the horses on Saturday. At the same time Artie has not been known to lie, especially these last years when we all have come to accept him and he has fallen ill with blood pressure so high that a stroke or heart attack is inevitable very soon. He has begun to explain himself a little, even hinted at calling up an attractive young woman he recently met, which comes as a relief since his mistress is the wife of an old friend of the family. The medication Artie takes depletes his sex drive, he is about to lose his mistress and finds himself telling saucy stories. At the party Nita Naldi sat in a rocking chair, crossed her meaty legs and fondled a breast, prompting everyone to gather around her. She had been drinking and talked freely. "It was a moment when one could expect the truth from her, even an indiscretion or two," Artie told me.

"Did you make love to Valentino off-screen?" someone asked her.

"No, no—we were friends, like brother and sister."

A young crooner in a tight brown suit and bow tie and with dark curly hair parted down the middle crawled up to her. "I would like to suck your cunt," he said.

"I've been sucked by the best, I'm tired of that, beyond it," Miss Naldi said.

The crooner said, "I'll do anything you wish if you will go on a promotional tour with me as Valentino reincarnated as a crooner and you as the woman he held so often in his arms."

"What's your name?"

"Rudy Vallee."

The tour did not materialize but the crooner kept the bastard-ized form of Valentino's name and went on to become a popular singer for many, many years. Valentino revealed through several mediums that he has been reincarnated as both men and women living in ancient and modern times and almost always as an or-dinary man, a hard worker with a family and a house. Perhaps Valentino was reincarnated as Rudy Vallee and perhaps in his role as Valentino, Rudolf Nureyev will transform into something other than a dancer, a painter or a poet or simply a man, an honest good man with myriad feelings, a human being instead of a talent.

The librarian said I could go up to his apartment the following evening, browse through the photographs and take the ones I want, and if he has time he would search among his pile of books for Rambova's memoirs. But I wavered, there was something in-judicious about applying another man's photos to my ideas. The librarian may not like what I say about Valentino, I thought, which could violate the good faith he displayed toward Valentino and Nureyev. In our hearts we know what Valentino looks like and many of us have imagined the heat and power of his muscle inside our mouths, our asses and our cunts, felt his lips driving against ours in an attempt to reach the core of our being.

But how many of us know what Valentino sounds like? He died in 1926, one year before the advent of the talkies. Whether he would have continued making motion pictures or retired at the pinnacle of fame is of course a moot point, but there was some discussion after he died about the quality of his voice. Some said it was high-pitched and unpleasant, like John Gilbert's, whose voice in comparison to his beauty was embarrassing. Others said it was soft and mellifluent. Toward the end of his life Valentino recorded a few songs, the kind you sing to children while they are falling asleep. Here his voice is filled with warmth and kind-ness, possesses the resonance of Ronald Colman's voice and the articulation of Cedric Hardwicke's. In all likelihood Valentino would have made talking pictures because at the time of his last film, *Son of the Sheik,* he was deeply in debt and also was eager to play the lives of great Italians like Christopher Columbus, Cesare Borgia and Benvenuto Cellini. Valentino was resourceful, adaptive, he would have made the most of the opportunity to speak. He would have placed less emphasis on the whites of his eyes and flaring nostrils and would have devoured the woman in his arms through his mouth.

There was a singer in Manhattan while Valentino was there who was sensitive to manners of speaking and accents. Maureen "Frenchy" Englen was her name and she sang at the Copacabana. Before she settled on a French accent, Miss Englen tried a host of others, including her native accent, Swedish, but none worked so well on her audience as the French. It had a way of penetrating the hard exterior, opening previously unexplored avenues to the heart. French was new: the time was before World War I, before any substantial wave of French immigration. Patrons listened raptly as if they were hearing about love and passion for the first time, and they left the Copacabana humming and singing songs that became American standards, like "Sweet Georgia Brown" and "Way Down Yonder in New Orleans." Between sets Miss Englen caught a fast bite at Giolitto's, where Valentino was a busboy, his last menial job before becoming a tea dancer at Maxim's. She made a point of sitting at a table attended by the busboy who did not speak, who stood in a corner waiting for someone to use a glass or a fork. From time to time he'd gesture toward Miss Englen with a crystal pitcher filled with ice-cold water or hold up a clean, shiny fork, entreating her with his eyes to allow him to refill her glass or replace a soiled fork with a clean one. She smiled at him and he smiled back. He tried to make her laugh by mimicking everyone, including the maître d'. One night, a busy one, a foghorn sounded. Red-faced, mustachioed men in tuxedos raised and turned their heads expecting to see a ship in distress. "The busboy in the corner did it!" Miss Englen cried. Everyone applauded, rose in unison and surrounded Valentino and begged him to teach them how to do the foghorn. He showed "Frenchy" how to do it but she could never do it quite so well as Valentino. Throughout her life whenever her thoughts fled to him, she would cup her hands, raise her thumbs to her lips and blow, and whenever she saw Valentino she'd say, "Please do the foghorn?" She left behind a few observations about his manner of speaking:

"Rudy would think carefully of how everything should be said before he uttered a sound. Sometimes he was ready to deliver but we were way ahead of him. He said it anyway, he was serious, but we couldn't hold back the laughter. As soon as he digested how inappropriate he sounded, he burst out laughing too, harder than anyone. He was forever asking what we had said. 'What did you say?' he'd ask, touching us on the arm or shoulder."

Valentino was in love with Maureen Englen's hair, which was long, straight and red. Late one night while he was setting up for the following evening, she passed the restaurant and he saw her hair in the light of the lamppost outside. He hurriedly un-locked the door and ran onto the sidewalk. "I would like to make love to your hair," he said.

"Come to my hotel later on."

"I want to go to Central Park, lie in the grass and hold you," and then he rested a cheek on her head and gathered her hair in his arms.

"I'm going to a party at the Plaza. You should have told me sooner."

Valentino felt the life drain out of his face, leaving it on the verge of tears. He was desperate to enter the life of someone respectable. A great deal had gone into the creation of his des-peration and at some point it became uncontrollable, fashioned a life of its own, tugged at his facial muscles and escaped with them, effacing his charm and beauty. His depression lingered for hours. He'd wander around the city and stop at telephones and ponder whether to call someone who might be able to help him. He'd pick up the phone, dial a number but while it was ringing put it down. Immediately his spirits began to climb. Rejection somehow moved him forward, and his desperation receded to a deep region where it lay dormant until the next provocation.

"What's the matter with you?" Miss Englen said, placing a hand on his cheek.

"I'm disappointed."

"All right, we'll have one drink but then I must go."

She cast a worried look in the direction of the Plaza and then Valentino placed an arm around her firm hips and led her into the restaurant to an unkempt table. He cleared a path so his hand could travel to hers. "I would like to hold your hand," he said, and she surrendered her hand. His fingers played along the diamonds in her ring. "Give me the ring so I don't have to work here."

She looked away.

"Are you angry?"

"I must go now."

"I'll tell you when to go—I'm the boss!"

She turned her head abruptly as if Valentino's face had suddenly grown grotesque. He was unable to translate her expression but it frightened and provoked anger in him at the same time. She wore on her face the difference in their worlds and her impulse was to put more distance between them, going so far away from Valentino that his existence was obliterated. She rose from her chair and made for the door but Valentino blocked her passage, letting her through only when he was about to strike her. Coexisting with the paraphernalia of desperation was a sense of decency; Valentino had a profound respect for other human beings and he had the uncanny knack of seeing in his mind what he wished to do in the real world. He saw himself slap her, and while he stood on the sidewalk outside Giolitto's his mind fought for the proper words to express an apology. He knew all along that at some point he would run after her, and he was convinced she would accept a sincere apology. The increasing distance between himself and her hair filled him with ecstasy. He felt each strand of radiant hair passing between his lips. He cherished the memory of what might have happened in her hotel room had he consented one day to go there. Valentino had grave doubts about whether he could satisfy Maureen Englen sexually. She might laugh at him the way she laughed at his impressions. She might look down at his penis and judge it insufficient compared to the penises of the carefree wealthy men she knew and so he would not take off his shorts until the very last moment, when she was so enmeshed in her own senses that she could not act as spectator to anything let alone to that tool whose heat and strength she had to consume in order to continue her journey. He would kick off his shorts himself or have her rip them off, then blindly grope for him with a bony, veiny hand, locate him, fill her hand with him and then skillfully guide him into herself. Now his penis was as much a part of her as it was a part of him. She did not carry it around all the time, that was all, she laid it down temporarily the way one lays down jewelry before going to sleep. The next day the moment he came through the door she would throw her arms around his neck and look up into his face with her eyes shining. "I thought about your penis all day," she would say.

He lost sight of Maureen Englen's hair and broke into a run without deciding what to say. He knocked people over. He saw her waiting on a corner for the light to change. He gained ground, risked his life crossing the street and arrived at her side huffing and puffing. She glanced at him, then returned her gaze in front of her, not saying anything and with no expression on her face of surprise or anger. It was as if they had been walking together all along and so Valentino believed there was still a chance of spending the night with her in the grass under the stars and moon.

"Phew!" He exhaled long and hard and wiped the sweat from his brow. "I almost killed myself running after you. Look, I'm sorry. There was a misunderstanding. I don't express myself too well in English but I know I would like you to buy me a drink now."

"You walk too slow!" she snapped at him. "At the next corner please go in another direction."

Suddenly, he had no desire to be with her. Her gratuitous attack extinguished any lofty feelings he had had for her. Her words pierced his skin, sought out those parts of her he loved and extinguished them. He walked in silence beside her trying to keep up, not announcing his intention to do exactly what she wanted, and so she exhibited a bit of surprise, doing a hop and a skip and yelping when at the next corner, without uttering a sound, Valentino tapped her taut behind and walked away.

He felt light as a feather, unburdened now not only of Maureen Englen but of his job as a busboy. He tore off his apron and tossed it into the street and vowed never to spend another moment on a menial job even if it meant starving to death. Since arriving in New York about a year before, he had worked as a messenger, clerk in an Italian grocery store and busboy at Giolitto's. Such labor warped his mind, numbed it for long periods after he quit, inflicted him like a disease from which he had to convalesce. Still, it was not clear what he wanted to do. He had a degree in scientific farming but in his heart he knew he would never be a farmer. Otherwise, he reasoned, he would stick it out on any job, scrimp and save until he had enough money to buy a Ford and then in a pair of overalls and with a song in his heart he would drive to a farm state, say Nebraska or Indiana. Nor had he as yet learned how to dance. Dancing was not popular in the poverty-stricken village of Castellaneta except on Christmas Day, when spirited young couples danced the tarantella around the village square and the old men danced a dance all their own, hopping around on one leg with a forefinger pointed at the temple and hooting and hollering like wild Indians, their eyes ablaze and unseeing. The dance of the old men frightened little Rodolpho and he ran away and hid, but when he grew older he realized that the dance did the old men a lot of good—it was a day off from pondering their dead. Once during a burial on the hill he ran up there and pushed his way through the mourners holding long-stem roses. He went up to the bereaved widower and said, "Why don't you do that dance, you know. . ." and he hopped around crazily on one leg, incensing the family, which converged and pounced on him, pummeling him with their ringed fingers, roses, rosaries, crucifixes. And if he was wandering over his beloved hills, the late-afternoon sun casting a red hue over the land, and he saw an old man down in the valley rocking back and forth in a simple chair, Valentino would approach him quietly, place a hand on his shoulder and say, "Why don't you do your dance, old man?"

"What dance? What are you talking about?" The path of the old man's grief required 364 days to traverse and it was only on the next day, Christmas Day, that he was allowed a respite. His heart was light and gay on this day, his body grew in harmony with his heart and he danced his crazy dance around the village square.

Sometimes his mother hummed while she was sewing. "Dance with me," she'd say to the boy, whose head barely reached her breasts, and he'd slip his arm around her waist and hold her hand high and tight, but after a few turns he'd begin stepping on her wooden shoes. "Don't you know how to dance yet, Rodolpho?" she'd say and then return to her stitch and smile, her thoughts fleeing to the tumultuous night when her husband, Giovanni, proposed to her standing beside his horses and then they danced a waltz around the village square.

Valentino decided to return to his room above Giolitto's to collect his things, including his standing oval mirror and wooden rocking horse. He practiced faces in the mirror and riding on the horse. Sometimes he positioned the horse in front of the mirror and made faces and rode and told outlandish stories. He considered explaining to Giolitto why he was leaving but the old man's response would certainly be that for an Italian to carve a niche for himself in America he had to work hard and it didn't matter at what. Giolitto had been generous but only so long as Valentino was an employee. The best he, Valentino, could hope for was becoming a waiter or maître d'. The old man's generosity was confining and so Valentino decided to eliminate him, leave in the middle of the night and never come back, and as Giolitto's existence was confined to his restaurant, Valentino was sure he would not see him anywhere else. He tiptoed past the front of the restaurant and went around to the back where an old linden tree stood beneath his terrace, which was bathed in moonlight. He took off his shoes, then his sinewy body weaved its way through the branches and leaves to the top. There he crouched, spread his arms, sprang into the air and with great strength and control hurtled over the low wall surrounding his terrace. He landed like a feather, then stood a while in the moonlight. He heard anonymous coughs, a late diner's fork hitting his plate. He looked around himself, at the tree, low and thick, at the darkened buildings where lovers slept in one another's arms, at his bare feet, up at the black sky studded with stars and a brilliant moon. He lowered his head in despair and tears fell from his curiously slanted eyes. "Forgive me, Mother," he said aloud. "I'm sorry, Father. Forgive me, Italy."

Valentino wanted a wife, a home and children for the same reasons my father wanted them. One reason was to have a child fight for his honor when he was no longer around. To walk up to a blaspheming writer and punch him in the mouth. Writers, his wives, juicers, extras—everybody said of Valentino that he was incapable of making love to a woman off-screen. As we never lied to one another, prefacing everything we said with, "Tell me man to man..." believe me when I say that Valentino made love to every woman he met off-screen, beginning with his mother, and if a man has courage enough to make love to his mother, he has courage enough to make love to a stranger. Valentino made love to thousands of strangers and was a gentleman with each and every one. Even if he knew the woman for years he greeted her warmly, spontaneously, as if he had just met her. After he made love to her, he thanked her the way a man dying of thirst thanks that person who lifts a cup of cool water to his scorched lips. Then he sent her packing with the same good humor he had displayed on greeting her, placing an arm around her shoulders as he ushered her to the front door.

Valentino had hundreds of children and I fancy I am one of them. It happened one wintry afternoon in Naples in a tenement near the railway station. Bundled up in a magnificent greatcoat with fur collar and cuffs, Rudy was walking briskly as he was late for a luncheon with the great Italian poet Gabriele D'Annunzio. Valentino knew he could not play the romantic lover forever and was looking forward to the day when as a man he would play Christopher Columbus, Cesare Borgia and Benvenuto Cellini. He wanted to consult with D'Annunzio about the lives of these immortal Italians, and to convince the poet that he was literate as well as beautiful, he brought along a book of his poems entitled *A Baby's Skin*. You could tell Valentino coming from a mile away by his gait and the musical swinging of his arms. He placed one foot directly in front of the other and swung his arms high in front and just as high in back. His walk reflected his determination. And he never looked you straight in the face, tilting his head slightly away to hide his cauliflower ear and his scar. It was a remarkable feat of nature how his head had evolved into such a perfect shape when at birth it was shaped like an eggplant. Upon seeing his son for the first time, Giovanni Guglielmi exclaimed, "My God—his head is shaped like an eggplant!"

Valentino tilted his head away from the street in case some Neapolitans recognized him, which was unlikely, for although he was famous in America, France and England, he was unknown in his native land. Mussolini had banned his films and Pope Pius IX had condemned the tango, instructing all priests to attack the savage dance. It was only after two Roman aristocrats danced it for him one Sunday morning in St. Peter's Square that His Holiness reinstated the tango as a respectable dance. Valentino was outraged at the choice of dancers. "The tango is a dance of the poor people of Buenos Aires!" he bellowed to reporters at the pier before boarding the ocean liner *Leviathan*. In the early 1920s one traveled to Europe by boat. There was no commercial airplane travel. The lack of any explains the wonderful reception Gertrude Ederle received upon her arrival in New York after swimming the English Channel. Her arrival coincided with Valentino's lying-in-state and it was while he was lying in state that Pola Negri, the sizzling siren of the Hollywood lots, contemplated hiring a mail plane to fly her to Campbell's Funeral Church, but then health officials in New York granted a delay in burial. Valentino's remains were packed in ice and Miss Negri took the train.

"The tango is a sad thought that is danced!" Valentino raged on. "And only I can interpret it the way it should be interpreted. I taught it to Nijinsky, surely I can teach it to the Pope!"

Also at the pier fielding reporters' questions was the daring Italian explorer General Umberto Nobile. The General had flown over the top of the world in his dirigible *Norge* and was on the last leg of a goodwill tour of the United States. He was short and bony but his cigar-shaped dirigible loomed high above everything, above the *Leviathan*, above Valentino and the reporters, above the skyscrapers of New York. The meeting between Valentino and the General was unexpected and they practically jumped into one another's arms, recognizing in one another their beloved homeland. They pressed close together, shoulder to shoulder, arm in arm, the leg of one inside the leg of the other. The ashes from their cigarettes blew off and drifted toward Italy. The General was Mussolini's right-hand man, so Valentino whispered in his hear, "Please talk to Mussolini about showing my films. He must know that I'm still an Italian citizen, that I'm like a conquering army on foreign soil, an Italian ship in neutral waters with our red, white and green hoisted high and flapping proudly in the wind."

At this point a reporter asked the General, "What did you do when you reached the North Pole?"

"I dropped the Italian flag and an oaken cross blessed by the Pope. Then I played the 'Bells of St. Giusto' on the gramophone and my crew and I toasted with wine-spiked eggnog."

Then a reporter asked Valentino, "Will you return to America, Mr. Valentino?"

"Reports that I will desert America for Italy are ridiculous. What can I play over there, Samson? I have made my success here and shall remain here. If I return to Italy, it is only to visit my parents' graves."

The General whispered into Valentino's ear, "Baron Fassini is making *Quo Vadis?* in Rome with Emil Jannings. Mussolini's apartment is directly over the Baron's in the Palazzo Tittoni. Tell the Baron I sent you and to set up an appointment with Mussolini. I'll be flying over Rome in two weeks. I'll see you all then."

"*Ci vediamo*," said Valentino, and he kissed the General's lips.

"Mr. Valentino," a reporter began, "during the day you wear a spiked platinum bracelet on your right wrist, and you wear a gold bracelet to bed. Are they slave bracelets?"

"No, not really."

"What is their significance, sir?"

Valentino smiled mysteriously, then hurried across the gangplank.

He was desperate for recognition in his homeland. Success was not complete unless his mother knew about it and although she was dead she would somehow know. He carried her around in his heart. Whatever he knew, she knew. If D'Annunzio liked his poems, he would present them to her at her grave. Standing above her remains, he would hold the book aloft, as she existed more in the air above her grave than anywhere else. His fame had brought shame to the family name, tormenting his mother's spirit. Dick Dorgan writing in *Photoplay* called her "a wop or something like that," when in truth she was French. According to Dorgan, it was this wop who filled little Rodolpho's head with romantic stories, something about fighting duels over a woman's honor. She was the Madonna and Valentino spent the rest of his life looking for Her in other women, searching far and wide for that serene face with calm, soft eyes. His marriages failed on her account. He became a queer on her account. She'd dress him in expensive smocks, then parade him around town so that the other wops could say, "Such a beautiful boy! He should have been a girl! I've never seen such long lashes on a boy, you should clip them, Mrs. Valentino. Close your eyes for us, little Rodolpho!" And one weekend when he returned home from Dante Alighieri college and forgot to take the condom out of his pantaloons and it fell out while his mother was straightening his room, she bent down, picked it up and examined it. She cried and told her husband, "Just tell him not to bring those things home anymore." But Giovanni Guglielmi locked the boy in a closet. He spent the night there, and after his father opened the door and ordered him to bed without eating, he discovered his mother in his bedroom and she cuddled him and made sure he ate the sandwich she had hidden in his bedclothes. At his school near the Adriatic, Rodolpho was placed in a barrel with only his head protruding from a hole in the top as punishment for not drinking the warm milk. The glass towered above him, still, enormous. His arms froze at his side, unable to rise and clasp the glass for fear it would engulf him. After school he ran home with a load in his pants and begged his mother to take him out of that school.

Valentino returned to his hometown from time to time and took leisurely strolls under the El with his dogs in tow. He passed my father's house, the large brick one on the corner, and doffed his hat at us huddled together on the porch. "He's the nicest-looking man I've ever seen," my father said, and saluted the Great Lover, who then continued toward the El until its shadows engulfed him. Upon seeing him the wops under there told him that in their entire lifetimes they had still not seen lashes as long and curly as the ones he had as a child, would he please close his eyes and display them one last time. Valentino laughed heartily, bending his body in the shape of a bow. "You are exaggerating, ladies!" he roared. He pitied them for not having anything more remarkable to remember than the lashes of a strange child, but as soon as he arrived at his suite at the Hotel Degli Artisti he went directly to a mirror, pressed his face against it and closed and opened and closed and opened his eyes. He stared at his face, remaining perfectly still. In time it lost its familiarity, the spirit having fled. Grotesque features and sounds surfaced. They flashed, then disappeared. At any moment, however, they might return and he would be staring at a hideous monster with bloodshot eyes, twisted mouth, smoldering, cavernous skin. He turned his head away just in time. After that he looked at himself only for the time it took him to shave. Valentino looked into every mirror he ever passed but now he glanced sidewise into them while knitting his brows, looking only to see that he had not grown old. At times he was inexplicably drawn to staring at himself for long periods and one day a remarkable thing hap-

pened—he kept staring beyond his worst fears and slowly, mi-
raculously, his mother's face replaced the face in the mirror and
looked out at him with kindness. Valentino's greatest pleasure was
having the door to the closet in which he was locked opened to
the light of the world and seeing his mother looking down at
him with kindness, tears of joy streaming down her cheeks. She
was naked and she picked him up and cuddled him in her soft,
thick arms. She lavished brief sweet kisses all over his head, on
his eyes, his nose and his lips. As she carried him to bed he
pressed his face against the red hide of her chest and looked
down at her breasts. Once he was safe and warm, she stayed with
him to make sure he ate the piece of lamb she had hidden in his
bedclothes, then she rocked him and sang to him.

Her name was Beatrice Barbin, and her father was a surgeon
practicing in Paris. She taught school in a one-room wooden
schoolhouse situated in a valley surrounded by tranquil, rolling
hills. In the spring and summer she held classes in the grass,
mingling among her children, reading and singing. The circumstances surrounding her flight from France are not known except
that her father had been involved in a scandal that would not
leave her life unthreatened. One day he was waiting for her,
holding the reins of his magnificent black charger and her linen
cape. His eyes were burning, and his full mane of silver hair was
blowing wildly around his face. He caressed her and spoke with
desperation. "I love you more than anything in the world, more
than myself and more than my work, and my wish is that you
save yourself."

"We will go together."

"No, I've lived among these people my entire life, and the
events that have arisen are my doing. But you must go now. Please
do this for your father. We will be together after this thing is
over."

She rode day and night through thick woods, over the Alps
and the Apennines, descending into Italy and then drifting south
until she reached the stony, sun-drenched fields of Castellaneta,
where she found a job as a teacher. She taught the children of

Italy with the same dedication and fervor she had taught the children of France. When the circus came to town, she gave the children the day off and accompanied them and their parents, mainly farmers, to see the animals and the clowns, performers in glittering costumes flying high above the town and scaling a wire extending from one end of the main street to the other. A flock of white pigeons was released, and balloons of various colors with long strings were tied around the children's wrists. There was an elephant and a camel as well as small animals like guinea pigs and gerbils, none of them caged. The happy children fed them, pretended to be bit by them, ran from them and chased them. Then the most beautiful Arabian horses with blankets of star dust and golden plumes were assembled by a tall, mustached man with eyes like an eagle and a finely chiseled nose. Giovanni Guglielmi had been a cavalry officer but had to resign his commission after killing a member of the House of Colonna in a duel over a woman's honor. One man against a powerful house, he sought refuge in a circus touring the continent. Now his horses galloped round and round the village square with their heads down, their long shiny tails unfurled behind them, occasionally darting a worried glance at the onlookers but never straying from their rhythm and line. The children mounted their backs and jumped off. Farmers and their wives, the village doctor and the mayor jumped on and off. Suddenly, cruelly, the sirocco arrived at the shores of Italy, hot winds and driving rain pelted the faces of the villagers, whose bewildered eyes turned skyward to ask God why He was punishing them. But then everyone rallied and an enormous tent went up over everything. The earth, however, was soft and the supporting rods began to slip. "Look!" a farmer screamed, pointing to the canvas high up undulating like a mainsail in a strong wind. "The tent is going to collapse!" There was a rush to get into the open air, some children were crushed underfoot and the elephant trundled through the town. Giovanni Guglielmi stayed behind with his horses, steadying them, embracing them, and he noticed a young woman watching him from the other side of the tent. "How about a ride!" he called out.

"Oh, no," Beatrice Barbin answered, approaching slowly. "They've had enough."

"Come, I'll help you up," and he gripped her slender waist with his huge hands and hoisted her onto the lead horse. She expressed her joy freely with the ride. "How wonderful this feels!" she cried. "I can go on and on!" When she passed in front of him, she smiled and waved, and he waved back, watching her closely. A voice inside of him said, "Now that's beauty," and all his resources gathered to preserve it. Later on, lying beside her in the grass under a brilliant moon, he said, "I will give up my horses and build a house with spacious rooms and a tiled roof. Mimosa and fruit trees will flourish in our courtyard, and we will have a vegetable garden. I know enough about animals to practice veterinary medicine. It will make me happy to serve as midwife to the farmers' cattle and care for their pigs when they get sick."

"And I will stay at home and bake black bread and care for our children," Beatrice said, and then they danced a waltz in the rain around the village square.

First they had a girl, whom they named Bianca, but she died at the age of nine. My father's twin, Edmund, died at childbirth. Then for the Guglielmis there was a son, Alberto, who when he stopped growing looked exactly like Valentino except for his nose, which was pudgy and dipped at the tip. My father had an elder sister named Carolyn. Valentino was born on May 6, 1895, and my father was born on May 5, 1907. Their mothers went to church and received a special blessing from their monsignors. As a boy my father had pigeons and was tough. Every day after school he fought the Irish. He punched a classmate who made fun of his real name, Nunzio. He shot crap on the high school roof. Carolyn told their father, who then smashed my father's bicycle to smithereens. In turn my father bought a hat and let it fly away while waiting for a train. His father went into the garage and killed the pigeons. Valentino went into the general store and charged goods to his father's account. Outside, leaning against a wooden column supporting the eaves, he waited for children to come up the road in order to sell them the goods. With the money he bought candy, stuffing his mouth and pockets. His father locked him in the closet.

Valentino refused to learn a trade or apprentice himself to the land. He refused to care for the farmers' pigs. He disappeared for days at a time only to turn up in a Taranto jail charged with vagrancy. He raided apple orchards and instead of going to school found adventure in the hills and caves of Apulia. Dressed as the bandit Mussolino, the Robin Hood of Calabria, Valentino leapt from rock to rock with his wooden sword raised and fought the King's soldiers. "Who is the most beautiful woman in Castellaneta?" was his cry. "Beatrice Barbin is the most beautiful woman in Castellaneta!" was the retort. Once, a soldier answered that his sister was the most beautiful woman in Castellaneta and Valentino would have drowned him in the fountain if the village doctor had not intervened. His mother's beauty was unparalleled in the town. She was the favorite of each and every one of the King's soldiers, even the King himself, and they each had their turn with her. She did not differentiate one penis from another, they were all the same to her—thick ones and thin ones, long ones and short ones. She did not differentiate her husband's penis from those of visiting princes from far-off kingdoms. It was normal that a soldier relieve himself inside of her. Her body was there the way a window was there, and it made little difference what the soldier had in mind, running his hands over the length and breadth of her gargantuan breasts, for example, or feeling the warmth at her thighs—because the end was always the same and it was the end in all things that mattered. The end in lovemaking was relief, peace, sleep, readying the soldier for the next day's battle. Beatrice Barbin's wisdom lay in minimizing the importance of everything. In the process she put everyone at ease. She put little Rodolpho at ease when one day he came home from school and between tears recounted what had happened in the shower. A school chum had pointed at his penis and laughed. Valentino said to his mother, "As a baby did something happen to my penis, stunting its growth?"

Beatrice Barbin threw back her head and laughed. "Someday that little thing will grow into a tool of pleasure and will make the ladies happy."

She minimized her husband's disappearance from the village, replacing him as veterinarian and in their garden under the scorching sun. Immediately, suitors came to the house with food, promise of free medical care, jewelry and tablecloths. She received each and every one with good cheer as if her Giovanni had gone off on a mission of such magnitude, such nobility, that it scoffed at infidelity. Even if he was gone forever she had known such happiness with him that it bequeathed an unexpected gift: she discovered a hairsbreadth of him in everything, including other men. One early evening in fall she was saying goodbye to Michele Converso, the village doctor, holding his head in her hands and kissing it all over, the immense sky filled with black, low-hanging clouds, the only light coming from a strip of bright orange sitting on the horizon, when a youthful rider with full lips and long, black serpentine hair brought his mare to a halt at the gate.

"Until tomorrow then, Michele," and the doctor rode off. Then she directed to the handsome youth, "And what do we have here?"

"I'm Giacomo Puccini of Lucca and I have a letter for you from my mother, Albina." He handed her the letter, then took up his reins.

"Where are you going in such a hurry?" A bolt of lightning lit the distant wooded hills, thunder cracked near and far.

"I promised my mother I'd return home as soon as I delivered the letter."

"In that case . . ."

"Why, what do you have in mind?" Puccini smiled from atop his horse, a magnificent specimen set against the tumultuous sky.

"I have a lot on my mind," Beatrice said, searching the youth's playful eyes and smiling too, whereupon he dismounted and with an arm around her waist walked beside her on the winding flagstones leading to the front door. They undressed, then she led him to a straight chair and sat him down. He looked up at her helplessly as she straddled his legs and sat in his lap, careful not to hurt him, stifle him. She dreamily scanned his body, then ran her hands over his broad shoulders and hard chest and flat stomach. He grasped her winglike hips and lifted her. His long, olive, uncircumcised penis found her wetness. He sighed, closed his eyes. She kissed them lightly and said, "I would like to stay like this and talk, do you mind?"

"I can stay like this forever," Puccini said.

The day her husband left the village, Beatrice Barbin began, had been the happiest day in her son Rodolpho's life. He had been selected to serve as head altar boy at the Castellaneta cathedral. The monsignor, a fanatic Hungarian, accompanied the boy home and said to his father, "Your son has a calling for the priesthood. One day I will take him to Hungary with me."

Her husband killed the monsignor and that night bid farewell to Rodolpho, who was asleep in his small room clothed in darkness except for shafts of moonlight on the ceiling, walls and the boy's coverlet. Giovanni stood at the door, sobbing uncontrollably. He approached the bed quietly and sat down. "I love you," he whispered and then caressed his son and pressed him tight against his chest so that on waking he would be greeted by warmth and strength. "Love your mother and above all your country," Giovanni said and then left.

But what had vexed him so that he was driven to lock Rodolpho in a dark closet night after night? He served the village well as veterinarian. He was respected, as veterinary doctor was one or two rungs above farmer and just one rung beneath physician, mayor and monsignor. Any deficiency in social position was more than compensated for by sweet memories of the cavalry and his love for his wife and children. But he didn't understand malice and so Michele Converso was able to torment him. The physician would ride past their fence tall and proud in the saddle, decked out all in white and high shiny riding boots. If Giovanni was at work in the garden, sweat pouring down his body, he'd stop his work and salute the physician but he ignored him and waved to his wife instead with a whip. Giovanni blinked and blinked his eyes in bewilderment as though an invisible hand were slapping his face. And if Michele Converso and Giovanni happened to be at the same farm, one tending to an animal and the other to a human body, and they met by chance at the well, the physician refused to acknowledge him. One day Giovanni turned to him and said, "What's the matter with you?" He asked her about it and she replied, "Beneath his hard exterior is compassion. When one of his patients dies, he locks himself in his house and cries."

"How do you know?" Giovanni asked her.

"It must be like that," she told him.

Her role as pacifier infuriated him, and he continued to say to the physician, poking his arm now, "What's the matter with you?" He began to feel that he did not exist, not only in the eyes of the physician but in the eyes of the other villagers and his wife and children. Enthusiasm for his work waned. He spoke of changing professions and moving to Spain. He began to gamble and lose. He committed murder.

"And now," Beatrice said, "I should like to read your mother's letter."

"Please wait until I leave," said Puccini, and he slipped himself out of her, got dressed and at the door amid numerous soft kisses said that he would like to visit again.

"Anytime, anytime," Beatrice said with affection. She watched him ride out of view, then opened the letter and read:

Beatrice, my sweet, I just wanted to let you know how bad I feel about your Giovanni, if there's anything I can do. As you know my Pietro departed from this world at the age of 33, leaving me to raise seven wild Indians, but do you know that Toscanini's grandmother gave birth to 22 children, went blind after the last one and shortly after died like a dog? And that the world would not know the voice of Caruso if a wealthy lonely spinster had not taken him away with her, sparing him the fate of his 19 brothers and sisters who all died of malaria?

What are we women supposed to do? Where are we to get money? On the one hand the Pope forbids birth control and on the other he has more money than anybody. He prohibits medical students from using the whole cadaver and then he imports his cardiologist from Texas. Women like us who lose their men at a young age and have children to raise should get together and talk the way alcoholics and gamblers get together and talk.

I'll tell you something right now: if you have to make it with somebody, make it with the physician or the mayor—they have direct lines to the Queen. If I hadn't been nice to a lady-in-waiting to the Queen, my Giacomo could not have gone to the Milan Conservatory. Even at that she allotted funds for one year. You'd think the fucking town itself would grant us the money seeing that seven generations of Puccinis served it faithfully as choirmasters, organists and composers. They have the nerve to tell me that Giacomo isn't serious, he's more interested in bird catching and skirt chasing than composing. Maybe it's so, I think, and I beg him to take a job in the olive oil factory—and do you know what he tells me? "Mama," he says, "you are an essential part of my magnificent destiny. No matter where I am, no matter how many years pass after you die I will have you before my eyes and speak to you."

How can you resist such a boy! I tell you, I just love being around him. When I serve him, I find myself running my hands over his chest and he reaches with a hand under my dress. Eternal damnation awaits me for thinking of making love to him, but what are a few moments of happiness compared to years of sorrow? If I have to fuck my brains out to get him through the next two years, I will and with all my strength.

Aren't men awful, Beatrice? I mean, you can't tell what they're like from their appearance. The scrawniest sometimes have a penis the size of a mule's! And the things they expect a woman to do! I was telling a neighbor over coffee how they like to put it in your mouth and your behind. She vomited all over the table. Giacomo was in the kitchen. He laughed then he went either to the house of ill repute on Via Dogana where he plays the piano for 75 lire a month or to the Cathedral of San Marco where he steals organ pipes in order to buy his Toscanos, those fat smelly cigars. You should smell his breath, and does he worry about the missing pipes? No—he changes the harmony to avoid the notes of the missing pipes. Last Sunday while playing the congregation out of church with a solemn *marcia*, he shifted to a lively Tuscan folk song. The priests, altar boys, parishioners—all stopped in the aisle and with mouths agape looked up at him bouncing and swaying.

Your Rodolpho, does he know what he wants to do yet? Talk to him about it, Beatrice, with the same tone you tell him you love him more than anything in the world. He may not know enough to search his heart. It's like this sometimes for those with more than their share of goodwill, decency, and honesty. They believe the world will recognize the grandeur of their spirit. They stumble through life like children learning to walk. Later on, disappointment dims the light in their hearts.

Perseverance, my sister. People say, "Life must go on." All right but let it go on the way we want it to go on, with every thought, every ounce of energy devoted to our loved ones, dead or alive. One way to keep a lost loved one alive, I found, is to continually think about him, talk to him, talk to others about him, cry over him as if he had merely fallen down and broken an ankle, take his advice and give him advice, apologize to him and admonish him. I'm beginning to cry. I'm about to throw myself on the floor. I must say goodbye.

Your Sister in Grief,
Albina

Some people today do not know where Valentino was born nor can they understand why their mothers and aunts made such a big fuss over him. One such person is an old friend of mine, a non-Italian editor of pornographic material who is leading a frustrated life as he's in his mid-sixties and his wife is thirty years younger and has breasts the size he had always dreamed of. For the past fifteen years this friend periodically has a piece of his bladder removed and the instrument's point of entry into his body is through his penis. It has been a durable, faithful penis, one he is rightfully proud of. "I'll live as long as I can use it to fuck my wife, she needs it," he told me, and he also ventured that Valentino was born in South America, Argentina, where the accent is thick and the tango is danced with passion in the streets, houses and cafés. It does not matter where Valentino was born, he is immortal, exists in the air everywhere, but when he was walking the earth he felt that he had left a part of himself in his hometown, Castellaneta, Italy, a part as real as an arm or a leg to which he joined himself whenever he returned home. It was a warm, intimate, secure feeling that he could not capture except at his birthplace and its vicinity, a feeling so strong that it displaced disappointments and expectations and elevated the commonplace to wonders of the world. He was content to sit in his garden and watch the road. Each passing carriage invoked in him great respect and curiosity: it was a faithful representative of all the carriages in the world. When a wind arose, he looked up at the tops of the tall trees and watched the branches rhythmically swaying and listened to the bristling of the shimmering leaves. He breathed in the sweet odor of honeysuckle and snowballs and was comforted by the familiar faces of passing neighbors.

Shortly after Valentino died, a reporter from the Chicago *Tribune* went to Castellaneta to discover what he had been like as a child. The *Tribune* had launched vicious attacks against him, calling him a sissy boy, for example, because he wore a wristwatch. A he-man did not wear the time on his wrist, he wore it dangling at the end of a chain pressed against his hard chest or muscular thigh. The paper's attacks on Valentino ceased with his death and it dispatched to his hometown a reporter who had once danced with him in New York. Valentino had liked Clair Honeycomb's carefree manner, the way she skipped along with the strap of her handbag over her shoulder, and she was playful and always had a ready smile, promise of some kind of a future. She had thick arms and legs, minuscule breasts and an oval face with features so large and set so far apart that every expression was unmistakable, rendering her more vulnerable than the majority of the other faces Valentino looked into while he danced and so he was careful not to hurt her in any way. Her skin was fair, they were like night and day in each other's arms, and although she had bad teeth she was not afraid to smile. They kidded one another about their birthplaces—he had never heard of South Carolina and she had never heard of Castellaneta. They were dancers without a nation gliding like feathers over the glistening parquet beneath the gigantic mirrored ball. One evening while resting her head against his chest she revealed her aspirations: "I have a girlfriend who went to Hollywood, slept with a producer and is about to get a starring role. I like to write and I'm thinking of joining my friend."

"That's all very well and good," Valentino said, "but are you aware that your teeth are cracked and stained, on some the roots have died and the teeth have turned black? You're such a pretty girl, my dear, but your teeth repulse every man who sees them. I know a dentist, I'll take you to him."

Clair Honeycomb also revealed a recurring dream that was so awful, inflicted her with so much pain, that Valentino put it out of his mind the moment he left New York. But later on when all the women he had danced with paraded across his mind and Clair appeared, he recalled some of the details of her dream. Her parents' farm had run down. A chicken toppled over dead and a starving dog scratched at the screen door. Clair's mother sat on the porch rocking back and forth, her spindly legs covered by a long plain dress, and she watched indifferently as her two daughters struggled at the well: Clair was trying to climb out but her diabolical sister kept pushing her down. Miles away at the depot a train was waiting.

"It's just a dream," Valentino had said to her. "Does your sister hate you?"

"No," Clair had answered.

"There you are," and they continued dancing.

Valentino believed that through hard work and a fighting spirit everything would come out all right. Clair's dream, for example, inspired a dream of his own, a pleasant one. The Honeycombs lived in a lighthouse. The father, fatigued and despondent beyond help, went out of his mind and one night his jolly wife hurled him out of the tiny window. Then she worked the beacon while her beautiful daughters swam naked around the lighthouse. Dressed in his white sailor suit and admiral's cap, Valentino guided his craft to the lighthouse, undressed and joined the merry sisters in a swim and then the three of them went into the lighthouse.

The idea of making love to Clair Honeycomb did not enter

Valentino's mind until years later when during a publicity tour he found himself on the Lower East Side of New York. He thought of her first in terms of her career—had she gone to Hollywood, made a go of it in New York as a writer or returned to South Carolina? If she was still in New York, he would walk to her apartment, they would have a quaint candlelight dinner, then make love. He stepped into a phone booth and looked up her name in the book. There was a C. Honeycomb in the vicinity. He called but no one answered. He called the next afternoon with the same result. The next day he called at eight in the evening and when no one answered this time he decided that she lived there and was leading the carefree life of a journalist or a novelist. He did not call her again.

The inhabitants of Castellaneta behaved toward Valentino in much the same way as the Chicago *Tribune*. While he was alive they despised and defamed him, and when he was dead they sought to perpetuate their measly existences by speaking fairly about him to strangers. They were a strange breed: in their dedication to work, their interdependence, their efficiency and absence of humanity, they resembled a colony of ants; in their savage support of one another (they attacked like a pack of wild dogs anyone who as much as spoke a word against them), their refusal to accept anyone who was not exactly like them, and their common mission to protect their true nature, which was that they were miserable, they resembled a colony of lepers. They visited one another throughout the day and night, and they all looked alike: low forehead, deep-set eyes, enormous mushroom nose. They were so familiar with one another's face and voice and dwelling that any outsider was peculiar. It was just fine with them that one of their own, Valentino, had gone to America for God knows what silly reason and who cared anyway as long as he left town with enough of the night remaining so that they could convene and derive happiness from feeling and thinking the same way about everything and everyone. What had gone wrong with Valentino and what was wrong with the world that it allowed such a person to exist? They showed him every hospitality, inviting him to their homes and playing the music he loved and cooking food he could not get anywhere else—all as a way of appeasing him. If he stayed beyond his welcome, their true nature surfaced: their skin turned red and they sweated, the women stuck out their tongues and bit them and the men growled. They turned their backs on Valentino and spoke of tomorrow's chores and the sick animals and the bandits ravaging the countryside. To press upon him that it was time to leave they prepared a package to take away, going into their gardens and picking fruits and flowers.

Valentino became a thorn in their side over the fate of his parents' house. They wanted him to sell it to them because if they knew his sort he would neglect it, it would become a retreat for bats and birds, he would make a bordello out of it and then lascivious women without families would parade around town with enormous free-swinging breasts, bouncing power-packed asses and long, hairless, ivory legs. They would go into the fields and distract the men, who hated their work and wondered what life was like beyond the hills. Some farmers took a liking to Valentino and he would go into the fields to talk to them, tell them that he was happy he had not planned his life carefully and tried to make the best of whatever came in his path. The wives of the unhappy farmers were wise and powerful. It was up to them to assure their disenchanted men that they had a beautiful job and to look out for the upstart, Valentino: when the women saw his bright-colored clothes and gesticulating arms through the tiny farmhouse windows, they sounded the bells and then all the women ran from their houses and across the fields to where the men were talking and stood among them with folded arms, stared them down and changed the subject. "We would like to buy your parents' house, don't we?" said the women to Valentino. "In a year your grief will wane and you will laugh again. Life goes on: everyone who has ever lived has lost loved ones. We need the work space, can utilize the rooms where Beatrice sewed and Giovanni kept his tools and cared for the sick animals."

"What are you talking about!" Valentino retorted angrily, waving his powerful left arm. "First of all, from wherever I am I will come back when it snows to clear a path for the passing carriages. With my massive shovel I will remove the snow from the winding path leading to the front door. I will come back for the garden, to trim the hedges and water the honeysuckle and snowballs, and I will clean the windows so that the sunlight will continue to shine in. I will come back just to sit in the chairs, move among the rooms where we ate, laughed and worked."

"Why, that little prick!" the people said on their way home. "He needs a kick in the ass!"

The opportunity to hurt Valentino presented itself with the mysterious appearance in the town of the February 22, 1920, issue of *Photoplay* in which Valentino conferred nobility on himself, presenting himself to the public not as the child of diligent, hardworking parents but as Signor Rodolpho Raffaello Pierre Filibert Guglielmi di Valentina d'Antonguollo. The Rodolpho Raffaello belonged to his father's house and the Pierre Filibert to his mother's. The di Valentina was a papal title and the d'Antonguollo indicated an obscure right to royal property forgotten now because one of his ancestors had fought a duel. Valentino did not figure that a copy of the magazine would find its way to his hometown. His movies were not shown there and the people did not read books or magazines. They knew about Dante because his works passed from generation to generation on a gene, and the works of Michelangelo hung on the walls of their minds. Even if they saw a copy, Valentino figured further, why should they believe what they read? What he said and did in America did not hold true for Italy, it was a way of getting on, thousands of immigrants with a flair conferred nobility on themselves as a way of competing with the American businessman. Valentino could not believe that a man like himself, a simple, formally uneducated Italian, was earning ten thousand dollars a week. "I don't believe it," he said to himself. "Millions of women adore me yet if they could see my penis they would know that it's not unlike millions of other penises." The public and the film studios elevated him to the stature of a god and god is an aristocrat, isn't he? a king, a king without a penis? For immigrants with or without fame and fortune it was easier to live in the realm of the myth, now their roots and the hunger and strife were forgotten, and so when *Photoplay* approached Valentino about an autobiography, rather than show them his penis he showed them a dream and agreed to collaborate with a certain Herbert Howe, whose uncle, a motion picture exhibitor, was a powerful man.

There was a moment of doubt. "Should I do it, Natacha?" he said to his wife. "It's not honest."

"Honest?" Natacha snapped. "How can you be honest with a stupid public?"

Three consecutive issues were devoted to a fabrication of Valentino's life. Extricated from his past, he felt free now to do some serious work. He liked his new self so much that he drew Herbert Howe aside and said, "No one must know you helped me. Here's enough dough to keep quiet."

The people of Castellaneta assembled in the village square with burning torches and with a translator read the articles, passing them from one waiting hand to another until the pages were torn and tattered, then the villagers searched their slighted faces for the method to inflict on Valentino the sting of reality. Agreement arrived unanimously and swiftly: their heads turned in unison to the hill of the dead and they began a slow march up there, chanting, flaming torches held aloft. Arriving at a grave on the side of the hill near the top, they encircled it and then a few men disinterred the body and reburied it on top of the hill along with the rest of the dead. Valentino had buried his father on the side of the hill so that he could be standing and facing the setting sun, recipient of its golden rays for all eternity, and in this position too, water would not linger on his body, it would naturally cascade down the mountain.

On the night of the disinterment, Valentino and Natacha were in Rome attending a production of *Aïda* at Caracalla. They occupied seats in a row hundreds of feet above the stage. Neither music nor voices reached up there, and the stage was a speck of light. Valentino was content with his position in the sky, he looked dreamily around himself at the endless space and nearby moon, and he bathed in the silence and the soft breeze. Then through the exotic calm his father's voice reached him: he was calling for help. Between Valentino and his father was a psychic connection the way there is between lovers and birds flying in a flock. The connection was not always direct: Valentino discovered his father in strangers and in inaccessible places like the sky. Feedback was a privilege, a gift conferred on him by the gods for offering himself to the universe. On this pleasant August evening the silence and the moon conspired to bring him an urgent message from home.

He turned to Natacha and said, "Come on, let's go. My father is in trouble."

"Your father is dead," Natacha said. "His troubles are over."

"I'm going. I'll meet you at your father's estate in France," and he rose quietly and tiptoed down the sharply elevated steps, passing row upon row of still heads arranged like beads along the arc of a bow. He descended through a cumulus cloud and gradually gained a plateau where there was music and voice but instead of registering in a pleasant way they assaulted his concentration on his father, he shielded his ears with his hands and practically flew down the remaining steps. The music was faraway again as he sat in his Avion Voisin, custom-built in France for fourteen thousand dollars. It had five speeds and four-wheel brakes and was upholstered in red leather. Valentino put on his driving gloves and goggles and with a roar of the engine began the journey home.

Natacha was afraid to drive with him. He ignored signs and impasses, burst through barricades and defied detours, hit hairpin turns at high speeds and accelerated along cliffs with no barriers. Once while he was driving the wrong way on a one-way street, the driver with the right of way indicated the black-and-white arrow in her favor.

"What are you talking about!" Valentino shouted, sticking his head out the window. "*You* are driving the wrong way!"

His friends were also afraid to drive with him, so for the few years the Great Maker allotted him to drive, he drove alone. He sang and laughed all the same, delighting in the knowledge that driving with him meant subsuming one's life to the pleasure of his company. Of the millions of people who professed to love him only two consented to drive with him: an aunt of Natacha's everyone called Auntie Turner and a minor director named Bernard Douglas who was so in love with Valentino that he preferred having his body maimed by a ton of steel rather than propose that his friend drove too fast.

"Douglas is a gentleman," Natacha used to say, and she encouraged her husband to go out with him. While they rode, Douglas kept his eyes glued to Valentino's lap because beneath the cloth was the penis of his dreams, the one he conjured up while making love to extras, grips and juicers, and in order for the mental picture to seethe with life he needed moments with Valentino in the flesh.

Auntie Turner was a robust, good-natured widow with broad shoulders, mammoth breasts and strong knotty legs who devoted her waning years to the happiness of her niece, Natacha Rambova Valentino. Every day Auntie Turner cleaned the house from top to bottom, shopped and cooked, planted flowers and greased the car. She took it upon herself to compensate for her niece's shortcomings in regard to heaping devotion and tenderness on Valentino. She made a point of being in those places where Valentino sought refuge after storming out of the bedroom. She was already in the den hiding in the shadows, naked and moist. She was in the car, her body draped across the back seat, or she was sitting demurely in the garden holding a picnic lunch and dressed in a flowing skirt with nothing underneath in case the sight and smell of his beloved roses moved Valentino to want to make love in the grass under a secluded yew or cypress or weeping willow. She did not disgust him. Propriety was nullified by a combination of her imminent old age and his desperation. She was fighting back the time when a man's touch would be a distant fond memory, and there were many, many hours in Valentino's short life filled with loneliness so desperate that it threatened his existence and could only be assuaged by a woman, a kind word from her, a caress.

MONA LISA

I N the middle of the night, while I was sleeping, Mona Lisa
rode in through my window on a mist. As she passed my
bed I bolted awake and reached out with my right arm to
touch her, but she was vaporous, of the texture of the mist en-
veloping her, transparent and damp, and by the time I got up
and cleared my senses she had disappeared through the door. She
left behind, however, her smell and the explanation of her smile.
Her words echoed in my ears for days, and I reveled in her smell
as it conjured up a memory of early love, that of my maternal
grandmother opening her front door and handing me a mozzarella and a Pepsi. The smell emanating from Maria—that's what
Mona Lisa smelled like. It can be explained in the following way:
the Italians of Brooklyn re-create the smell of their ancestors'
homes by cooking in a low-ceilinged basement with the windows
closed; garlic and olive oil simmer free of America's air, and then
this smell combines with the body's natural odors of sleep, sweat
and love, which also remain pure, free of America's water. The
emerging smell is sharp, acrid, stale and offensive to the untrained
nose—nevertheless, this is what Mona Lisa smells like.

She first gave me a clue to the mystery of her smile. She said she had no idea how she came to be called "La Gioconda." For some reason art historians had feminized her husband's cognomen, Giocondo, while it was the custom in Italy to feminize the woman's first name.

"My best friend, for example," she said, "was Bianca Bennini, and we called her 'La Bianca,' not 'La Bennina.' By the way, Leonardo did not name my portrait nor did he sell it or give it away. He carried it with him the rest of his life to keep me near him always, for he loved me."

Unconsciously, she went on to say, art historians had pointed to her husband as the key to the mystery of her smile.

"'Leonardo is fifty-three years old,' my husband remarked, 'past the prime of his life, and in addition I've watched him for years parade around in long robes and shoulder-length hair, holding a staff, followed by an entourage of beautiful young men, and he travels from city to city so that the neighbors cannot discover how he is—he's homosexual and for this reason I will allow you to sit for him.'"

Leonardo had been studying Mr. Giocondo as hard as Mr. Giocondo had been studying him. "In fact," said Mona Lisa, "Leonardo chose me as a subject precisely because of my husband's prejudice. Leonardo told me, 'Your husband believes I am homosexual and before I begin work I should like to tell you two interrelated things: first, I desire to capture a smile aware of the boundaries of human knowledge, specifically, your husband's boundaries, those of a narrow-minded, ignorant man; and second, before I set paint to canvas, your image must undergo a long gestation in my spirit,' and with that Leonardo approached me with open arms—I was sitting in the chair you see in the painting— he let down my hair, gathered it all in one hand and kissed the back of my neck.

"I wrapped my arms around his waist and pulled him close to me. His body was hard, there wasn't an inch of fat on it. He whispered, 'Now we will create the smile.' With his soft hair falling around my face, he kissed my lips, my teeth, my tongue, my chin and my cheeks and the sides of my nose and under my

eyes. He fluttered his eyelashes around my forehead, like a butterfly. He said he was pleased that I had shaved my brows—they
would not obstruct my smile's journey to my temples.

"He kissed my lips so long and hard that they began to bleed.
They are pressed together in the portrait because if I had smiled
according to the joy I felt, they would have bled again, and
Leonardo did not want to capture blood, he wanted to capture
the blissful repose of a woman in the wake of intense love.

"He knelt at the foot of my chair and slowly lowered my dress.
He looked so long at my breasts that he took my breath away.
To my great pleasure he finally touched them, then he buried his
head in them and kissed and bit the nipples until I cried with joy.
Oh, how he adored my breasts! He painted only a hint of them,
a fraction of an inch of cleavage, but it was enough, he said, to
keep them with him forever and in their full glory.

"He stood up, slipped out of his robe, then with his strong,
gentle hands guided me to my feet. He sat in the chair and took
me in his lap, where we consummated our love.

"We repeated this scene day after day, week after week. My
image, my body became one with his. 'My portrait will also be
a self-portrait,' he said one day, and then he began to paint.

"He painted first the landscape, unreal and dreamlike yet pre-
cise as a map so that I could find my way along the serpentine
road to the dampness and dissolved mists. On these mists I travel
around the world.

"Then Leonardo painted the cartoon for the portrait. We looked
at it, holding hands. I could see how it was going to turn out,
and after I said, 'I must go now, my husband is waiting,' we threw
back our heads and howled with laughter."

GIOVANNI
VALERIO

L EONARDO spent a great deal of time and money in the
courts trying to reclaim his ancestral property, and when
he died the "Mona Lisa" was in his room, and so I believe
that he would have liked the painting to hang in the Uffizi in
Florence or in a shrine in his home in Vinci, rather than in the
Louvre in Paris. I decide to confer with my son. Giovanni is an
art historian. This past year he graduated from a prestigious New
England college and now he works in a fine art gallery in the
city. At his suggestion we meet in a Chinese restaurant on Catherine Street. I arrive first and moments later Giovanni walks in
swinging his arms, he looks up at the tin ceiling, then at the
glazed ducks hanging in the window. He shakes my hand and I
run my fingers through his hair. Over shrimp on rice, I say, "How
did the 'Mona Lisa' wind up in Paris?"

"Leonardo died in France, in Boise. At the time, he was the
court painter of Francis I. The King claimed the painting."

"Why did Leonardo go to France, do you know?"

"I guess he was offered the job and needed it. So, Daddy, what
have you been doing?"

"Thinking about Italians."

"Any women?"

"Well—"

"Marie de' Medici is interesting. She was the Regent Queen of France during the seventeenth century and introduced Italian fashion and taste in art to the French. She also introduced the Italian court structure, which developed and expanded into the huge proportions of Versailles under the direction of Marie's grandson, Louis XIV. She was the great patron of the Flemish painter Peter Paul Rubens, the most 'Italian' of the northern painters. The Medici cycle by Rubens is pro-Marie de' Medici propaganda and anti-Richelieu. She wanted her son Louis to take power in France. Marie introduced northern Italian cuisine to France, which subsequently became the basis for French crème-sauce cooking."

"I'm not surprised."

"Artemisia Gentileschi was remarkable as a painter of Bible stories. She concentrated on images of strong women, illustrating stories of Judith and Queen Esther. You know who Judith was, don't you?"

"Yes, but tell me again."

"She was the Jewish woman who killed the leader of the enemy forces, Holofernes, by sneaking into his tent at night, getting him drunk and finally cutting off his head. Gentileschi's work is very gutsy—it matched Caravaggio's blood-spurt for blood-spurt. Both she and Caravaggio concentrated on images of vigorous violence, especially beheadings. Psychologically, this is interpreted as castration anxiety on Caravaggio's part but aggression against men on Artemisia's part. She was raped, and at her trial they put thumbscrews on her to find out if she was telling the truth."

"Was she?"

"Yes."

"Well, Giovanni, I find this all very interesting. So, tell me, how have you been doing? Seeing anybody of late?"

"You always ask me that and I think it's rude!"

"You're right. I won't ask again."

"I'm not trying to hide anything!"

"I know—"

"I've had two girlfriends in my life, Sylvia and Françoise, and it just didn't work out," and then he breaks down and cries.

I get up and go over to him and press his head against my chest.

"I'd like to have somebody to love. . . ."

"You will, you will."

He had wanted me to visit with him up at his college while the leaves were changing. During the summer of his second year I waited with great expectation for the onset of fall, then I made a reservation on a bus. From my window seat I would see the change in season reflected in the miraculous colors of the leaves. Vivid reds and brilliant yellows would blanket the land, and up ahead I could see the Berkshire Mountains on which Giovanni skied and ran. I'd picture his nose nipped red by the cold, feel the warm breath steaming out of his mouth.

When Giovanni learned that I was going up by bus, he said, "Can't you rent a car or borrow your sister's?"

His father would emerge from the Greyhound bus in a rumpled suit, with a shadow of a beard, and he might also feel tired and lost, desiring some rest. The entire student body would be gathered at the terminal, including the Shah of Iran's son, George Steinbrenner's son and the son of the man who invented Tylenol. How could Giovanni show such a father the inside of the Shah's son's house or have him kiss the Shah's hand or shake hands with Mr. Steinbrenner and Mr. Tylenol? Giovanni knew that I didn't fly and spoke to my sister only in emergencies. He also knew that I didn't aspire to own a ball team and that any hope for an aristocratic strain was dashed a century ago when the Kingdom of Sicily confiscated our ancestors' holdings in Messina. Giovanni was born in Italy and so he cannot become President of the United States, but I did not want to hold him back from becoming President of the World—I did not see the changing leaves of New England, I sat tranquil and still in my modest beach chair of green and yellow stripes and looked out at the calm waters of

the Hudson River, up at the sun making its way across the sky.
Occasionally, my attention was captured by the buzzing of a
small plane making short runs for the fun of it. I looked up at
the sky and experienced the thrill the novice pilot must have felt.
At sundown I felt peaceful, and I thought. The air was still, time
itself stopped, and with the colors of the waning day growing
darker and deeper, I resurrected from them other places and times,
Giovanni's first day, for example, and my daydream renewed my
love for him.

Giovanni was born in the ancient city of Bologna, Italy, on
December 13, 1964. The onset of the day witnessed the season's
first snowfall, which Nicoletta and I watched from our bed. We
had never seen the snow of Italy. It transported us to the snow
of our childhood, the fun of rollicking in it, burrowing through
dark tunnels made of it, standing in triumph on a mound as the
newly crowned King of the Mountain. It was as if the heavens
had let go a phenomenon that when it touched the earth erased
the names of cities and countries. We prayed for a healthy child,
as Nicoletta had been ill from drinking too much new wine. She
developed a bad case of the runs, losing pound upon pound until
her weight dropped below one hundred. Lying naked in bed she
looked like she had been reduced to the swell of her belly, and
we wondered whether she had the strength to bring our child
into the world. Nicoletta got her first labor pain at seven o'clock.
I had gone to the window and thrust my head outside for a close
look at the snow. Snowflakes swirled around me, landed lightly
in my hair, tickled my face like an infinite number of playful
feathers. My face reddened from the sudden blast of cold and
from my excitement, and I laughed and let go an ecstatic yelp.
It was then that I heard from deep inside the room, *"È tempo!"*
disorienting me because like most couples living in a foreign land,
Nicoletta and I spoke our native language when alone, in this
case English.

I swung into action. The public hospital was located far beyond
the confines of the city, beyond Bologna's landmark, *le due torri*,
the two towers erected by the Etruscans two thousands years ago
as a lookout for invading marauders. An American friend, Donald

Segers, had promised us a ride when it was time, and now I had no other thought except fetching him and his car. I slipped on a pair of pants but neglected to put on a shirt and my shoes. My naked torso and bare feet entered the falling snow. The cold did not penetrate my nakedness, nor did the snow pile up or melt upon hitting the ground, and my feet did not get wet as they scurried to Donald Segers' house. As I passed the café where the old men met every day to be together and play cards, I pictured them playing on the outdoor tables under the falling snow. They played with gusto, discarding with the velocity and snap of a whip. Every card that was played ushered in new life. The old men reared with laughter and they bantered. They were happy. Frozen in that moment, they would always be happy. Whenever I thought back to that time, I would be happy. My American friend with the car, Donald Segers, he would be happy. He would be happy to know that another American was about to be born. He would recognize my face at his door and immediately re-member his offer of a ride. He would get dressed in a jiffy while singing a song, then the three of us would ride to the hospital with an aura of goodwill in the car.

I knocked at Donald's door, softly at first. Beyond it his apart-ment had never been so attractive, everything was in place and the Segers family slept blissfully together. After a while I screamed, "Donald! Donald!" waking up the other tenants on the floor, all Italians. The harsh, alien sounds penetrated their unconscious, recalled them from their dreams. They threw off their blankets and scrambled from their beds and glided over the marble floors while ridding their eyes of *l'uomo della rena*, the Italian sandman. They swung open their doors and stood there all in a rage, dressed in funny-looking nightclothes, the kind you read about in books, long gowns and caps with tiny balls at the end. The Italians screamed at me, "You Americans think that just because you're Americans you can wake anybody up at any hour of the day and night!"

Donald's door opened a crack and a pair of sleepy eyes peered out. "Yeah?..."

"Nicoletta is having labor pains."

"Be right there."

I looked up to Donald. He was older and had successfully completed three years of medical school. He gave his exams orally in Italian and did not complain. I surmised that the Italian language posed no problem for him. He showed me where to have a good winter coat made. He took me to the fine cafés and bars of the city, introducing me to bitters and real hot chocolate. He knew the cheap trattorias that served good food. In addition, Donald had made love to countless Bolognese women, discovering whether it's true that they are experts at making oral love, enough to earn them a worldwide reputation. He was searching for one of these carnivorous women the night he offered the ride. His battered Ford crept up and down the dark, narrow streets. From the passenger seat I turned and looked at him and was struck by the desperation on his handsome face. With one hand on the wheel he strained his eyes upward in search of a lighted window.

"Are they that good?" I asked him.

"All I know," he said, "is that they devour me like a piece of rare *bistecca*. My kinky hair stands on end and I fly home over the red roofs."

"But what makes the women of Bologna such great cocksuckers? What about the women in nearby cities like Modena and Forli? Do you think there was once an Etruscan woman living within these walls who developed such a talent for making oral love that she raised the practice to an art which was then passed down through the ages on a gene?"

Donald smiled. He didn't know. He was married and had a son. "I tolerate my wife but I love my son," he told me. Bolognese women just made him feel good.

We drove through the snow to the hospital, passing the two towers, then acres of barren farmland. The Grattacielo, a highrise apartment building, loomed high in the middle of nowhere. When the professor who was going to deliver our child saw Nicoletta, he threw up his arms and said, "Oh, no, not another American!"

We learned that an American woman had given birth the day

before to a stillborn baby and so the professor faced the prospect
of two Americans dying on Italian soil on consecutive days. What
would the Ford Foundation say? Nicoletta said to me, "You're
going to stay with me through the whole thing!" With my
mask and gown on, I discovered what a woman has to go through
to bring a child into the world, the courage she displays in the
face of great pain. Bologna was the center of Communism in
Italy, and the medical profession was influenced by a recent Russian study that concluded that there's no such thing as pain for
a woman giving birth. But while I was standing beside Nicoletta,
holding her hand, I saw her grit her teeth from all the pain, and
I also saw her emaciated body racked with it as she pushed and
pushed. She raised her head and cursed the professor in English,
"You fuck!" Later on she apologized in Italian. My respect for her
increased a thousandfold, and I vowed that from that moment
on nothing she could say or do would undermine that respect.

She needed an episiotomy. When the professor was about to
cut her without anesthesia, I reached into the pocket of my
American-made pants and withdrew a fifty-dollar bill. "Please give
her a little anesthesia," I said to the professor while handing over
the money.

He threw up his arms again and shouted, "You Americans think
that just because you have the almighty dollar you can push your
weight here and there!"

His assistant approached me. "Don't worry, she won't feel any
pain."

"How would you feel if I cut your balls with that scissor!" I
raged. "What do we men know? What do we contribute to all of
this? Just another night's fuck, that's what!"

I was staring at Nicoletta when Giovanni was drawn into the
world. I heard him cry, then looked up and saw him held aloft
in the professor's hands. A nurse dipped him in a bath, dressed
him in swaddling clothes, then placed him beside his mother. I
walked beside their bed as it was wheeled to our room. There
was no artificial milk, mothers breast-fed their babies but Nicoletta's nipples were not long enough: the boy wasn't eating. The

nurse told me about an apparatus I had to go out and buy in the pharmacy up the road. Night had fallen. The road ahead was pitch black, and no lights indicated a store. Snow was still falling heavily.

ANITA
GARIBALDI

OW wonderful it is for a man to have his woman fight beside him the way Anita Riberas fought side by side with Garibaldi! They were married on deck facing the setting sun and spent their honeymoon waging amphibious warfare along the Brazilian coast and in the lagoons. During Anita's first sea battle she was knocked down by a cannonball onto the bodies of three dead men. Garibaldi rushed to her. "I'm all right, I'm all right," she assured him.

She was an expert horsewoman, having hunted as a girl with her father, and she galloped beside her husband at the head of the Republican army. They ranged the hills together, slept under the stars. She talked to the soldiers around the campfire, nursed their wounds and sickness, rallied their broken ranks.

"You are my treasure," Garibaldi told her, "and however things turn out the future smiles on us, and the vast deserts unrolling before our eyes are all the more delightful and beautiful for their wildness."

In a fierce land battle her horse was shot and she was thrown. She scrambled to her feet and ran. The enemy cavalryman hurled his *boleadoras* around her legs and she went down, rolling, bruising her face and arms and legs. Her captors told her that her husband had been killed and allowed her to search the bodies. She turned over one after another, expecting to see the lionlike mane. At night, while her guards slept, she fled into the tropical forest and ran for four days and nights, eating berries and food some peasants gave her. One peasant gave her a horse. She rode across fifty miles of desert, without food, swam rivers holding on to her horse, flew through hostile pickets posted at the passes of the hills and fords of the rivers. She reached the town of Lages, where her husband joined her.

She gave birth to a son practically in the saddle. The Brazilian Imperialists prevailed, and she had to ride with her twelve-day-old son across her saddlebow. They wandered the high sierras and primeval forest during the rainy season. Food was short, and rain fell continuously on the slowly marching column. While climbing steep hills and crossing flooded rivers she carried Menotti in a handkerchief slung around her neck and kept him warm by clasping him to her breast and with her breath. In 1842, Garibaldi sought a peaceful life for his family in Montevideo, the capital of Uruguay. His wages for six years of fighting for Rio Grande do Sul was a herd of six hundred cattle. Anita drove them, along with her husband and the drivers. The drive covered two hundred miles, and the rivers and mountain streams were flooded. Half the herd drowned in the Río Negro in Uruguay. The remaining cattle were exhausted, and there was little fodder to feed them. Garibaldi slaughtered and skinned them, and the family arrived in Montevideo with two hundred skins, which sold for very little.

The Garibaldis shared a five-room white granite house with two other families. Garibaldi tried to earn a living by teaching mathematics and selling restaurant supplies, mainly macaroni, to the Italian restaurants going up in Montevideo. One hot summer night he came home with his head hanging low. Anita said to him, smiling, "Well, Peppino, how many pounds did you sell today?"

"Two," he answered, "to two Italian friends. I saw a man from the United States trying to sell ice. He put a few lumps in a drink and told the Uruguayans that on hot days like today his ice turns the drink cold. The ice melted, the Uruguayans drank and still they refused to buy. If that man couldn't sell his ice, how am I going to sell macaroni?"

Anita embraced him, pressing her dark skin the texture of leather against his cheek. "You don't have to," she said. "President Rivera was here today. Uruguay has gone to war with Rosas and the Argentine invaders. Rivera offered you the rank of colonel in the navy. It was getting dark and he saw that we have no candles. He left a hundred *patacones*."

"I don't know, with you and Menotti—"

"And the new one growing in my belly . . ."

He picked her up and whirled her around.

"Go to war, my husband. In peacetime you're useless."

Garibaldi nodded. "I'm not accepting the rank. I must set myself as an example of Republican virtue and also leave myself free to lay down my arms and return to my homeland when it beckons."

"Can we keep the money?"

"Half, and give half to the widow down the road."

While Garibaldi was away fighting, Anita cared for the house and children. She gave birth to a second son, Ricciotti, and to two daughters, Rosita and Teresita. Ricciotti was named after the Italian patriot who had been killed with the Bandiera brothers, Attilio and Emilio, when their conspiracy in Calabria failed. A defrocked priest informed the Governor of Otranto, and instead of insurgents joining Ricciotti and the Bandiera brothers, Neapolitan troops arrived. The brothers sang as they were about to be shot: "He who dies for his country has lived long enough!"

The soldiers misfired.

Ricciotti shouted, "*Coraggio!* We too are soldiers!"

Garibaldi refused land and wealth as well as rank but Anita managed to save a few coins from his soldier's pay. She hid them in a gourd. One day they were missing and she threw up her arms. "That man! He orders traitors and thieves shot with his cigar in his mouth, but when it comes to his daughters he's soft as shit!"

Rosita had wanted a toy and her father took the money to buy her one. He had a meeting that day with Suárez. Garibaldi dressed the same as his soldiers, in the red shirt and white poncho, and during the meeting Suárez said, "Why do you not take off your poncho?"

Garibaldi lifted off his poncho, revealing a red shirt stiff with dried blood. On the way home he forgot to buy Rosita her toy and the girl sat on her doorstep and cried.

She died in a fire. She had been playing with a lighted candle and her bed caught fire. Garibaldi was away, and by the time Anita burst through the jammed door, the child was dead. In a wild rampage Anita threw down all the doors in the house, including the front door. Years later a guest in Garibaldi's house on Caprera remarked that his room had no door. Garibaldi told him, "You have nothing to fear in the house of Garibaldi."

He kept in touch with his revolutionary society, Young Italy, corresponding under the name of Borel. In 1844, he received the news that the tricolor had been raised in the Neapolitan Kingdom. Then in 1847, Garibaldi learned that a reforming Pope had issued a decree of universal amnesty. Soon the whole peninsula would be rising in revolt against the Austrians and Spanish. The time was right to return home. Garibaldi's Italian Legion wanted to follow him. Not knowing exactly what awaited them once they landed in Italy, Garibaldi decided to send ahead Anita and the children. They would be safe in his mother's house in Nizza. Anita agreed. "Before we go," she said, "I would like to go to the cemetery and place flowers for the last time on Rosita's grave."

Pius IX's liberal policies catalyzed revolutions over the whole peninsula, from the northern Kingdom of Piedmont, where King Charles Albert raised an army of sixty thousand to drive out the Austrians, to Sicily, where thirty thousand inhabitants expelled the royal troops of King Ferdinand. The King granted a constitution to his Neapolitan subjects to prevent them from joining the Sicilian revolt. The people of the Lombard-Venetian Kingdom boycotted tobacco and the lotteries, two important sources of Austrian revenue. The Milanese waged a bloody five-day street battle, driving out the Austrians. The city of Venice proclaimed a republic and installed a provisional government. In Rome, the Pope found that he had unleashed forces which threatened his temporal powers. Romans called for the expulsion of the Jesuits, who acted as spies for the Austrians and the Neapolitan Kingdom. The Pope insisted that the Jesuits be dealt with by legal means, which did not exist. He refused to join Charles Albert in the fight against the Austrians. The Papal ministry resigned, and the Municipal Council called on the Pope to refrain from interfering with the army. To strengthen his temporal powers, the Pope appointed Count Pellegrino Rossi as his Prime Minister. An Italian by birth, Rossi had been the diplomatic agent for France, and his dismissal was a major step toward liberty. He was against Italian unity and aligned himself with King Ferdinand by driving Neapolitan refugees from the Papal States. Rossi squashed agitators with a strong force of carabinieri who marched day and night along the Corso. He sneered and spit at critics, making some formidable enemies, including a burly wine merchant, Angelo Brunetti, and his son Luigi.

On November 15, the new session of the Council of Deputies opened in the Palazzo della Cancelleria. Rossi had prepared a law-and-order speech, as the city was on the threshold of civil war. His tall, gaunt figure emerged from his carriage. The piazza was packed with angry citizens, and soldiers returning from the Lombard campaign shouted execrations. Rossi was warned. "Rome cannot wait!" he responded. "Let me through the rabble!" He pushed his way through the entrance hall to the staircase. "Stand aside, peasants!" Angelo Brunetti was on one side of the staircase and his son was on the other. As Rossi climbed the lower steps, Angelo hit Rossi and as he turned, his face contorted in contempt, Luigi Brunetti plunged a dagger into his neck.

Margaret Fuller Ossoli wrote to her mother from Rome:

"For me, I never thought to have heard of a violent death with satisfaction; but this act affected me as one of terrible justice."

On November 24, the Pope, disguised as a servant, fled to the Neapolitan Kingdom. On February 18, he called for the armed intervention of Spain, Austria, France and Naples. France alone sent twenty thousand troops. Austria and the Neapolitan Kingdom added another eight thousand. General Avezzana, the Minister of War of the newly formed Republic of Rome, summoned Garibaldi to its defense. On April 27, the General entered the Eternal City at the head of his thousand legionnaires.

A sculptor named Gibson was sitting in a café. He described the warriors:

"The men, sunburnt, with long unkempt hair, wearing conical-shaped hats with black, wavy plumes; their gaunt, dust-soiled faces framed with shaggy beards; crowded round their chief, who rode a white horse, perfectly statuesque in virile beauty."

Garibaldi carried her across the maize field, setting her down now and then to wipe away the cold sweat and froth at the sides of her mouth. "Ricciotti," Anita murmured, "he has nightmares about the Christ on the cross in his school... take him out of that school... Teresita needs you... Menotti will make a fine soldier..."

She was delirious from the malaria she had contracted in the independent Republic of San Marino, where Garibaldi discharged his remaining troops, freeing them to return to private life. He had also left behind his horse with the order to shoot him if the Austrians occupied the Republic.

Just ahead was the Guccioli dairy farm, a spacious house standing among vineyards, and about a mile beyond the house was the pine forest of Ravenna and safety. Major Bova arrived with a doctor.

"You cannot imagine," Garibaldi said to the doctor, "all that this woman has done for me, and how tenderly I love her."

"We must make a shift to get her to bed."

"I brought a mattress," said Major Bova, and they carried her on it into the house, to a room at the head of the stairs. While laying her down in the bed Garibaldi saw the death-look on her face. He staggered to the window and wept while looking out at the tops of the trees.

She had written to him from Nizza that she wanted to join him in Rome. He wrote back, telling her to stay, she was pregnant and should care for the children. Then in late May she heard that he had been killed in a skirmish with the Neapolitans. He had ridden out of Rome with his cavalry to drive back the Neapolitans. Their cavalry charged, putting the Italians to flight. To halt the retreat Garibaldi faced the fleeing riders in the middle of the road. The stampede knocked him and his horse down and they were trampled. Anita traveled to Livorno by ship, then rode in a coach to Rome. She arrived at dusk on a hot Sunday, and less than a mile from the city walls she could hear the reports of muskets and cannon peal, the clashing of the campanile bells and drumbeats, a broken beat, signaling alarm. She directed the driver to take her to the Porta San Pancrazio, for she saw men on foot and on horseback rushing to this gate. Beyond it, rising high on the western side of the Janiculum Hill, was the Villa Corsini, and she saw the French soldiers' gun barrels flashing on the balcony. She left the coach at the base of the steep, shady path leading up to the city gate. On both sides of her were old palaces and gardens. She hurried up the steps, stepping aside for riderless horses galloping wildly through the archway and for the wounded being carried out in wheelbarrows and slung in scarves. Women as well as men, as the women helped build the barricades and spread sand over the streets to make sure footing for the horses. Anita passed under the archway and two hundred yards ahead of her, at the garden gate of the Villa Corsini, she saw her husband reining in his horse, and he was shouting, *"Orsù! Questa è l'ultima prova!* [Let's go! This is the last fight!]"

The road to the garden gate was exposed to enemy fire from the Villa's upper stories. The road was strewn with bodies and limbs. Anita picked up a cavalry pistol, then crouched low against the orchard to her left. She inched her way forward, bullets hissing all around her, and when she was within earshot she cried, "Peppino! Peppino!" He turned and saw her and galloped for her. He swept her up behind him and made for the corn field behind the orchard. She wrapped her arms around his stomach, pressed her cheek against his poncho riddled with bullet holes. His thigh was bandaged, and his saddle was soaked with blood.

"I heard you had been killed. . . . "

"Horses and riders piled up in the road and then the Neapolitans rode in, sabers drawn. But I had stationed a regiment of infantry in the orchards. It ambushed the Neapolitans, then my fourteen-year-olds ran out and dragged me to the side of the road. I'm taking you to the Villa Spada."

"You want to leave me."

"We're all dead men here."

"Then I'll die too."

"We're mounting a last charge. If we don't take the Villa, all Rome is lost."

The French could establish their full complement of field cannon on the ridge of the Villa and bombard the Janiculum Hill, Garibaldi's headquarters, the San Pancrazio Gate, and the heart of the city itself, killing civilians and demolishing buildings. The Villa Corsini rose four stories high, its decorative stoneworks exposed to the winds. Thus it was called *la Casa dei Quattri Venti*, the House of the Four Winds. The two lower stories on the side facing Rome had no windows and were also masked by a wide, marble outer staircase which had to be climbed by troops storming the Villa. Its flanks were protected by statues, bushes and trees. In the orchards and pine woods behind the Villa the enemy massed their reserves, sixteen thousand strong. Running in both directions from the foot of the staircase was a two-foot-high wall on which stood large orange-tree pots, good cover for the troops holding the hill. The downhill path between the staircase and garden gate was lined with stiff box hedges six feet high and triangular in shape and at its apex was the sole entrance to the Villa. It was a murderous angle: the enemy's fire from the half-open upper-story windows, from the balcony and from behind the orange-tree pots was trained on the bottleneck—yet for the past twelve hours Garibaldi, mounted on his horse in the open road, had sent in wave after wave of infantry, cavalry, workers and students, all crying, *"Avanti!"* They were mowed down charging five abreast through the garden gate and along the two hundred yards of open slope to the Villa stairs.

The last charge consisted of the remnant of Garibaldi's Legion, five hundred strong, Luciano Manera's three hundred *bersaglieri*, sharpshooters, young men of aristocratic families who had fought with King Charles Albert in Lombardy. Their uniforms were spotless, and they wore high shiny black boots and the cross of Savoy on their sword belts. Finally, Angelo Masina's forty lancers. They waited in a column outside the Porta San Pancrazio. Garibaldi rode out to join them, Anita behind him. She saw soldiers who had fought in Montevideo. Sacchi, Montaldo, Major Bova saluted her. Garibaldi ordered the cannon on the city wall to bombard the Villa as cover, then he rose in his stirrups, drew his saber, and the bugles sounded the charge. Led by Garibaldi and Masina, the column advanced three abreast through the archway, picking up speed they charged the garden gate. Masina was shot in the right arm. Garibaldi hit the Villa gate at top speed, Anita firing from behind him. One close behind the other, the horsemen sped through the gate, then spread out right and left along the box hedges, jumping over corpses of men and horses. Manera's sharpshooters knelt on the path and opened fire. French soldiers collapsed dead on the balcony, fell out of the upper-story windows. With the flat of his sword Garibaldi drove the riderless horses to the staircase. He struck about with his saber and Anita shot the defenders behind the wall of orange-tree pots. The stairs were swept by bullets. Masina was hit. "I'm a dead man," he said, falling onto the stairs. Garibaldi galloped up the staircase, survivors behind him, and they charged into the drawing room on the second floor and fought with bayonet, lance and saber. They succeeded in driving out the French. Anita helped pile up the bodies of her dead comrades in the open loggias, then from the barricade Anita and the sharpshooters opened fire. They couldn't station themselves on the upper stories, as they were in flames from the cannonade. Garibaldi had to move his defense into the gardens on both flanks. The Italians lay low among the brushwood, easy prey for the French counterattack from the west and north, regiment after regiment pressing forward through the orchards and pine woods. Night fell with the French in command of the Villa.

All forty lancers were killed. Manera lost two hundred of his Lombard Brigade. Garibaldi lost three hundred of his Legion, including forty officers. He lost one thousand of his total force of six thousand. The French had sent sixteen thousand against the Villa, and even if their casualties were half that number, they still had twenty-two thousand to take the Janiculum Hill and from there bombard the eighteen-mile circumference of city walls and the city itself. It took one month.

A twenty-four hour truce was called for the gathering of the dead and wounded. Garibaldi was summoned to the Capitol for his opinion of three plans: surrender, die fighting in the streets, or flee into the country districts with the government and the army. He would not discuss surrender. "There will be no further destruction of the buildings," he said. "I will carry the army into the wilderness."

The next day fourteen thousand Romans gathered in the Piazza of St. Peter's. They stood on carriages, on each other's shoulders. They heard cheers form Via del Borgo, then saw his black feathers. He was surrounded by citizens waving handkerchiefs and cheering. Anita was beside him on a white horse. She had cut her hair and wore a green uniform with a broad-brimmed plumed Calabrian hat. Slowly, they made their way to the Egyptian obelisk, stopped and turned their horses. Garibaldi waved his hand and there was dead silence.

"I am going out from Rome. Let those who wish to continue the war against the stranger come with me. I offer neither pay nor quarter nor possessions. I offer hunger, thirst, forced marches and death. Let he who loves his country with his heart and not with his lips follow me."

Four thousand chose to follow. As night fell, Garibaldi gave the order to march, and the two-mile column of men and wagons and one cannon passed through the Porta San Giovanni.

They were pursued by thirty thousand French, twelve thousand

Neapolitans, six thousand Spaniards, fifteen thousand Austrians and two thousand Tuscans—but Garibaldi managed to reach the independent Republic of San Marino by employing tactics he had learned and developed in South America. Orders were passed down the line in whispers. The men were not allowed to smoke. Wagons were changed for beasts of burden—thus, the food walked, allowing the column to leave the roads and range the Apennines. Marches were of irregular length, by night and by day. Camp was broken up at irregular hours, often at sunset. The feint was followed by a second feint in another direction. Garibaldi leaked false reports, exaggerating his numbers. His cavalry's system of scouting kept him informed of the enemy's movements. The horsemen's moving screen confused the opposing generals as to his position and movements. Several cavalry detachments were always on the move, miles away from the column.

Peasants were often hostile, supplying the French with information. Anita went into the fields. "What are you afraid of?" she said to the peasants. "Do we speak German? Do we burn and pillage?" Desertions were by the hundreds yet she was cheerful, chatting with the soldiers during the marches. In the Papal State of Citona, she bought a dress. She received the women of Todi in a straw hut the soldiers made her amid laurels, cypress and fruit trees. The column stopped for a siesta of six hours in a cool, wooded place along a tributary of the Tiber. Anita made their tent. She bathed in the river. She helped the soldiers slaughter eight of the twenty oxen and gathered wood for the fire. After dinner, Garibaldi spoke of better times and told stories of their South American adventures. Especially Anita's escape into the forest, swimming the rivers holding on to her horse, her ride across the desert, alone and without food. Anita sat under a rock, tossed a stone, and smiled.

ELSA RODARI

LSA and I hadn't seen each other for about a month, since she had gone to Brooklyn to see her friends' puppies. Chuck and Tom lived in the Park Slope section. "Come and see our beautiful puppies!" they invited her, and she left me behind and traveled to Brooklyn for the first time, and so my heart went out to her and my eyes were on her shoulders as she boarded the F train at the West Fourth Street station, hopefully the first car because the Seventh Avenue platform has two exits leading to two entirely different places: from the lead car she would exit onto Eighth Avenue, where she wanted to go, but from the end car she would exit onto Seventh Avenue and from there to the park block where Chuck and Tom lived was a long uphill climb.

Once at Chuck and Tom's, Elsa calls the puppies, "Puppies! Puppies!" and all seven of them run to her in a pack, fight each other as they jump on her and lick her all over. "Such sweet things," she murmurs, and then tears come to her eyes as she recalls the dog she had left behind in Argentina, Clotilde, "pure dog," Elsa described her, meaning she had no pedigree. Clotilde was ten years old when Elsa saw her the last time. Elsa's bags were packed, and her family was out in the hall waiting to drive her to the airport.

"I looked around the apartment, whispered, 'Goodbye,' and Clotilde looked at me and she knew she was never going to see me again."

Clotilde died exactly six months later, while Elsa was working for a Mrs. Mayer in Queens Village. "Did I ever tell you about that job?" Elsa once asked me.

"No."

"Do you want to hear?"

"Of course!"

Ten days after her arrival in New York, she was riding in a subway with her girlfriend Delia, and they were going to meet Delia's Aunt Flora, who knew about a job. Elsa didn't know where she was or where she was going, but she trusted Delia the way a child trusts his parents during his first train rides, freeing him to spin around the poles, count the naked light bulbs flashing by in the tunnels, count the steel girders on the bridge. Elsa looked around at the filth and thought of the subways in Buenos Aires. They are immaculate, have wood-paneled walls and dainty little chandeliers, and the platform walls are decorated with *mayólicas*, tile mosaics depicting men at work and historical events such as General San Martín crossing the Andes. But the filth of New York subways amounted to very little compared to the excitement Elsa felt for her new life. The day before, she had ridden in a bus with no destination in mind, just a ride downtown, then back uptown, taking in the sights from her window. The bus had pulled up to the yellow line, and Elsa stepped up holding a dollar bill.

"Change! Change!" the driver shouted.

Elsa stepped down and went into a fish store. "Have you change?" she asked the vendor. She boarded the next bus and rode downtown, taking in the sights and also noting the street numbers. The bus sped through the Fifties, Thirties, Twenties. With the approach of the Teens Elsa panicked at what lay beyond Zero Street—the end of the world? Argentina? She pulled the cord and got off at Zero Street.

Elsa and Delia got off the train, and Flora appeared out of the crowd on the platform, smiling, arms outstretched. She spoke over the roar of the departing train.

"You just got to the United States?"

"Yeah."

"Do you speak English?"

"No."

"You need a job?"

"Yeah."

"Would you take a job caring for an old lady—a witch, a bitch?"

"Yeah."

"One-fifty plus room and board."

"O.K."

Flora went to Mrs. Mayer and told her about a wonderful young woman, Elsa Lydia Rodari, thirty-six years old, warm, hard-working, practically single-handed had run a store in Buenos Aires, like a delicatessen.

"I bet she don't speak English," Mrs. Mayer said. She had short white hair and blue eyes.

"She arrived only ten days ago," said Flora, "but she's taking an English course at NYU."

"A hundred a week plus room and board. Take it or leave it."

"One-ten," Flora bargained.

"A deal, but tell her no late-night radio or telephone calls and three showers a week."

Two days later Elsa took a downtown Lexington train to Fifty-ninth Street, switched to an N train and got off at Continental Avenue for an F train going to Jamaica, 179th Street. She exited to the street and in front of the Burger King boarded the Q-33 bus which ran along Hillside Avenue. Flora had told her to sit in the front of the bus, in a seat across from the driver, so she could see out the front window. Flora was waiting on the corner of Francis Lewis Boulevard. Mrs. Mayer's house was two blocks away, and as they walked Flora coached Elsa: "Close your door at night so she can't see the light. When you go to the supermarket, buy what you need just for that day, a few potatoes, a brick of butter—like that."

"Why?"

"This way you get out every day. And don't do windows! If she tells you to do windows, faint!"

"Who does the windows?"

"Nobody. In the United States nobody cleans windows."

Flora introduced Elsa to Mrs. Mayer, then showed Elsa around the house, the upstairs bedrooms, three of them, but Mrs. Mayer slept on a folding cot in the parlor so she could see her companion lady's light under her door, hear the rush of the shower, the sounds of music. Before Flora left, she told Mrs. Mayer the reasons why:

"In Argentina I was a woman of property. I owned a store which I sold for a lot of money. I was married to a hardworking man and his work brought him to the United States, Queens, where he died and I became a companion lady—but this was no reason to change my style of living. I've prided myself on my cleanliness, my dress, I use the best perfumes and love to read Borges and listen to tangos. I would never stoop to cleaning windows or bending to the unreasonable demands of an old crow! Goodbye and God bless Elsa!"

Then Flora left Elsa alone with a strange lady and with things to do: fix breakfast, do the dishes, give Mrs. Mayer a sponge bath, then while she was napping go to the supermarket and shop and learn the names of things. As time passed and Mrs. Mayer saw that Elsa was not reading late into the night, talking on the phone or running the water, Mrs. Mayer expected Elsa to complain, but she did not, and Mrs. Mayer took a liking to her. On Saturdays Elsa went to her English course at NYU. It ended at 3:30 and she didn't have to get back until 9:30, but she didn't want to travel in the darkness, so she returned immediately after class. Mrs. Mayer was so happy to see her. She made Elsa tea and sat her down and spoke to her like an old friend who had stopped by unexpectedly after a long trip abroad. Mrs. Mayer asked Elsa about her life in the United States thus far, always coming around to a subject that pleased her but was out of reach now, romance.

Yes, there had been romance, with a native New Yorker, Bud, a fabric designer who twice a year traveled to Mexico, Europe and South America. She had met him in Buenos Aires. He sold her bolts of silk, cotton and wool for the *vinchas* she made, headbands of twenty different colors, silk and cotton in summer, wool in winter. They had conducted an affair in Buenos Aires, then when she wanted to go out with somebody in the United States, she called Bud. She called him at his office because he was married. They arranged a rendezvous in a motel. She asked him to help her with her permanent residence, and he told her he would talk to his friends, even his mother, an aging woman in need of a companion lady.

"Wouldn't it be exciting," Bud said, "if you cared for my mother and while she's sleeping I steal into the house like a forbidden lover, climb in through the window in the servant's quarters, surprise you in your bed, throw you down and molest you, persevere until you surrender to my kisses—"

"Sounds like fun!" said Mrs. Mayer.

Well no, because while Bud's friends were deciding whether to sponsor her, the problem arose over where to make love. His place was out, and you get tired of making love in motels, and she had just moved in with Delia in Lefrak City. Bud wanted to go there to make love.

"I live with somebody," Elsa told him. "Am I supposed to ask her to leave?"

"Yes, you can ask her," said Bud.

"I can't do that!"

"Can't you ask her to do you a favor? Can't you do *me* a favor? After all, I'm doing *you* a favor!"

That was it—the romance was over.

Elsa and I got together to talk things out. She said she hadn't asked me to go to Chuck and Tom's because she knew I didn't like homosexuals and went to Brooklyn only to visit my parents' grave in Greenwood Cemetery.

"But I never met Chuck and Tom!" I objected. "If anything, I'm afraid of dogs. As far as I'm concerned, Chuck and Tom are a couple just like a man and a woman are a couple. They're human beings like everybody else. All I know is that Chuck is a bartender, a no-nonsense bartender—when he insisted on a share of the waitresses' tips and they refused, he quit. He's a man of principles. Tom—he's an itinerant waiter and first-rate gardener. I like that, he loves flowers. You describe him as thin, frail—he's the feminine component of the couple—"

Elsa's black eyes smiled at me.

"You have to understand," I continued, changing direction, "that where I come from, Bensonhurst, Brooklyn, there was no such thing as a homosexual. Nobody lived alone or with just another man or woman. The houses were too big, two- and three-story brick and shingle. Married couples lived in them and they had kids, the kids I played with in the street. Each member of the couple had known the other since they were kids. The prospective brides hung around while the boys played ball in the lots. They built their houses on these lots. Oh, yes—one man raised our suspicions that something was wrong. Bob Taura had been a priest, then left the calling. He moved in with his mother and cared for her instead of a parish. His skin was pink and he was very thin, and from my kitchen window I watched him walk to the six-thirty Mass, his head tilted, prayer book in hand, his thin lips moving in silent prayer. He played knock-hockey with the boys at the YMCA across the street from the church. The only time I heard about a homosexual was in a story my father liked to tell. Would you like to hear it?"

"Sure."

"His poker group met every other Wednesday, and one Wednesday he happened to sit next to an old friend, Rosario. They had played ball together. As was my father's habit, he placed his arm around the player to his left—on this night, Rosario. A newcomer to the group, a skinny attorney, noticed this and said, 'Hey, there, take your arm off Rosario!'

"Red with rage, my father retorted, 'Just shut up and play cards!'

"After the game, in complete disbelief that what had happened really happened, my father approached the skinny attorney and said, 'Now will you tell me what that was all about?'

"'I apologize,' the skinny attorney said, realizing my father's ignorance.

"Then while riding home with my Uncle Mike, my father turned to him and said, 'Did you see that?'

"Mike snapped, 'You stupid ass! Everybody knows the man's a fairy! Rosario's his chauffeur! They've been living together for twenty years!'"

Elsa said, "Do you know what happens in Argentina if two men are caught living together? They're dragged to jail, beat up, fucked in the ass and blackmailed. Their families are sought after and they have to make a clean break. Children are watched extremely closely. Girls are taught macramé before they walk. Boys are given soccer balls. Argentina's homosexuals migrated wholesale to San Francisco and here—do you know what it's like for them to walk down Christopher Street arm in arm in broad daylight?"

"I can imagine."

Though the homosexuals in Argentina were in hiding, Elsa was introduced to them at an early age. One lived next door. "Mariquita, everybody called him, and I see him perfectly: skinny, tall, wavy black hair, painted cross-eyes, and every morning at ten he stood at his door waiting for his lover to arrive on the tram. An old man in a business suit and eyeglasses and carrying a suitcase got off the tram, then looked around for police and unfamiliar faces. He approached Mariquita with a faint smile. The lovers talked rapidly in the shaded doorway, arranged a rendezvous, then the old man boarded a tram and disappeared. Nobody squealed on Mariquita, because he was gentle, especially with children, and the children loved Mariquita's older brother, an invalid confined to a wheelchair. His only view of the world was the one outside his window. He'd call the children and they'd gather outside the window. Their favorite story was about María Luisa and the lieutenant. Would you like to hear it?"

"Of course!"

"One day during Carnival, María Luisa, dressed as a butterfly, picked up a lieutenant in the military. In all his days this lieutenant had never seen such a gorgeous woman: long, shapely legs, plucked eyebrows, sensuous white arms. María Luisa and the lieutenant drank and sang, and he melted in María Luisa's arms as they danced. He looked into her beautiful eyes while his hands played along the smooth white skin of her arms, then his hands caressed her broad back and then moved down to her muscular buttocks and then around to her chest and then—and then the lieutenant felt María Luisa's manhood bulging! The lieutenant drew his revolver and pressed it against María Luisa's temple. 'I'm not going to kill you,' the lieutenant said, 'because you're just a child.'"

Elsa's first love was a suspected homosexual named Fito, her best girlfriend's brother. As a teenager Elsa loved to dance the tango, and Fito was the best tango dancer in Buenos Aires. His family was happy to see him go out with such a lovely girl, but Elsa's family questioned her about the boy she was often seen dancing with.

"I like Fito! We're like brother and sister. We dance the tango!"

"Fito—he's a *maricón!*"

"No, you're lying!" Elsa protested. "He's not a *maricón!* I tell you, he's not!" Then she ran into her room and cried.

Elsa said to me, "Years later I realized he was gay, but as a teenager it was enough that I enjoyed dancing with him. We were like brother and sister, and he never asked me out."

I said to Elsa, "I'd like to ask you out."

"Where to?"

"My place."

"Let's go."

THE

DIGEORGIO

GIRLS

ALL the DiGeorgio girls are nearsighted and flat-chested, and since the DiGeorgio boys go in for big breasted women with good vision we have written off our female cousins as uninteresting, with no goals in life other than marrying and promulgating other nearsighted, flat-chested women. With bowed heads and heavy hearts our cousins have dispersed not only from Bensonhurst but from the whole of New York State. Cousin Nancy bought a big corner house in New Jersey, Butler, New Jersey, and recently I discovered that she likes to garden. Every spring I will picture her turning over the earth and planting seeds, her glasses on, wearing a pretty smock and a sun hat. She devotes her life to her two small children, Guy and Arlene. Guy is a promising left-handed batter, he has a natural swing, and at the age of six Arlene already wears glasses, but we will have to wait a few years to see if her breasts will bud. The best Nancy could do by way of a husband was a half-Sicilian, half-Irish sales-man with venereal warts. He picked them up before the marriage from a woman up in Spanish Harlem. They were removed sur-gically but they've grown back. Fortunately, one of the DiGeorgio boys is a surgeon. He operates on Sunday afternoons, a discreet nurse in attendance. Cousin Nancy's sex life is reduced to a few episodes every six months or so. In her sorrow, in her adult silence, she takes pleasure in planting flowers and watching them grow.

Cousin Antonia is the only DiGeorgio girl with blond hair and she's also the shortest. Her mane of odd golden hair barely reaches the top of the stove, but during her formative years she stood beside our grandmother and learned the recipes. She carried them off to Rhode Island, where she fell in love with a full-blooded Irish accountant, a real nice guy because he comes from a family of fourteen children. His greatest attribute is tolerance. He eats everything Antonia cooks and tolerates his four daughters, believing that one day he will have a son.

Cousin Diana is the ugliest DiGeorgio girl. We call her "Dead-eye" because for the first twenty years of her life a smile did not break on her homely face. She's legally blind, and her sloppy ass accents the flatness of her chest. But Diana surprised us by marrying an intellectual, an Irish linguist just as ugly and nearsighted as she. They found happiness in Kentucky amid the horses and bluegrass, and they're raising a brood of contented, ugly intellectuals.

Cousin Gloria once entered a nunnery up in Canada. She took her sabbaticals in Bensonhurst and we saw that she smoked and cursed. A new breed of nun we have nowadays, we whispered. When the news reached Bensonhurst that Gloria left before taking final vows, we suspected that smoking and cursing had been the least of her vices. In the dead of night, in the sacred silence of the convent, a wavering nun creeped into her bed, and Gloria also fucked one or two of the lecherous priests who lived in the rectory across the street. Secretly, we were relieved: now she could curse and smoke all she wanted, shed her habit for a dress, let her hair grow and fuck her brains out with a normal guy.

She lived a while in Manhattan, alone, in an overpriced apartment in the East Forties. It was worth it because she had a doorman to protect her against the coloreds. She was within walking distance of the theaters, yet she was not known to take in a show or stroll from time to time along the East River. She never appeared in Bensonhurst with a man. What was she doing in New York? She was going to a school, and she attended this school as long as it takes to become a doctor. She became what was called a physical therapist, using the love and strength in her Italian hands to soothe the ailing spines of people of all races. Her hands worked over the paralyzed spine of the great Italian Joe Columbo after he was shot during one of our Columbus Day celebrations. Our hats go off to Mr. Columbo for having the courage to try to organize us. Some of us frowned upon his leadership because of his purported links with organized crime. But what manner of man among us is going to pick up the gauntlet? A Mario Cuomo? A Lee Iacocca? I cared about Joe Columbo and so at the first funeral after the shooting I collared Cousin Gloria, led her out to the vestibule and said, "How's Joe doin'?"

"Forget it," she said. "He's a vegetable."

"We mustn't give up hope," I said. "You come from good stock, good blood—use it to help Joe back to his senses. And you of all people know the power of prayer. Pray for him, Cousin Gloria. I say the Lord's Prayer for him every night. I fall asleep saying it, and I vow to God that if He pulls Joe through I'll say a rosary every night. I'll even work for Joe—I'll help him board up Little Italy, sever the tongues of Italian crooners. Joe is alive, Cousin Gloria, and as long as a man is alive, especially an Italian man, there's hope. Every minute of every day his family whispers words of encouragement into his ears. They dress him in a colorful sports shirt and wheel him to the window to look onto the light of day. Out the bay window is a scene of beauty: manicured lawns and hedges stretching to the horizon; tall, sighing pines; acres of snowballs and honeysuckle vines. The odor of honeysuckle wafts in through the window. A cool breeze rustles his thinning black hair."

While my father was dying, an amusing story unfolded in the life of the youngest DiGeorgio girl, Cousin Sylvia. Future generations of DiGeorgios, boys and girls, may look back upon it and a smile may break on their glum faces.

In Italian families, perhaps in all kinds of families, saying farewell to a dying member is a special occasion, much like a wedding or a birthday. Each member begins preparing his clothes and arsenal of thoughts and behavior the moment the invitation arrives, and in my father's case invitations were sent out the day he underwent surgery on his brain. A brief, misleading period of convalescence followed during which we could all cry, saturate ourselves with sorrow. Family members came over to the house to say goodbye, for we Italians die at home. To die in a hospital is a disgrace. A hospital is a place for people with no family to care for them, an alien place populated by black nurses and bland food.

My father would die in his bedroom and live out his days in his living room. His chair was there from which he watched the ball games and counted his money. I dressed him in a nice sports shirt and slacks and placed his walker beside his chair in case he had the desire and strength to walk.

Cousin Sylvia's mother, Aunt Tessie, was the first DiGeorgio to visit. What a wonderful person she was to come over that way, dressed in a pretty blouse and black slacks and all made up with lipstick, rouge, and powder! She truly loved my father over the forty years she knew him. In the summer he liked fresh fruit, especially peaches and cherries, and so when Tessie knew he was going over she pictured his mouth watering as he crossed beneath the El and prepared a heaping bowl of juicy red peaches and big black cherries. Sometimes she made him manicotti. "The best manicotti in the world," he'd say. "So light they melt on your tongue."

She had no choice other than to make light manicotti because her husband suffered from diverticulitis and a bad bowel—the DiGeorgio bowel, we call it, characterized by excessive flatulence and intermittent diarrhea. If the dough was heavy, if the ricotta wasn't exactly the right texture, he'd fart and shit for weeks and blame her.

She came on a day in late December. It was snowing. Father insisted it was August, the month he had taken for his vacation.

It was August. He asked for a cigarette, and I lit a Chesterfield regular and placed it in his lips. He dragged on it, screwing up his face, then he gazed out the window and was sane enough to see that it was snowing. Not only was it snowing outside but it was snowing all over the world, including in his living room.

"Jesus Christ! In August we have snow! How the hell did it snow? Let's go into the kitchen, Anthony—you can't smoke in the snow."

"Pa, Tessie has come over to see you. She brought a box of pastries."

"Oh, shit. . . ."

Our pastry boxes are white and smooth to remind us of the cream in the cannoli, and the string is thin yet strong. Aunt Tessie laid the box on the kitchen table, it was forgotten, then I ushered her into the living room. She sat on the couch and stirred uneasily, unaccustomed to wearing nice clothes and looking pretty at four in the afternoon on a weekday. She usually wore a housedress and slippers in order to make a fluid transition between her position in front of the stove and lying on the couch in the living room while the food cooked. She rested her elbows on top of the couch. The action lifted her breasts and I could see that they were still appealing, expansive and firm. Once, they had been inviting to the youngest of the second generation of DiGeorgio boys, Mario. During the Second World War he was stationed in Texas. Thoughts of home included a vision of his house on Seventy-fifth Street, the sunlit porch with cane chairs, even the tiny copper hat that served as an ashtray. Looming high above everything, above the tall, sighing trees, above the El, was a picture of Tessie's breasts. He called her and told her to come down. She took a train. The happiest moments in Mario's life were those first moments alone with Tessie in a hotel room in Texas. The door was double-locked and the family was a thousand miles away in Bensonhurst. There was no need for secrecy or restraints of any kind, yet Mario shut the lights in order to intensify his desire by touching Tessie in the darkness. Turning pale from the expectation, his mouth open, he fumbled with the buttons of her blouse. She sighed, her eyes shone like stars, her breasts heaved like a swell in the tide. "Now take off your brassiere," Mario commanded.

After the war, Tessie became the last of the in-laws and in the time it takes to say Giuseppe Verdi she acquired a reputation: she was a lazy good-for-nothing, ate too much and after Sunday dinner sat on her ass while the true-bloods did the dishes. At the same time, in order to live with Mario, it was said that she was a good mother to Sylvia, which she was, and made the best manicotti in the world. In the final analysis she and she alone was responsible for Mario's wavering between becoming a dentist or a lawyer. He chose the law. Then he decided to become a pianist. He moved his piano into his law office and played until midnight—all because during the war Tessie had forced herself on him, calling him over and over from Brooklyn when he was in Texas, breathing huskily into the phone. He was living peacefully in the barracks, but then Tessie flew down, stretched her breasts in his eyes, dragged him to some fleabag hotel, then fucked him until he couldn't think straight.

Trying to pinpoint exactly what had gone wrong in their marriage, over the years we have kept our eyes glued to Tessie's breasts. By her fiftieth year they were still appealing but Mario played later and later into the night. Tessie's breasts no longer held a fascination for him, so we looked elsewhere—her legs, for example. Mario had converted his backyard into an Italian garden: terraced rows of carnations and alpine roses, mimosa and fruit trees, statues of the saints and a replica of the Fontana di Trevi. He attached speakers to his fiberglass awning and piped up arias and folk songs from the hi-fi in the cellar. The pièce de résistance was a swimming pool slightly larger than a bathtub. From my deck chair, drink in hand, the sun shining on my face and my heart swooning from the melodies, I scrutinized Tessie's legs as she jumped in and out of the pool. They had once been shapely. Tessie giddily scurried to my chair, placed one hand on her hip and one hand behind her neck. She forced a smile, feeling young and beautiful again.

"Do I still have a nice body?"

"You certainly do."

"I have a lover, you know. . . ."

In the living room with Father and me, Aunt Tessie exposed a part of herself she had not exposed before: a mind of her own. No one would know. Soon her brother-in-law would be dead and his son would return to his world of penury and ideas. She leaned forward and directed to me, the only other sane mind in the room: "What is it about me that nobody listens to me? My daughter wants to go out with the Javel salesman and won't take no for an answer. Don't you think she should find somebody else?"

"About yourself first," I said. "Nobody listens to you because you don't assert yourself. See how you're talking here? Talk that way in your own house. Don't cook, clean or shop unless you're given a genuine response to your question: What is it about me that nobody listens to me? The abuse you get from your husband is based on your doing everything he wants despite your dissatisfaction, and the abuse you get from your daughter is based on the abuse you get from your husband. If your husband respected you, so would your daughter."

"Why didn't I think of that, Anthony?" Tessie said.

Father said, "I have to pee." He reached for his walker, his body shaking, pain surfacing to his kind hazel eyes.

"Just a minute, Pa." I wasn't about to step out of the limelight just because he had to pee. "Tessie," I said, "you're absolutely right about Sylvia and the Javel salesman. She has to find somebody more suitable."

"Would you talk to her?"

"I'd love to. Tell her to call me."

Javel is a bleach the women of Bensonhurst used in their wash. Light blue in color, it came in gigantic bottles too heavy to carry home from the supermarket, so it was delivered to the doorstep by a salesman. The salesman who serviced Brooklyn was a young Italian named Pasquale. Son of immigrants, he lived on Fifteenth Avenue among the stores, and every morning he drove in his horse and wagon to the supply house on Avenue U, loaded up with bottles of Javel, then rode happily around Brooklyn. On his way to Tessie's back door, he passed Mario's garden. He had never been to his parents' homeland and said to himself, "Italy itself couldn't be this beautiful." He rang the bell. Tessie was in the kitchen cooking. Cousin Sylvia was in the living room dancing. She's the thinnest of the DiGeorgio girls, suffering from acute gastroenteritis, but she put every ounce of remaining energy into her dancing, jerking, shimmering, flailing her arms to the frantic rhythm of the music. She smiled when she danced, enjoying it.

Pasquale presses his face against the screen door. Tessie opens it and takes the bottle. "Can I have a glass of water?" the boy asks.

"Of course, sweetheart. Come in."

He goes into the living room, sits on the couch and watches Sylvia dance. "You're the best dancer I've ever seen," he says.

From the kitchen: "Sylvia, shut the music!"

"She's very good!" Pasquale says.

"See, Ma, he says I'm very good! Know how to dance?" she asks him.

"A little."

"C'mon, then," and she reaches a writhing hand down to him.

"Let's go out," he says.

"Ma, he asked me to go out!"

"You'll have to wait for your father!"

"Why, Ma?"

"You know why—now don't ask me."

"I'm calling Cousin Anthony!"

"Do that!"

She calls me: "Cousin Anthony, this is Cousin Sylvia."

"How are you, sweetheart?"

"Not so good. See, the Javel salesman asked me for a date and my mother said I have to ask my father. But I don't want to. If I hesitate, he may think I don't like him. You should see him— he's gorgeous!"

"Where is he now?"

"Downstairs in the living room."

"Listen," I whisper, "if you want to go out with this guy, go out with him. Arrange a secret rendezvous."

"A what?"

"Meet him on the sly. Maybe you can go with him on his rounds. There's room for two in the driver's seat. It should be fun."

"I love you, Cousin Anthony!"

She brings the subject up over dinner. "But *he* wasn't born in Italy, his parents were. It's not his fault."

Mario says, "I don't care. You're not going out with him."

"But why? I have a right to know."

"He comes from the lower classes. He has no future."

"I can't stand this!" and she throws her fork into her plate. It bounces into the center of the table among the myriad side dishes. Mario swings, Cousin Sylvia bounds from the table, runs up the stairs and sulks in her room. She hears the funny words again, "secret rendezvous," and they're confluent with her desires. She prepares an outfit of pink tank top and white short-shorts and goes to sleep.

She gets up early and has breakfast with her father, the DiGeorgio standard of a cup of coffee and one piece of toast. She looks at his lips for any aftereffects. There are none. He places his cup emphatically in the saucer and goes to work.

She runs to New Utrecht Avenue and hidden in the shadows beneath the El telescopes the winding avenue as far as the Seventy-seventh Street station. She sees the horse, a tired old colt, and he's waiting, scraping one shoe against the tarred street. She hesitates: "Should I?" She hears my voice, "Do it!" Crouching behind the cars, she slowly makes her way to the horse and carriage. She pets the horse, climbs aboard, takes up the reins and with the happiness she feels while dancing drives around the block.

Pasquale comes out from his delivery. "Somebody stole my wagon!"

"Around the corner!" a pedestrian yells.

He runs around the corner. "Hey, come back here!"

Laughing hysterically, Cousin Sylvia snaps the whip. Pasquale sees who it is, recognizing her lean torso and swanlike neck. Inspired by love, he picks up speed, hops in among the crates and crawls to the driver's seat. They hug and kiss and just for fun race a train to Coney Island.

From that day on until they married they delivered Javel to the Italian women of Brooklyn, racing over the back roads of Bensonhurst, East New York and Canarsie. After work they drove over the Verrazano Bridge and made love in the marshes of Staten Island. In winter they went to a motel, where sometimes Cousin Sylvia danced. One night, Pasquale suggested that they visit my father. Sylvia gave him a special hug and kiss, not from feelings for my father but from relief that her Pasquale was acquainted with the notion of respect.

THE
DIGEORGIO
BOYS

———

THERE comes a time every day in the lives of the Di-Georgio boys when we like to set aside our guns and rest our heads on the bosom of a woman. We insist on a big bosom, expansive and firm, so it can provide a welcome similar to the welcome our mothers gave us when they first drew us to their breasts and coddled and suckled us. Our mothers and aunts had thick arms and knotty legs, natural hair and a mushroom nose. We prefer sinewy arms and shapely legs, an aquiline nose and bleached hair to remind us that the flesh is real. Skin the color of Italian bread and a face that reflects the mind, that is, blank, a stupid-looking face that harbors no treachery. If our luck runs low and a comforting bosom also comes with a mind, we tolerate it as long as possible: we allow her to go to work, listen to her talk, visit her parents on Sundays, forgoing a plate of spaghetti smothered by our grandmother's sauce.

Of the six DiGeorgio boys only four of us count: Big Johnny, Captain Frank, Carmine and myself. We count because we are aware that our behavior points to the image of our family, and as a result we are close, first-cousins-closer-than-brothers. No matter how many years pass, how different our lifestyles grow, we stay in touch, bringing one another up to date on the tasks we are undertaking and, most important of all, the women in our lives, the possibility of marrying one and promulgating the blood.

Big Johnny owns a string of pizzerias. He makes ninety pies a day with his rings on. The diamonds glitter through the flour. At the end of the day he hops into his red Coupe de Ville and brings us leftover slices and calzones. He's about to marry after a ten-year engagement. "Why?" we ask him. "Why?"

"I'll tell ya," he says. "You guys ever see the program 'Bowling for Dollars'?"

"Of course."

"So you know how before you bowl the MC asks a few questions. He asks her, 'Your husband in the audience?'

"'I'm not married,' she says, then the idiot says, 'but I've been engaged for ten years and I have ten diamond rings to show for it,' and with that she holds up her hands to the camera. The next day she's robbed. We got most of the rings back but I'm still afraid for her. We're getting married, and I'm going to live in her parents' basement."

"Please, Big Johnny, don't do that."

"You don't understand," he says. "I'm smart. If I come home late after a poker game and she doesn't like it, I'll tell her, 'Go upstairs to your mother!' And another thing—you don't pay alimony if your wife lives with her parents."

Big Johnny believes that cocaine curbs his appetite, so Cousin Carmine supplies him. Carmine gets around a little more. He works in New York and is a college graduate. It took him sixteen years to graduate, as he attended night school, going surreptitiously in the dark so his father wouldn't know. Carmine became a builder, so before we pick up a hammer we consult with him. He's been going out with the same woman for eight years, a true enough Barbie with big tits, but she has bad teeth and hammer toes and wants to get married. Carmine has been forthright about his intentions, so much so that even the jewelers in the diamond district know about them. Around the holidays Carmine wavers. For some peace he either proposes or flies to the Bahamas. One Christmas season he tells Barbie, "Go get a ring—we're getting married."

She goes to the diamond center, picks out the diamond of her dreams and puts down Carmine's money. A month passes, two. Carmine calls the jeweler. "Where's the ring?"

"Forget it," says the jeweler. "You don't really want to get married."

Barbie loves children, and so on Sunday afternoons Carmine takes her to an orphanage in New Jersey. He waits in the car while she plays with the children. Lumps begin appearing in her breasts. The doctor tells her that they'll disappear once she gets pregnant. She tells her mother, who in turn calls Carmine.

"I don't care if you marry my daughter, but I want her to have a baby!"

"Fuck you!" Carmine says, and decides to end the relationship. He calls me.

"I'm in total accord with your decision," I say.

"I'm afraid," he says.

"Of what?"

"Barbie was free of herpes, and now that I'm going out with other women... Two million people have herpes, you know. It's an epidemic. How can you tell, Cousin Anthony, especially if she doesn't offer the information?"

"Let's go up to City Island and ask Captain Frank. He'll know."

Captain Frank is a surgeon and a sailor. He removes the veins that surface at the base of our mushroom noses and takes us sailing under the Throgs Neck Bridge. He's known not to be too quick to operate. A widow walks into his office for a breast enlargement. A proper-looking lady, around fifty, and she sits down and says, "I'm starting a new life. I'm going on a cruise to meet a man and I'd like to look nice. I want a breast enlargement."

"Take off your blouse," Captain Frank says.

The woman stands up, removes her blouse and waits. Captain Frank takes one look. "Sorry," he says, "there's nothing I can do."

She sued him for discriminating against older women. Ever since then Captain Frank has been going out with one young flat-chested woman after another. He insists on nudity while sailing. From a passing ship it's impossible to tell him apart from his women.

Carmine and I drive up to City Island on a beautiful day in August. No wind, just perfect to sit around and talk. We park at the marina and see hundreds of sailboats stacked one beside the other, lolling in the calm sea, bells ringing, masts of all sizes punching holes in the sky. Carmine says, "You know the name of his boat?"

"No need to," I say. "Just look for the biggest stick in the harbor."

We find it, moored at slip 87, an impressive sloop around fifty feet, all fiberglass, and sitting on deck with a drink in one hand and *The Life of Thomas Jefferson* in the other is our beloved cousin Captain Frank. He's tall, 6'4", and when he sees us a smile breaks behind his full beard. He helps us aboard, telling us to take off our shoes, which we don't like. We hug and kiss, then he leads us down to the staterooms, all oak, custom-built by a bunch of poor Portuguese bastards in Rhode Island. On the oak table in the sitting room Carmine lays out a dozen lines of cocaine. We snort a few and then Captain Frank says:

"I'm expecting a Hawaiian woman. Actually, she's half Hawaiian and half French. What a body—the most fantastic breasts you guys have ever seen!"

"We thought your derangement was only temporary," Carmine says.

"I can almost see them now," I say. "You're anchored off Gardiners Island, an isolated island, and there's not another boat around or a cloud in the sky. Our half-breed is tall and she leans against the mainmast, face to the sun. Her breasts are magnificent and free, yellow as lemons, big lemons, and they rise and fall gently with her breath."

Captain Frank and Carmine laugh nervously, but I go on: "Listen, Captain Frank, our young cousin here recently split up with Barbie. She was free of herpes and now Carmine is going out with other women. As you know, twenty million Americans have herpes, it's an epidemic. You're a scientist, tell us—what do you look for?"

Captain Frank vacuums the remaining lines of cocaine, licks his fingers, smiles and says:

"I want you guys to remember two things: one, tits are for kids; and two, if you can't eat it, don't fuck it."

A few words about the two prodigal DiGeorgio boys, Skinny Billy and Bobby Boy. If we passed them on the street and looked them square in the face, we wouldn't know who they were. We see them fleetingly at funerals, and thus far only our grandparents have died and my mother and father. After my father's funeral, Bobby Boy came to the house with his new bride. He wore the same tortoise-shell glasses he had worn when he was nine years old, and he was the same height, too. We call him Bobby Boy because he's the youngest DiGeorgio and in our hearts will always be a boy. Only his voice had changed, and he used his manlike voice to say with some conviction, "I'm a school psychologist. My wife is a psychologist, too."

We were all surprised. We had remembered him solely for two things: he had a basketball court in his backyard and for years stood beneath the hoop waiting to grow closer to it; and at one Christmas dinner when he was nine, sitting beside his father, he had said, "When my father dies, I want his job."

Why, the brazen little bastard! we all thought. His father had slaved thirty years inching his way up the ladder of a big pharmaceutical company. His ass thirty thousand feet up in the air, the man flew all over the world overseeing the building of satellite pharmaceutical plants, bringing the wonder of American drugs to the peasants of Mexico, Sicily, the West Country of England. When he wasn't flying, he was driving to headquarters in Connecticut, a long commute from Bensonhurst. He has little time to spend with his son, who grows quiet and sullen. The old man decides to move near the plant, buys a property in the middle of nowhere. It was the first time in the history of the DiGeorgio family that one of us lived under foreign skies. We lament that branch of the family, it's as if they had died. We lose track of Bobby Boy. He stands beneath his basket. The years pass. An old engineer now caught in the recession, his father is fired, leaving Bobby Boy without his childhood dream. Instead of look-ing back to Bensonhurst for a new way, he goes to a college up

in Buffalo. Here his voice deepens, his genitals flourish, he dis-
covers psychology. In the laboratory one day the aspiring psychologist next to him, a girl who sitting on her stool looks about
the right height, is fitting two test tubes together when they slip
and one pierces her hand between two knuckles. Blood pumps
forth as from a fountain.

"Oh, look," she says nonchalantly, "blood."

Bobby Boy doesn't panic. He wraps the hand, then, taking
hold of her waist, leads her gently and swiftly to the hospital.
The wound requires six stitches, that's all, and afterwards she
invites him back to her dorm. She's kind and warm. The love she
showers upon him relaxes him, frees his DiGeorgio mind to think.
They go outside and knee-deep in snow Bobby Boy says, "You
Italian?"

"No," says the girl. "A problem?"

"No. I've been through enough upheavals without insisting on
a cultural link."

"Well, thanks a lot," the girl says, affronted.

"There I was," he goes on, "about to be an engineer, we move
to Connecticut, my father gets fired, and now I'm up to my ass
in snow, surrounded by nervous laboratory animals."

"I love you, Bobby."

"You do?"

"Yep. You know, we could make a life together concentrating
on the abnormal personality."

"Think so?"

"Yes, I do."

They hug and kiss. His eyes soften, his cheeks flush with
health. He commits himself to the girl and in the privacy of his
mind decides to exercise the DiGeorgio spirit amid the mountains, fresh air and psychotics of upstate New York.

Skinny Billy is slightly older than Bobby Boy and is the tallest
DiGeorgio boy. As a kid he refused to eat. He stared at his food
with his mouth open, a stupid look on his face. He grew so tall
so fast that his mouth remained open. He still looks stupid, and
if he isn't careful he's going to get a fist down his throat.

One Friday after work he hops on a West End train, his destination his mother's house in Bensonhurst. He gets a seat and starts reading the afternoon papers. Standing directly opposite him against the door is Carmine. He tells me: "Would you believe Skinny Billy sees me and turns his eyes away? He didn't want to know me."

"Are you sure, Carmine?" I say, giving him time to think.

"Anthony, I'm positive. He looks at me and just as we recognize one another he turns his head away and pretends to read the papers."

"Why, that little prick," I say. "He deserves a belt in the mouth."

Skinny Billy's parents are the kindest, most generous people on the face of the earth. Their little brat wanted trains, so the father, a struggling inventor, takes up his savings, boards a real train and goes to the Lionel store in New York. He buys the most elaborate setup Bensonhurst had ever seen: the black engine with a smokestack emitting real smoke and a real whistle; coal and cattle cars with bits of coal and little calves; coaches with the shadows of passengers in the windows; an adorable caboose; a network of tracks that traversed every room in the house; sidings with old, abandoned cars waiting to be overhauled; crossings with semaphores; tunnels and mountains; a corral in which horses and cows graze; a green station deep in the bayou, lit by a gas lamp, a man in black waiting to board; a transformer that only a genius of an inventor could operate.

Still the little pain in the ass refuses to eat. He's sent over to our house. My mother cooks him a lunch fit for a king. My father yells at him, "Now eat!" He swallows a few morsels to appease us. Tall and gawky, he goes to a Catholic high school in another neighborhood. The priests ruin his mind. His childhood love of trains extends to a desire for a real car. His father brings him home one, a Ford, after checking out every showroom in Brooklyn. Skinny Billy drives off to a college somewhere. He returns to Bensonhurst with a woman in the passenger seat. His wife, he says. Up at college he must have pursued a business course, because he lands a job on Wall Street. Nobody knows exactly what he does. And nothing is known about his so-called wife except her name, which we forget, and that her mother is a divorcée who lives on Staten Island. She's lonely, frightened and confused, so Skinny Billy buys the house next door, which he can't afford. His parents make up the deficit. His mute wife is administrator of a high school, so she needs a car, too, a little something to run around in. The parents buy him a second car, a Rabbit. And the wife has to look nice for the principal. She goes to the hairdresser's twice a week. The parents pay for her hair. They tell us:

"Every Friday night Billy comes to dinner with his wife and pain in the ass of a mother-in-law. But in all the years he's been married he's never come over alone to see us. We're very hurt. After all we've done for him, he's never come over alone—why?"

"Let's ask Bobby Boy," I venture.

"Good idea."

We call him:

"Yo, Bobby Boy!... how ya doin'?... wife?... kids?... good ... good... lots of snow, huh?... listen, Bobby Boy, we have a situation down here..."

After we fill his ears, Bobby Boy says, "At least he's being consistent."

"Explain a little, will ya."

"Well, the force-feeding, expensive Lionels, the house, cars, hairdos—they're all part 'n' parcel of the same thing."

"What might that be, Bobby Boy?"

"Who knows? But what's for shit sure is that it's worth all your while to keep paying the little prick to stay away."

DR. SANTO SPADARO

———

I AWOKE this morning hugging my pillows and laughing, tit-illated by the image of my paisan, Hector Belvederi, out in California lying naked beside his "other woman." I rolled over toward the wall, clasped more pillows and continued to laugh. Hector's other woman was also naked and the nearness of her nakedness, its desirability, transformed my paisan into a "sexual motor," as he calls it. Then in the shower the thought entered my mind that friendship aspires toward immortality. A friend provides an optimistic view of the world, buoys the spirits. Hector and I speak over the phone every other Sunday evening at nine o'clock California time, twelve o'clock New York time, and this past Sunday evening he told me that he's drinking two liters of wine every day, is in debt twenty thousand dollars on a short-term loan and is torn between his wife and the "other woman." I told him to cut down on the drinking. At times I've thought it would be all right if he drank himself to death—immortality would be that much closer. I offered him money, which he re-fused, knowing my financial condition, and I also offered him the peace and joy of my home, my Castro convertible.

"That would be running away," Hector said.

"What's wrong with that?"

"You don't understand," he said, "if I had my way, I'd live with the two women."

"No problem there," I said. "Become a Mormon, marry the other woman and bring her home." Then to give Hector a meaningful point of reference I told him about a second cousin of mine who had lived for thirty years in perfect harmony with two women, up in Albany next to the Governor's Mansion.

Dr. Santo Spadaro was one of America's foremost skin specialists and he was also a fine amateur violinist. Every early evening his house was filled with beautiful music. His two women sat close together, inseparable in their rapture. They wore pretty dresses and their clear, smooth faces beamed as they listened to their man playing. The time arrived when Dr. Santo was in the market for a new violin. He wrote to me in Bologna that he wanted a new violin made and of all the violin makers in the world the one he had in mind lived in my town. Price was not an issue, he wrote, and he gave me the violin maker's name and address. It was not too far from me, so I walked, but no violin maker lived or worked at the address, and the phone book did not list his name. I wrote to Dr. Santo telling him about my efforts. I felt that I had let him down and that the opportunity to be a small part of his exciting life had cruelly escaped me. I am the only DiGeorgio in the history of the family to be divorced, but none of us has ever lived with two women under the same roof, and so when I heard that Dr. Santo was coming to New York for my sister's wedding, I looked forward to discovering what qualities made it possible for three lovers to live together in complete accord. I pictured the sparkle in the women's eyes, their worldliness, generosity. Dr. Santo arrived at the church with only one of his women. She was a scrawny blond not of Italian extraction, and she was giddy and slobbered all over her man. The family also agreed early on that she was an ordinary floozy, but I believe Dr. Santo had invited the judgment as a way of keeping his way of life separate and apart from the branch of his family in New York. During the wedding ceremony the lovers sat in the last pew, laughing hysterically, then when my sister marched out of the church beside her husband, Dr. Santo and one of his women were already far up the block. From the church steps, through the shower of confetti, I glanced at them—they were doubled over with laughter, then he rested his head on her chest and she embraced him. I received no further news about him until after he died.

My paisan, Hector Belvederi, said, "I bet he left his women in good financial shape."

"No," I said, "he left everything to a third woman, his violin teacher!"

MARIO LANZA

O UR cultural station, Channel 13, recently aired a program called "Mario Lanza: The American Caruso." Mrs.
Richard Tucker must have been extremely upset, refus-
ing to tune in, because her husband was touted as America's heir
to Caruso. "Richard Tucker: A Brooklyn Caruso," he was once
tagged. Mrs. Tucker pitches for Channel 13, bringing in Jewish
money, but she must understand the channel's need for Italian
money, Italian money not only from the tri-state area but also
from outlying areas with a heavy concentration of Italians like
South Philadelphia, where Mario Lanza was born. There are only
so many good dead American tenors to dig up, and even at that
Italians don't care what Channel 13 calls a program or who shows
up to host it or do the commentary—they talk during the credits
and eat during the commentary. In the case of "Mario Lanza:
The American Caruso," they might have stared long and hard at
Zsa Zsa Gabor. Italians tuned in to hear Mario Lanza sing a few
songs, for it is his voice that lives on in our hearts.

"Forget about the Caruso thing, Mrs. Tucker," I'd like to tell
her. "Caruso was Caruso—it's intimidating, even contemptuous,
for a good tenor to be compared with him. It's a good thing your

husband and Mario Lanza are dead, I say. I mean, do you hear Luciano Pavarotti calling himself 'Luciano Pavarotti: The Italian Lauritz Melchior? The Italian Jussi Bjoerling'? Or Plácido Domingo calling himself 'Plácido Domingo: The Spanish Luciano Pavarotti'? Nor do we hear Mrs. Leonard Warren calling her husband 'Leonard Warren: The Bronx Titta Ruffo.'"

Mrs. Tucker persists: "My husband's voice was just as powerful as Caruso's!"

"Your husband had a fine, fine voice, and he had courage, giving up a career as a cantor to sing on the opera stage. I believe Jan Peerce was also a cantor. Leonard Warren was a tailor from the Bronx. Men like this don't exist anymore—do we hear nowadays of cantors or tailors with great voices? Men like your husband, Jan Peerce and Leonard Warren belong to another age, the age of my father, when singers like your husband did not forget their humble beginnings and sang from the heart."

For the Mario Lanza show, I imagine the Met says to its principal tenor, Plácido Domingo:

"Thirteen is doing a thing on Mario Lanza. They want you to host it. You won't have to go out of your way—one afternoon after rehearsal we'll set up a camera in the orchestra pit, you stand on an empty stage, and in your best accent you say, 'Mario Lanza, he wanted this—the stage of an opera house, but he never got it. He was born in 1921, the year Caruso died. Mario Lanza believed that Caruso's voice passed into him.' Stuff like this. You won't be alone—we're sending over Robert Merrill, Anna Moffo, Rosalind Elias, and there'll be clips of Kathryn Grayson, Ann Blyth, Frances Yeend, Lanza's physical instructor, even Zsa Zsa Gabor. Then we'll shoot you down to Lanza's childhood home above his grandfather's store in South Philadelphia—"

"I'm not going to South Philadelphia!" Domingo might have said. "You want another young dead tenor?"

"All right, all right. You have a fireplace in your condo?"

"Five of them."

"We shoot you in front of a mantel with a photo of Lanza on

it. Nobody'll know—a mantel is a mantel. Look, you played *Madama Butterfly* and *Tosca* on 13."

"Well, okay..."

The key to Mario Lanza's tragedy was his belief that his nose, his neck and his weight were interrelated. He was born with his mother's nose, a finely chiseled, uptilting nose, but Caruso, Gigli and even Richard Tucker had mushroom noses. Mario Lanza could change his name from Alfredo Cocozza, which translated means Alfred Eggplant, but there was nothing he could do about his nose. And his neck was thin, while the golden voices, including Richard Tucker's, had thick necks, like a bull. Mario Lanza believed that an appropriate nose dwelled somewhere inside his body and that it would surface to his face if he bloated that body. And so he ate and ate, and he grew fat around the midsection, but his nose stayed fine and his neck stayed thin.

Early in his career Mario Lanza sang the role of Pinkerton in *Madama Butterfly* in a minor opera house in New Orleans. He sang with a fine nose and a thin neck, and when he got paid—a small amount because unfortunately Pinkerton is viewed as a minor role—Mario Lanza said to himself, "Fuck this!" and he went to Hollywood. Joe Pasternak took one look at his girth and black curly hair and said to the studio beautician, "Take the kinks out of his hair, reduce him by eighty pounds, and I'll put him in *That Midnight Kiss.*"

The point is—he wasn't fat enough! Or he couldn't add weight where he wanted, on his nose and on his neck. But he kept trying. After *That Midnight Kiss*, he sent for his mother and she brought to Hollywood her recipe for spaghetti sauce. As long as his mother lived she would make the sauce, and as long as she made the sauce there was the chance that it would stir the nose inside of him. It would rise up through his stomach, into his gullet, and then one morning he would look in the mirror and there would be his operatic nose.

He paraded his mother around Hollywood in her apron, and he said to everyone, "Look at my mother. Look how great she is." He was so intent on changing his body permanently that he didn't understand the rivalry between his mother and his wife Betty. He'd say, "We have a big house in Bel Air, servants, custom-built kitchen—I don't understand what's going on!"

Betty made a good plate of spaghetti, but her sauce came nowhere near his mother's in taste. After Maria Cocozza died, he would relish his wife's sauce. But then Betty gave up eating entirely, let alone cooking. She drank and swallowed every pill in sight, including her husband's phlebitis pills.

Mario Lanza found some peace in the recording studio, away from mirrors and the viewing public. Except for a few technicians he was alone with his voice, and he recorded immortal songs, as well as a few pretty good arias. But he grew more and more frightened of singing live with his fine nose and thin neck. He reneged on a Las Vegas contract. His voice was dubbed on a supposedly live TV show, creating a scandal. In *The Student Prince*, Edmund Purdom's full nose stood in for his. Mario Lanza broke down and moved to Italy in order to be near millions of mushroom noses and thick necks. Nothing happened. He submitted himself to the cure of a twilight sleep lasting twenty days. His true nose would drop out of the twilight. He was fed intravenously—the true nose was lodged somewhere in his veins and would be drawn up to his face along with the fluid.

Lucky Luciano found the answer. He was going to attend a benefit in Naples, and he asked Mario Lanza to sing a few songs. But Mario Lanza went instead to the sanitarium for his twilight sleep. Mr. Luciano in his widsom hit on the idea that the tortured young man's ultimate peace lay in dwelling permanently with the twilight, leaving only his voice behind. A few trustworthy Neapolitans were dispatched to the sanitarium on the twentieth day, the day Mario Lanza was supposed to come out of his sleep with his new self. The men waylaid the chauffeur and the nurse and in the last intravenous bottle introduced a few bubbles of air.

ENRICO CARUSO

O H, why didn't we listen to Caruso on Christmas Eve? I
sigh from my exile in Manhattan, now that there are
no more Christmas Eves in Brooklyn. They were held
at my house even after my father died, and then my mother died
and now her body, those beautiful hands, is rotting atop her
husband's ashes regaled in his new blue suit and pink carnation.
On Christmas Eve the DiGeorgios of Brooklyn ate exactly what
Caruso had eaten: eel prepared five different ways, hot and cold
octopus, little fishes fried in oil and dried. The DiGeorgios also
put a roast beef on the table for the Irishmen some of the girls
were marrying. After dinner, with the linen tablecloth of holly
wreaths stained with wine and sauce, and with their intestines
swollen with gas, the men retired to the living room for a record
concert of arias and songs. Gigli sang and DiStefano and Bjoerling, even Richard Tucker and Perry Como—but no Caruso! Was
it the quality of his recordings?—no amplification except for the
resonance chambers inside his barrel-like body, the orchestra
straining to be heard, and so Caruso's voice would arrive practically a cappella, bald and as from a great distance, from Naples
itself, as if he had sung at the mouth of the Bay and Victor's

recording machine picked it up in their studio in Camden, New Jersey.

Did my father and my uncles object to Caruso's friendship with the head of Victor's recording department, Calvin Goddard Child, a Wasp?

Did the elder DiGeorgio men, all experts on the voice, know what I know now—that Caruso hated to record and his recordings suffered for this? He recorded in the morning, the Victor Company believing that the voice is freshest in the morning, so close upon sleep, but Caruso slept poorly and once told his beloved American wife, Dorothy Park Benjamin: "My voice is cold and 'eavy in the morning and I don't feel to sing." And he had to sing into a short, square horn instead of projecting his voice into the length and breadth of the opera house, up to the rafters, or into the black infinite night lying atop bull rings and glittering racetracks. Between the horn and the recording machine the Victor Company erected a partition so that no one, even Caruso, could steal its secrets, and in the partition was a small window in which appeared the ridiculous face of the operator, whose eyes signaled frantically for Caruso to raise or lower his voice, distracting him from the memory of his mother, to which he sang.

A major portion of the evening's concert was devoted to Puccini's La Bohème because it was only in the presence of all of her blood that Aunt Julia could unabashedly shed tears of joy and sorrow while singing along to Mimi's death aria in the Fourth Act. It didn't matter who the soprano was, let alone the tenor, and we played the whole opera so that the death aria wouldn't come as too much of a shock. We were worried about Julia's state of mind: if she was crazy, others of us could also be crazy. She was the second of three sisters, sandwiched between my mother, Margaret, and the youngest, Elvira, and Julia carried to extremes her sisters' opposing inclinations. My mother worried enough for everybody while Elvira was lighthearted and playful, leaning forward now and then to give her husband flash views of her breasts. Julia fainted at the slightest of our misfortunes and at the table would suddenly grow red as a beet, titter, "We're having a pah-dee!" and then throw chestnuts at us. They were hard and so we ducked under the table, where our faces simultaneously lost their smiles. Cysts were breaking out all over her body, including her head. One daughter wanted to become a nun, another was so homely that marriage was practically ruled out and Julia's son had decided to study psychology up in Buffalo. Her husband, Leo, was such an intensely private man that the only things we knew about him after forty years in the family were that he had given up cigarettes for an occasional cigar, sprouted hair white as snow exactly like his mother, who was somehow elegant and articulate, and Leo was also smart, otherwise he would not have risen to managing engineer of a big pharmaceutical firm in Connecticut. Leo's insanity was confirmed when without hesitation he uprooted his family from Brooklyn and dragged them to an isolated, sunken home in Hartford Lakes, Connecticut, and then from there he left them alone and traveled to even more exotic lands—Mexico, London, Sicily—where he supervised the building of other pharmaceutical plants so that the godforsaken inhabitants could have access to American drugs. You just don't sing La Bohème to such a man! He might think you're crazy, quit his job, plunging his branch of the family into penury and disgrace and setting them to wander to more remote regions. When Julia heard her husband coming home, heard the grinding of the gravel beneath the weight of his car, she put on a bright false face and ran outside as though young and beautiful again, wrapped her arms around her man and gushed into his bemused face: "So good to see you again, my love. Do we have a week together? Oh, never mind that now—come inside so I can comfort you, put up a little something to eat."

When the Fourth Act of La Bohème began, my father, uncles and male cousins signaled to me to turn up the volume and then our eyes turned toward the kitchen. Julia appeared in the doorway with her mouth wide open, white as a ghost, tears welling in her small, deep-set eyes. While wiping her hands on her apron, she succeeded in making it to the edge of a chair, and then the house grew quiet as a church as the Bohemians Rodolfo and Marcello attempt to write and paint in their garret overlooking the roofs of Paris. The Bohemians are poor and young, at the beginning of their artistic careers, witnessed by their idle chatter and reminiscences of lost sweethearts. I'd like to see a libretto where the Bohemians are old and still poor—they'd be working their butts off every day of the week, holidays included, scared shitless and alone. Rodolfo had seen Musetta, Marcello's old flame, riding in a handsome carriage; and Marcello had seen Mimi, Rodolfo's heartthrob, dressed like a queen and also riding in a carriage. Here the librettists are on target: it's a rare woman who wouldn't trade her struggling artist for a regular paycheck, a kitchen with room enough for a table and chairs, a bureau just to hold the linen. Our poor old Bohemians not only understand but they also grow pale with shame at seeing an old flame walking up—they turn quickly away, dart across the street. Rodolfo had shouted after Musetta's fleeting carriage, "Hey, Musetta, you look gorgeous today decked out all in velvet!" Our downcast fellows are at a loss at what to say to a friend's former love; she's one among hundreds of the lost: wives, girlfriends, children, homes. During their apprentice years Puccini roomed with Pietro Mascagni, composer of the much-loved *Cavalleria Rusticana*, and Emile Zola roomed with Paul Cézanne, but once they all achieved fame and fortune they didn't want to know one another. Our lonely fellows keep up any old friendship and number among their new friends the Oriental greengrocer, Indian jeweler, Greek baker. Rodolfo finds a pretty blue bonnet Mimi had left behind and sings to it. Our old lechers come upon satin, lace-trimmed panties and cry into them. Two more youthful Bohemians arrive, Schaunard and Colline, and they bring food, three rolls and a herring. All indulge in a mock feast fit for a Caesar: water turns to champagne, the herring becomes oysters and salmon. Our gaunt characters put up plain white rice fit for a starving Chinaman and it stays rice, and for their after-dinner leisure they sit quietly in a corner until sleep descends upon them. Puccini's Bohemians have the strength to dance a Gavotte, Minuet, Pavanella and Fandango. They assume quadrille positions, choosing their ladies, one another.

Schaunard calls Colline a clod. A duel ensues with pallets from the fireplace. The clanging of armor is suddenly interrupted by an orchestral ostinato: strings, brass, woodwinds combine to harbinger an ominous situation—Musetta arrives and sings with alarm:

"It's Mimi and she's sick! She whispered, 'I'm dying and I want to die near him. . . .'"

Through the open garret door Mimi is seen sitting on the top step. She's consumptive, coughs and convulses. Before Julia moved to Connecticut, the three sisters occasionally stole an evening and went to the opera together. They lived within walking distance of one another and the New Utrecht Avenue El, and they met at the central location of the Seventy-first Street station along the West End line. It was cold on the elevated platform, but they bundled up in their mink skins which piled on their shoulders made them look like furry angels with multiple heads and dead peering eyes. The sisters had in common big breasts and thick arms, and except for Julia, who was a tree trunk from her toes to her hair, shapely calves and sharp ankles. It was also dark and silent up there, but the sisters formed a close happy group. It felt so good to be together, with ultimate happiness awaiting just across the bridge in the form of *La Traviata* or *La Bohème*. They looked so clean and pretty in their long glittering gowns, high heels and stockings attached to tight girdles, white gloves and pretty little hats with black-mesh veils. All made up for a change with bright red lipstick and rouge, brows and upper lips plucked. Their gay youthful spirits surfaced to their familiar faces, and their eyes shined in anticipation of the glorious melodies. Their lively chatter filled the air atop Spagnoli's Pastry Shop. Earlier in the day they had done one another's hair.

"Mine's too short," my mother says, running her fingers through the ends of her graying hair.

"Oh, Maggie," says Elvira, biting her tongue, "you're always finding fault."

"Yeah, Maggie, you never have anything nice to say," Julia chimes in coolly, her behavior between holidays held in check by her quiet, intelligent husband.

"I can't say anything—you two are always picking on me!"

Tears come to my mother's eyes, and the subject abruptly changes.

"Who's singing tonight?"

"It doesn't matter."

"As long as there's the music!"

The train approaches low and serpentine out of the southern horizon, Coney Island, and carries them across the bridge to New York. They get lost temporarily among the skyscrapers, look up at them and marvel:

"I can't get over them!"

"Imagine the men who built them!"

"I admire the men who work in them!"

At the old Metropolitan they occupy orchestra seats, and if the soprano isn't very good and in time becomes the object of jeers and hisses, the three sisters turn and look at one another in disbelief, shrug their shoulders, spread their arms and say in unison amid smiles: "What do they want—she's dying of tuberculosis!"

In my dining room in Brooklyn, Julia is transfixed. . . . Rodolfo rushes to Mimi and sighs, "Ah!" jolting Julia from her reverie. Schaunard and Colline, basso and baritone respectively, carry a bed to the door. (Bassos and baritones are usually bigger than tenors—the lower the natural register of the voice, the bigger the man? The uncircumcised penis have anything to do with the predominance of Italian singers? Were there any big castrati singers?) Rodolfo and Marcello support Mimi and guide her to her deathbed. Julia's enormous lungs fill. Mimi exclaims, "Rodolfo!" Julia spreads her thick arms. Mimi raises herself slightly and embraces Rodolfo. Julia looks up at the crystal chandelier, lets loose an avalanche of tears. Mimi gives Rodolfo a sweet smile, opens her mouth to sing, and Julia opens her mouth at the same time, and then for one moment out of the year she lets it all go—rotten kids, strange husband, house in Hartford Lakes with no picturesque lakes around—her pure coloratura voice dips and soars to the dying flower maker's refrain and forms a link between all of us, each in our respective place: on the couch, wing chairs, poised motionless at the sink, refrigerator, cabinets. We lower our heads so as not to see Julia yet we are immensely proud of her. Tears come to all our eyes, our blood boils, our hearts rise to our throats as Mimi and Julia sing:

It's so wonderful to be here again.
I feel alive,
I feel alive,
You will never leave me!

Or was it that Caruso's was such a distinctly manly voice that we feared it would exclude the women? They were in the kitchen doing the dishes and shuttling back and forth setting the table again with nuts, fruit, coffee and pastry—still, Caruso's powerful voice would reach them. One uncle, Mike, had married a Czechoslovakian, Olga Lendl, who after growing accustomed to money and her elevated social position, wife of a prominent cardiologist, found the courage to yell articulately from the kitchen, "Would you all lower that, please!"

It had taken Mike years of hard work to teach Olga Lendl how to make the sauce, be an efficient nurse, take care of the house and kids and at the same time be quiet about it all, and so he wasn't about to sabotage his efforts for one night, one tenor. As the years passed, Mike realized that he needed his wife more and more, with the result that he convinced himself that all singers who sang in major opera houses and recorded were more or less the same. "They're all good," he'd say to us on Christmas Eve and then sigh and lower his head. To keep the peace we made little distinction between one singer and another, and toward the end, the last Eves at my house, we played Perry Como's Christmas carols and Mantovani's orchestrations.

Mike DiGeorgio was the eldest of the five second-generation brothers and sisters, and he was the first to hear all about Caruso. Mike's father, Don Salvatore DiGeorgio, had been a budding baritone with Salmaggi's troupe, which sang at the Brooklyn Academy of Music. Sometimes Caruso came to Brooklyn to sing, and before the performance, through a crack in the dressing-room door, Don Salvatore espied the Master of Song smoking Egyptian

cigarettes in a long, black, diamond-studded holder. Don Salvatore was also a chain smoker, but he smoked Camels in his fat,
stubby fingers.

"There he was," Don Salvatore would tell his first-born, "sitting
at his makeup table surrounded by his wigmaker and dresser, and
Caruso insisted that his woman stand behind him with her hands
on his massive shoulders. His last and greatest love was the
American Dorothy Park Benjamin, and Caruso would smile at her
reflection and she'd smile back. 'Is it really you, my Doro?' Caruso
would say.

"'Sì, Rico, it's really me,' his wife would say. Her words had
the effect of soothing him and then he'd ask playfully for a
cigarette: 'How 'bout a schpomp?' 'Schpomp' being Neapolitan
slang for cigarette. He smoked one after the other until a thick,
bluish-silver fog went up, I couldn't see a thing, but I could hear
them all coughing, and when the veil lifted, Caruso called im-
patiently for his washstand filled with warm salt water. He inhaled
the solution into the great bellows that were his lungs and then
he gargled, he gargled until he practically strangled and, Mike—
even his gargling was beautiful! I'll tell you something you'll never
forget: Caruso had musical bones—that's right, his bones were
musical! If he was in a jocular mood, he'd let us tap his mastoid
with our fingers, or tap his earlobe, which tapped his mastoid—
and boing! the tone was mellow, velvety and sustaining, carrying
all the way to the stage.

"His beloved Doro then placed snuff at the base of his great
flaring nostrils—one sniff and the snuff was sucked up as fast as
you can say Giuseppe Verdi! Caruso downed a wineglass of whis-
key without blinking an eye and then chased it with a glass of
charged water. Doro peeled him a quarter of an apple. Slowly,
majestically, Caruso stood up to digest it. The dresser sewed two
pockets into his costume exactly where his hands dropped, and
into these pockets the dresser slipped small bottles of warm salt
water in case Caruso had to wash out his mouth onstage. Mike,
I'll never forget the time I was onstage with him and I saw him
suddenly turn his back on the audience, fill his mouth and spit

a long stream, a perfect arc, into the shadows backstage. Doro handed him his charms: twisted coral horn, religious medals and ancient coins, all linked together on a gold chain.

"I felt a tugging on my arm—it was Carboni, the assistant stage manager: 'Don't you have anything better to do, DiGeorgio!' Then Carboni called meekly into the dressing room, 'May we begin, Mr. Caruso?'

"'*Ah, sì, comincia,*' Caruso would say and then I'd hear, 'Shoo! Shoo!' and the wigmaker came tumbling out followed by the dresser and Dorothy Park Benjamin.

"The door closed slowly, deliberately. I pressed my ear against it and heard what sounded like a boy's voice, shrill and desperate, call upon his mother for help and courage. '*Mamma mia,*' Caruso choked, '*aiuta mi.*'"

Caruso exacted such a high fee that all the other singers suffered, including Don Salvatore. In addition, Caruso's voice knew no registers, it spanned the entire range of the operatic voice, from basso to tenor, and when he came to Brooklyn Caruso often replaced Don Salvatore as baritone. To raise his fledgling family, Don Salvatore became a tailor and in time had enough money to buy a house with a porch and a backyard, a three-story limestone half a block from the New Utrecht Avenue El. As a general practitioner, Mike practiced in the basement. Out the back window, beyond the pantry where the wine was stored and the olive oil and canned tomatoes, Mike could see his sister Elvira gathering her roses while biting her tongue. He had to listen carefully to his patients' heartbeats due to the continual roar of the trains. Mike soon discovered that of all his patients his cardiacs were the most helpless and so he decided to devote to them all his knowledge and wisdom and courage. He became a master of the heart and a sought-after diagnostician. He could tell a cardiac from across the room. He was the first doctor in Bensonhurst to convince Italian cardiacs that they might have to leave Bensonhurst a while in order to go to the Mayo Clinic in a place called Minnesota for what was called a bypass. Mike himself traveled alone to Texas to witness experiments on a dog's heart. Mike DiGeorgio was also the first doctor in Bensonhurst to convince Italian cardiacs that they had to spend a little time in a hospital— it wasn't a disgrace, their families could come. He became affil- iated with Brooklyn General, where we all go to die. The back rooms afford a splendid view of the Hudson River and Manhattan skyline. My father lay dying during a furious snowstorm in Jan- uary. He wanted to live until the Christmas holidays and got his wish. Falling past his bay window were snowflakes the size and action of feathers, and each one carried on it a bit of my sorrow. And so when I discovered my mother dead in her back room on a November Sunday morning, I looked out her window for the same snow. I saw instead a bird in flight and remembered what she had recently told me: "Don't forget to give fresh water to the sparrows." First thing every morning I place on my window ledge a white scalloped bowl filled with cool water, and I will continue to do this until the day *I* die, here in my room on Charles Street, alone, the door locked, a last vision from my bed of the sparrows perched on the rim of their bowl, and then I'll turn my face to the wall and die.

Soon Mike had enough money to marry and buy a house. Don Salvatore advised him: "Look here, Mike, I have a letter Caruso wrote during the last tour of his life. He was in Denver, Colorado, staying in the Brown Palace Hotel, and at eleven p. m. on October 19, 1920, about a year before his great heart stopped, he wrote to his beloved Doro, who had stayed behind in New York: 'I envy you,' Caruso wrote, 'in going out and eat nice spaghetti, because is very difficult to have some. Everybody which I meet say, "I wish to give you a nice plate of spaghetti but my cook is in vacation." They make me make water in the mouth and swallow down.' It's sad, Mike, and a tragedy when you think that Caruso's wife didn't know how to make spaghetti either! So marry an Italian girl, *figlio mio*, and live in Brooklyn—otherwise, what will you eat?"

Mike was tall and thin, and in the corridors of Brooklyn General he noticed a tall, lively nurse in training. They fell in love, and

Mike proposed to Olga Lendl in the hospital utility closet, promising her a long, happy life in God's country, Bensonhurst. Olga Lendl was dressed in her white uniform, white stockings and white shoes, and in the dark closet she let down her hair the way I used to see her let it down as she came out of her bathroom after her shower, wearing a white terry-cloth robe that failed to conceal the hills and valleys of her body. She strolled dreamily to the kitchen, all the while brushing out her hair, which was so long, black and fine that it reminded me of an Indian's. It unfurled lightly around her waist, caressing it, and then to my wonderment extended to her knees and slightly beyond. In the small, dark utility closet Mike and Olga kissed and caressed, and then they threw open the door and danced a lively polka up and down the corridor.

Mike went halves on a house with a boyhood friend, Eddie, who was courting Mike's sister, Margaret. The friends had a house built on the lot where they had played ball. A big brick house ideally located in that it was within walking distance of Don Salvatore's, one block from the El on the other side, and around the corner from Eddie's father, Don Antonio. There was a secret double wedding, and then my mother and father moved into the top floor and Mike and Olga moved into the bottom. Every morning at seven o'clock, Mike walked up the block to visit with his family. As he emerged from the shadows beneath the El, stepping into the sunlight on Don Salvatore's side, Mike pulled back his shoulders and pressed down his fine suit with his hands. At Don Salvatore's, Mike had the standard DiGeorgio breakfast of coffee and *one* piece of toast. His parents wondered why there had been a secret wedding and also why after five months of marriage Mike had still not brought his wife to meet them. Mike had intuited that it's unwise, perilous even, to seek the family's approval of one's woman. He was out in the world and had carried away all he had been given, all he had learned in his father's house. Mike recalled Caruso's attitude toward his family and toward the Italians in New York—he simply didn't care. Caruso was forty-five years old when he married Dorothy Park Benjamin and he loved her more than anything in the world, and he was wealthy and still at the top of his voice. Mike DiGeorgio had a promising future, half of a house and a beautiful, faithful wife. Before he brought her to his first home he wanted their love to congeal into an impenetrable barrier against the Italians in the neighborhood, his insulated family, the mixed group at the hospital. Mike remembered one particular letter Caruso had written during an opera season in Mexico. The letter began with Caruso trying to translate an Italian proverb: "The good day beguinning at the morning and the same at reverse." October 22, 1919, had begun with Caruso listening to an impresario's sister. After she sang, she knelt at Caruso's feet, kissed his hand and said, "Please sing a benefit so I can pay for my singing lessons."

Caruso told her, "Signorita, you save your money and I save my voice."

True to the proverb, the day ended badly. At half past nine, he was ushered into a theater to hear one of Mexico's leading sopranos. He sat in a box decorated with flowers, and after the soprano's performance she announced that the world's greatest singer was in the audience. The spotlight found Caruso and he stood up and smiled and waved amid thunderous applause and hundreds of hats and fans and flowers and walking sticks flying into the air. Caruso wrote that he suffered because he was losing time in being alone with thoughts of his beloved wife.

One morning after Mike had gone off on his rounds, Don Salvatore took the pins out of his mouth, put on his white suit, white shoes and white fedora and strolled to the corner. There had been a heavy snowfall but now the sun was shining, bouncing off the fresh whiteness and filling the air with silver clarity. The mixture of gold and white bathed Don Salvatore's great nose, a perfect giant mushroom with a tributary of prominent veins at the roots of the flaring nostrils, the veins flowing riotously northward toward the soft, bulbous tip and southward deep into the thick upper lip. Except for this fleshy, corpuscular appendage, Don Salvatore blended into the snow, was one with the row of snow-covered tree trunks. On reaching the corner he stepped into the shadows and was able to stand in the street, traffic being light because of the deep snow. He had heard that Olga Lendl had assumed the role of caretaker of his son's house. During the hurricane in August she had braved the gale-force winds and driving rain to sweep the leaves away from the sewer. She trimmed the hedges, manicured the lawns, planted honeysuckle vines and bushes of snowballs, and when it snowed she shoveled the walk. Hidden in the shadows, Don Salvatore saw her come out of the house, smiling and singing, she took up the shovel on the porch and lifted and tossed, lifted and tossed. The sunlight caught the tip of her nose, which shined like a star in a black night sky and radiated its brilliance all the way to the El. Neighbors passed her on the way to the train, turning their heads away, yet Olga Lendl greeted them and spoke of the beauty of the virgin whiteness and the hard work involved in getting rid of it. The shrill timbre of her spirited voice carried to the shadows. Don Salvatore nodded, then returned home.

The very next morning as Mike was about to leave, Don Salvatore said, "I know why the wedding was secret—Maggie was three months gone, wasn't she?"

"Yes."

"But that's no reason not to bring your wife here! What did we ever do to you? Your mother is sick in bed!"

"Pa, I'd like her to get used to me first, our Sicilian ways. And the other day we received a package in the mail, gift-wrapped, with a pretty ribbon. It was a box of shit. I don't want shit coming over here."

"I don't care about shit! People are talking!"

"What are they saying?"

"The way she pronounces her r's. . . . "

"You're supposed to pronounce r's!"

"Her nose is pointy, stuck up, like a ski jump. . . . "

"Look who's talking about a nose!"

"And you go dancing in New York, the polka instead of the tarantella, and she whoops and hollers and kicks up her heels. You can see up her dress!"

"Give me a little more time, Pa. Yesterday a Chinese couple moved in up the block."

"No!" Don Salvatore took his son by the hand, led him outside and practically dragged him to the corner. As they reached the sidewalk's edge bordering New Utrecht Avenue, a train roared overhead. Don Salvatore pointed into the street and his baritone voice boomed, "If by tomorrow night you haven't brought your wife to my house, this street between our houses becomes a deep hole, and we won't hear screams from the opposite sidewalks— I'll disown you!"

Mike brooded a little that day but kept his somber thoughts to himself, just as he kept his great love for his wife to himself. He acted the same with the hospital parking lot attendant: polite. The same with the nurses: playful. His bedside manner was the same: forceful, unswerving. Over the lunch of *pasta e fagioli* Olga Lendl made him, he was as usual dead serious. After lunch, Mike made love to her, they made love at least once a day, and from the age of sixty onward at least kissed before going to sleep. Before losing themselves in sleep, in dreams, one or the other recalled their vow of at least kissing before going to sleep and then pressed forward, pursed and extended the lips and kissed. I know all this because Mike and Olga told me. At Mike's fiftieth birthday party I went up to him and said casually, "How ya doin', Uncle Mike?"

He bolted as if I had struck him. He had to look at me a long time before recognizing me. It was a time when he was coming to terms with the awful things neighbors and colleagues were saying about him. His family wondered what he had done down through the years to have gained such a bad reputation: ruthless in the political infighting at the hospital? He was the only Italian in Bensonhurst to accumulate a stock portfolio worth millions. Only the Syrians in Bay Ridge accumulated that kind of port-folio—was he keeping information from his landsmen? He had bought into a loan company—was he squeezing debtors? After Don Salvatore died, Mike became Head of the Family, and we cared about his reputation. His reputation was also ours. One

Sunday afternoon my cousins Big Johnny and Carmine and I corralled our uncle in the gazebo behind his country house. The gazebo faced a lovely stream.

"Do you know what people are calling you?"

"Who cares! What was I supposed to be? A bricklayer with dignity? A mafioso with the reputation of being a good family man? A smiling, sweet-talking barber who doubles as a bookie? A longshoreman who drives his kids crazy because he wants them to become professional men? A housepainter who plays a good game of pinochle? I became a doctor, a good doctor, and if they want to call me a prick, let them! At least I'm a consistent prick!"

"We understand, Uncle Mike, and respect you for that. But why won't you go sailing with your son, who loves you?"

"Wait a minute here! Here's a kid who has the world by the balls: top surgeon, a house, boat, apartment in the city—and what does he do? He sails naked drunk as a lord with women young enough to be his daughter! He gets laid, so what! I get laid every day! I want him to settle down with a good woman, I want to see him step onto my lawn hand in hand with my grandchild."

"But you're a grandfather four times over. Your daughter has four children."

"Theresa? Well, yes, she has four beautiful children and of course I love them, they're part of the family, but I have that husband of hers to contend with. You know, I spent forty thousand dollars on her education and she becomes a housewife."

Mike DiGeorgio was my godfather, and so whenever I saw him I went up to him with an open heart. At his party, after I said, "How ya doin', Uncle Mike?" he said peremptorily, "Fine, how else?—I get laid every day." And then years later Olga Lendl told me, "We at least kiss before going to sleep."

Their bedroom was directly beneath my parents' bedroom, and in the middle of the night of Don Salvatore's ultimatum Mike's sobs filtered up through the floor. When one of his patients died, he went into his parlor and cried. My mother said, "Who is it this time?" waking up my father. They got up, waking me up, and I began to cry. My mother picked me up, soothing me, then the three of us went to the landing of the staircase that led down to Mike's apartment. We huddled together, listening. We heard Mike crying. A light flashed on, then a moment later we heard a voice, a round, golden voice, it rose slowly over Mike's distress and carried out into the hall and up the stairs. We waited a while, thinking that Mike would return to bed, but the arias continued. We went downstairs. Mike signaled us to come in, sit down. He wore a crimson robe and sat beside his wife, wearing a pretty yellow petticoat threaded in violet. They held hands. As we listened, tears flowed freely down Mike's cheeks. He had learned about death through Caruso's, and sooner or later the majority of Mike's patients died, adding to the graveyard he carried around in his stomach. We listened to Caruso until the first light, then Mike packed the records and gave them to his old friend, his brother-in-law, Eddie. Olga made breakfast, and the new day's golden rays shined onto the table from the skylight. Then we watched from the porch as Mike and Olga walked hand in hand up the block to Don Salvatore's.

Don Salvatore's wife, Filomena, was ninety-four years old on the last Eve at my house. She sat at the head of the table, rocking back and forth in her straight chair. "Now put on *La Traviata*," she sighed. "It was Don Salvatore's favorite opera."

I put on the opera, then ran my hand over her smooth crown of silver hair. I had often slept with her and in the morning watched her put up her hair and in the evening watched her take it down. I watched her hair over all the years it took to turn silver, and I watched her light her votive candles, then we went to sleep. She had been the only one of nine children to survive infancy. Embodied in her were the aspirations of eight prematurely dead brothers and sisters, and she possessed the wisdom and courage of nine people. She raised five children practically on her own, teaching them how to pitch in around the house, the boys, too, and she taught her daughters how to stand before the kitchen sink with elegant aplomb: pelvis pressed gently, gracefully against the sink, one leg slightly raised as if about to begin a dance. Over the twenty years since her husband had died, she searched her mind every Christmas Eve for a sweet memory but she heard only her father's words: "See what kind of a man you want to marry—he has to go out into the hall and fart!"

Their courtship had been oh so short due to Don Salvatore's chronic condition of uncontrollable flatulence. He would arrive at her house at seven o'clock. Her father opened the door and Don Salvatore swept in dressed all in white. He removed his hat, then raised her hand to his lips. She sat in a corner of the sofa, hands folded on her lap. Within moments she saw his face turn red as a tomato, he squirmed in his chair, lifting himself slightly. In mid-sentence he excused himself and ran out to the hall.

"Hurry up, Filomena—shut the door!" her father would say, and then he added, "See what kind of a man you want to marry— he has to go out into the hall and fart!"

If only she had had the courage to say, "We understand, Salvatore, it could happen to anybody, so relieve yourself here and now—yes, in the living room in front of my father, I want to hear you tell him how much you love my chestnut hair, my defiant jaw," then maybe she would have other memories, sweet ones to console her and pass along to her children and their children. He wasn't circumcised and spoke with no trace of an accent—had he been born in Sicily or New York? He had told her that he was a baritone but she never heard him sing. He prohibited her from going to the Brooklyn Academy of Music, saying he was a budding baritone and wanted to wait until he became a principal. One night when he said he was singing she put Mike and Maggie to bed, then rode in the train to Atlantic Avenue. "I know it's around here," she was saying to herself when a husky young man wearing a black hat approached her. "Can I help you?" he said.

"I'm looking for the Brooklyn Academy of Music."

"Come, I'll take you," and he motioned to take her arm.

Her heart pounded with fear. She felt herself grow dizzy and small. "That's all right—just tell me where it is."

"I'm going to save you a trip, lady—there's nothing playing tonight."

"No *La Traviata?*"

"No *La Traviata*, no *Aïda*, no opera at all. I've lived in Brooklyn all my life and I love the opera and know what's playing where and who's singing. I'll tell you something else about myself: I roam the streets at night searching for people who are lost. They're easy to spot—a word or two of a foreign language, mouth open, looking at a map, eyes searching the sky. I say softly, 'Can I help you?' Some people get frightened and rush away, but some allow me to give directions. To these I sometimes say, 'Come, I'll take you,' and their pleasure at reaching their destination becomes mine."

"Do you have a home, young man?"

"Many, I've had many homes, but I'll tell you how I feel right now—my home is where I was born, where I suckled, stopped crying, learned to walk, saw my first sunlight. It's the one place I remember exactly how to get to, the only place I can resurrect in a split second, not only the rooms and their space and light, but the outside, too, the streets, back alleys, trees, the neighbors' faces. You know, I haven't felt quite on balance since I left, but I carry this home with me in my heart and it has blessed me with an understanding: how easily, how unknowingly one can get lost. Do you know what my prize possession is, lady? My keys. That's right, my keys, no matter what door they fit into. I gotta go now. Believe me, as I just came from there—the opera house is closed."

MARIO CUOMO &
LEE IACOCCA

———

ARIO CUOMO'S *Diaries* and Lee Iacocca's *Autobiography* arrived in elegant shopping bags suspended on my doorknob. They were left by my neighbor to the north of me. Our apartments were contiguous save for the wall between our bathrooms, yet I had never heard or spoken to or really seen this neighbor. From my desk when my door was kept open by my dagger, I often glimpsed a shimmering pole fleeting by. It made no noise but then I heard a door softly close, the one just up the corridor on my side. I left a plate of spaghetti in a shopping bag around my elusive neighbor's doorknob in the hope that he or she would materialize. The next day I found Lee Iacocca's *Autobiography* along with the dish, which was sparkling clean, in a shopping bag around my doorknob. My neighbor enjoys a good plate of pasta, I thought, and then the next few days I watched for a more substantial form but again only a vibrating shaft flashed by my open door. The next Sunday I left another dish of spaghetti and on Monday discovered Mario Cuomo's *Diaries* and the dish, licking clean again. My neighbor may be Italian, I thought further, or believe that I am Italian, seeing that I make good pasta. It may feel the Italian in me with its sensors as it flashes by my door. Yes, it has an acute rudimentary nervous system, but how does it know that it is I who leave the pasta, unless its embryonic eye is pressed against the peephole when I leave the shopping bag. Then I focused on the choice of books. I was immensely proud of the two foremost living Italians in America, but I did not own a car nor was I in the market for one or plan to work for somebody else, let alone a Ford or Chrysler. Nor had I aspirations of waging a political campaign and at six in the morning, instead of writing in a diary, I gravitated toward Elsa's warm, soft body. And so the following Sundays I alternated pasta with stews, chicken, pieces of fresh fruit pies Elsa bakes, and much to my delight found on my doorknob novels by Italo Svevo, Elio Vittorini, Carlo Emilio Gadda; *Stories of the Great Operas;* the *Moral Essays* and *Pensieri* of Giacomo Leopardi. My neighbor is preparing me for a cabinet post, I decided— cultural minister in either Lee Iacocca's presidential cabinet or Mario Cuomo's. In 1992, I estimated, and I envisioned two pans of lasagna on every table and a Chrysler mini-van in every garage. Caruso singing in all the parks and from loudspeakers attached to buses and trains, GPO manuals on all the great Italians. I stopped giving my neighbor pasta altogether. A week passed without any kind of book around my doorknob, then another week. I found myself searching my mind and heart for Lee Iacocca and Mario Cuomo. The problem arose over which great Italian should run for President first. I read their wonderful books, stared at their faces. I studied their names for symbols they give rise to that could go to the heart of the American public. I pronounced the names aloud: "Iacocca, Iacocca, I-a-Coca-Cola, I-a-Coca-Cola, I-cocaine, I-cocaine. Cuomo, Cuomo, Uomo [man in Italian], Uomo, Om-m-m, Om-m-m, Home, Home." Tradi- tional values abounded: Man wrenching control of his destiny from machines and implements of war; Home and Family again the underpinning of our society; the Coca-Cola Company had returned to its earlier formula—maybe Lee Iacocca could per- suade Coca-Cola, in return for higher tariffs on imported soft drinks, to go back to its original formula when there was a slight amount of cocaine in Coca-Cola. The symbols painted a bright picture of the future: to embrace the growing Asian population Mario Cuomo after his campaign speeches would chant like a Yogi, and all America would join in: "Om-m-m, Om-m-m . . ." If Lee Iacocca promised a free lifetime supply of Coca-Cola laced with cocaine to all levels of management and workers, the unemployment rate would drop to zero, the Gross National Product would soar, American business would put a substantial dent in foreign competition—the best foreign workers would come here! Short of such a drastic measure, the Iacocca Campaign Committee could issue an olive paper, stating that around the time when there was cocaine in Coca-Cola, the early 1900s, women were drawing in their waists with corsets, the wasp waist was the rage, the hourglass the shape women aspired to. The Coca-Cola Company hired a man named Loewy to design a bottle. He couldn't take his eyes off all those pinched waists, what they did for the rest of a woman's body, her hips, her breasts, and while Loewy was swilling his brandy the glass felt like a woman's breast in the palm of his hand—thus the hourglass shape of the Coca-Cola bottle. If Lee Iacocca's candidacy resurrected in men's minds the image of the Coca-Cola bottle, then he might appeal to American men, given their infatuation with breasts, but I was solidly convinced that Lee Iacocca would appeal more than Mario Cuomo to Wasps, especially those of the South. Before embarking on his first trip through the South as a salesman, Lee Iacocca was told that Southerners wouldn't take too well to his name. Lee Iacocca had the presence of mind not to change one letter of his name, he merely reversed it, and so now Iacocca Lee conjured up for Southerners their great General. With the simple reversal of his name, Lee Iacocca made Southerners forget that a century ago their forefathers paid good money to see a dead Italian's body laid up inside a circus tent. Mario Cuomo or Cuomo Mario would amount to the same deficit in the South—what to do with the musical O? Cuomo Mar, Mario Cuom, Cuom Mar, Mar Cuom . . . But after recalling the *Diaries*, a testament to a brave, patient, reflective man committed equally to public service, to his family and to his vision of our nation as a family, I doubted seriously that Mario Cuomo would consent to change or reverse his name, as one important way a family is held together is by taking pride in its name. As far as names alone were concerned, Lee Iacocca got off to a flying start.

Next I studied their faces again, their physiques, and Mario Cuomo emerged with a slight edge. His skin appeared more olive than Lee Iacocca's and with a little sunshine up at Camp Dante would turn yellow. Lee Iacocca's skin reflected a perennial tan rosy in hue. Mario Cuomo wore a pensive, faraway look, tortured even, the way the prominent son of immigrants should look. His face was also capable of slyness, which non-Italians are accustomed to seeing in an Italian's face. Lee Iacocca wore a look of repose, contentment. His face was open, amused, searching for the wisecrack. Mario Cuomo had been a professional ballplayer and now he jogged, fighting his weight, while Lee Iacocca appeared to be growing portly. This was a crucial point in deciding between them. Mario Cuomo had kept his weight down even though he was married to an Italian and on the holidays his family convened for the great feasts. Lee Iacocca was not married to an Italian—how had he gotten out of shape eating roast beef? Did he eat out a lot in Italian restaurants, compensating for the memory of his mother's cooking? And how far would the memory of his mother's pizza parties sustain him? Mario Cuomo had the overall look of the battling father, the pioneering brother, while Lee Iacocca looked like the jovial uncle, the prosperous, smart next-door neighbor. Lee Iacocca would have trouble gaining the Italian vote in Brooklyn, I decided, not so much because he was a Democrat again or had been raised in a distant land called Pennsylvania and worked in an even more remote region, Detroit, but rather because he had worked for somebody else, was salaried, had to answer to a boss. I remembered Mr. Volpi, our prosperous neighbor who lived across the street. At six o'clock every morning my mother walked up the block to visit with her mother and sister. She descended the brick steps leading down from our porch, watching her step, holding on to the black steel banister.

She circled our garden of honeysuckle vines and bushes of snow-balls. She crossed the corner with the light and when she stepped onto the sidewalk, she was in front of Mr. Volpi's house. Mr. Volpi held himself tall and proud and spoke with a great stentorian voice. He was an official with the Port Authority and one of his sons played chess on the stoop. These things kept us at a distance. From his parlor windows Mr. Volpi could see that my father and my uncle made money in their house, while every morning Mr. Volpi had to drive to work, ending his journey along isolated avenues leading to the waterfront. We didn't want to alienate Mr. Volpi any further, because my Uncle Mike and his wife, Olga, were beginning to travel abroad by ship and after the voyage home didn't want to wait at customs in the darkness and cold, surrounded by immigrants' prancing chickens. And so when the opportunity arose for a relationship with Mr. Volpi, we grasped at it. I used to see him come out of his house early in the morning carrying his golf bag. One morning I had the courage to go up to him and say in my best English, "Hi, Mr. Volpi, I live across the street."

"I know," he said.

"I see you play golf, and I'd like to tell you that I play too. I caddy at Dyker Beach."

"I play there several times a week. Why don't we go out one day?"

A few days later I found myself sitting beside our neighbor as he drove toward the ocean. There were so many things I wanted to say to him, like how did it happen that he became an official with the Port Authority when there was not another one in the neighborhood? Whether it hurt him that his family had to watch him contend day in and day out with a boss, surrounded as they were with self-employed doctors and dentists, not only in my house but also Dr. Bruno, who lived across the street from their kitchen and bathroom windows, and if the Volpis stuck their heads out far enough, they could see Dr. Pico's shingle waving on a post planted in the garden in front of his house? The only thing I managed to say to Mr. Volpi the entire outing was: "We can start on the back nine. There's no wait on the tenth tee."

It was still dark when we arrived, yet there was a long wait. Dyker Beach was the only public links in Bensonhurst and its duffers saw the fairways and greens in their sleep. Mr. Volpi added our names to the big blackboard, but I didn't want him to be late for work, so I scurried to the tenth tee. It was empty and I was elated and ran back to Mr. Volpi. "We can start on the back nine. There's no wait on the tenth tee."

But no, he wanted to do things right. "While we wait," he said, "let's practice putting."

We walked side by side to the putting green. I watched his stroke, a good one, and tried to match the accuracy of his putts. Of the actual round I recalled only that I had taken a good swing with my driver on the back nine. Mr. Volpi did not ask me out again, nor did I see him again. In the back of our minds was an all-seeing eye that kept track of the comings and goings of the neighbors. One day I said to my mother, "See Mr. Volpi lately?"

"Who?"

"Mr. Volpi—you know, the official with the Port Authority who lives across the street."

"Oh, he died."

"When?"

"Last year."

"How?"

"Heart attack, I think."

"Was he a patient of Uncle Mike's?"

"No, no," my mother said.

Winter arrived and I had to close my door, as frost blew down from the open roof door. But then I found outside my door boxes filled with a wide assortment of books representing an international array of authors: plays by Arthur Schnitzler, Milan Kundera, David Mamet; autobiographies of Paul Robeson, Truman Capote, Margaret Fuller, Tennessee Williams; *Glitz* by Elmore Leonard, *The Sicilian* by Mario Puzo, *Opium and Other Stories* by Géza Czáth. My neighbor was sanctioning the path I was on, and the next step was rehearsing a meeting with President-elect Cuomo:

"Mr. President, your *Diaries* are a breath of fresh air. You speak of love, concern for your wife and children. You expose your doubts and fears, address the subject of money, keeping up with the Joneses—but I believe you made a mistake publishing them so close upon the heels of Mayor Koch's book, which as you recall was a runaway bestseller."

"How so, Valerio?"

"We need look no further than the name: Koch, Koch, Scotch, Scotch, Hop-Scotch, Hop-Scotch. In your fantastic campaign for governor, sir, you were outspent in the primary and then in the general election by more than two and a half to one, the same odds Garibaldi overcame during the fight in Rome for Unification—still, Koch's book outsold yours. And isn't it also ironic that Mayor Koch styled himself after an Italian, the great Fiorello La Guardia, and emerged with flamboyance and charisma, and here you are an Italian itself and at least in your *Diaries* emerge a bit morose, lackluster? Maybe you looked back over your shoulder and didn't see another great Italian politician to style yourself after. After all, there had never been an Italian governor of New York, and you didn't feel quite comfortable styling yourself after a Rockefeller or a Lehman. You say yourself that you inherited very little of Roman sculpture and law and opera and philosophy. That's what I'm here for! Leave it to me to tell you about the Medicis, Machiavelli, Caruso, Petrarca, Benedetto Croce. I fully understand how you feel culturally starved. Sons of immigrants like you and my father and Lee Iacocca and my Uncle Mike— you didn't have the time or motivation to study your culture. You were expected to improve on your parents, uneducated and, as my girlfriend Elsa says, ignorant; to take advantage of the college education they never had by using it to enter the mainstream of American life, blinding you somewhat. But isn't it wonderful, Mr. President, how God created us Italians in such a way that we complement one another so perfectly? Remember your delight in going to the beach of a Sunday with your parents, the delicacies you took along: the salami, prosciutto, bread and fruits? Well, I also went to the beach with my parents. We brought sandwiches wrapped in wax paper but I wouldn't eat them—somewhere along the line, I suspected, sand got into them. Worse than that, I wouldn't touch the sand. I had to be carried to and from the blanket and I sat the whole time with my ass on the blanket and my hands and feet up in the air."

"Guard! Guard! Please escort this fellow to the door. How did he get past the talent search?"

I conferred with my closest adviser, my sister Concetta, Ph.D. in political science. "Concetta, I'm going to work for Mario Cuomo."

"I don't like him. He reminds me of Daddy's friends. I have to catch a plane to Atlanta. I'll call you as soon as I get back."

"Wait a second! Which friends? Hello! Concetta?..."

While I waited for Concetta to return from Atlanta, I turned my attention to Lee Iacocca. Dressed in my woolen overcoat, hat, blue suit, white shirt and tie, I traveled on the West End line to the Bensonhurst section of Brooklyn with the idea of canvassing from two strategic places: in front of the Hollywood Terrace, a catering hall located beneath the Seventy-ninth Street platform; and in front of Pino's Photography Studio, three blocks from the Hollywood, on the corner of the busy intersection of New Utrecht Avenue and Bay Ridge Parkway. The Hollywood Terrace used to be a movie house and its choice as one of my sites had been inspired by Lee Iacocca's memory of his father's movie house in Allentown, the Franklin. Lee Iacocca attributed his instinct for marketing to his father, who had been an imaginative promoter: the ten kids with the dirtiest faces were admitted free to the Saturday matinee. Today the Franklin showed porno films and so no special offers were necessary. For the first six years of his life, immediately before the Depression, little Lido was captured by the family photographer wearing satin shoes and embroidered coats, holding a silver rattle. Ted Pino was the DiGeorgio family photographer, and the hardest part of his job was getting us to smile. He acted the buffoon and convinced us that he was a cheerful fellow. While focusing his camera on its tripod, ducking in and out of the cloth mantle, he'd say, "Now smile big!" and then he'd smile the way he wished us to smile, from ear to ear, showing all our teeth. When I was old enough to cross beneath the El alone, I liked to step into the sunlight on Don Salvatore's side and watch the wedding parties drive up in a procession of black limousines, horns blaring, joining the roar of the trains. The limousines double-parked, tying up traffic, and these horns added to the cacophony. I watched for the bride— could she get out with the long train of her veil intact? She emerged from the lead limousine on the street side, her veil bunched up in her arms. Her maids of honor dressed in blue and sad assisted her. The bewildered groom got lost in traffic. The glum DiGeorgio look came over my face as I thought: Ted Pino is inside waiting for you with his phony smile. Before he became a photographer, Ted Pino was a violinist. His sister worked with him and I remembered her: very dark, especially her eyes and brows, and she was beautiful and possessed a bright, elusive spirit. When I was old enough to go inside the studio for a chat and look around, I'd ask her, "Your brother still play the violin?"

She'd turn away with a worried look. "He practices a lot," she'd say. He died of a heart attack in his darkroom at a young age.

Mike DiGeorgio had originally brought home his boyhood friend Eddie for Julia, as Margaret was going out with Ted Pino, a violinist with a neat mustache and flashing eyes. Eddie was the Beau Brummell of Bensonhurst. He rang the doorbell. The door was open but only the DiGeorgios walked in without ringing. Elvira went to the door and, seeing the man standing there, she blanched, bit her tongue and gasped, "Oh, my God!" and then she ran inside to Julia and said, "No, Julia—you never saw anything like him! He's better-looking than Cary Grant!"

Ted Pino had given up the violin for photography and had opened a studio across the street from Don Salvatore's, on the corner in the shadows of the El. Too close to home for Maggie. At the dinner table she discovered that Eddie was doing postgraduate work up in Halifax, far enough away, and she also learned that he was engaged to a beautiful blonde up there. Margaret accidentally cut her hand, drawing blood and tears. Eddie felt sorry for her and took her out. He took her out once her hand healed. Julia was happy for her sister and was secretly heart-broken. She decided that a man as handsome as Eddie and with such a promising future would never take an interest in her. To fortify her decision she ate a pound of spaghetti before going to sleep. At the same time her idea of a life with Eddie had stirred in her a feverish longing for a man. Each added pound caused her breasts to swell another inch, much to the delight of the very next man to see them: a short, pale pharmaceutical engineer who took pride in his dress and also assured Julia that some types of engineers, like the kind he was, earn as much as a dentist. When they were alone, Julia was delighted to discover that Leo's swings in mood matched hers in their severity. One moment he was saying, "I like to read and spend time alone," and the next moment he was tearing at the buttons of her blouse. Julia embraced his wide range of behavior by surrendering her chest, dropping her arms at her side and saying with earnestness in her voice:

"You like 'em, Leo, my tits?"

Leo guffawed, pleased and shocked by her directness. He lived amid his family four long avenues from the El, the absolute outer limit of walking distance to Don Salvatore's.

"Promise to buy me a car right away?" Julia said.

"We'll go to the showroom tomorrow."

They fell back onto the sofa, Julia on top of him, and she maneuvered herself until her breasts hovered above Leo's face.

"Promise we won't move further from the El?"

"No, no..."

"Wee, they're all yours!"

I was born six months after the secret double wedding, and for my first five years I cried. Night and day I cried, sometimes for eighteen hours at a stretch, and the day I was administered morphine, I cried twenty hours. They held down my arms and legs and I peed on their laps and cried. Uncle Mike agreed to have me see a pediatrician in New York, Dr. Mueller. Elvira and my mother bundled me up and took me on the train. I stopped crying. "He likes the train," my mother said.

"What are we gonna do, Maggie—live on the train?"

Dr. Mueller examined me from my toenails to the follicles of my hair. "This child is in textbook health," he concluded.

"But, Doctor, he cries twenty hours a day."

"And for no reason—he eats and shits like a horse!"

"Let's see . . . he's not circumcised—have you been cleaning it?"

"Cleaning it? Twice a day we roll back the skin and oil that little dingle of his with a Q-Tip."

"What does your brother say?"

"He says he's a crybaby and one day will stop crying."

"I concur," said Dr. Mueller, then the sisters brought me back to Bensonhurst.

I stopped crying while I suckled and as my appetite was ravenous, I was breast-fed on demand in plain view of everybody, as my mother sat on a straight chair at the entrance to her bedroom. I stopped crying when I was rocked, and so my mother rocked me throughout the day and night, stopping only to put up dinner. I bolted from my reverie, stiffened and kicked my cherubic legs, and I waved my little arms wildly and twisted my wrists and screamed. I stopped crying for longer periods outside than in, and so every mid-afternoon, my mother wheeled me in my carriage outside in the sun. If she wheeled me away from the El, I cried, but if she wheeled me toward New Utrecht Avenue, I stopped crying even when my carriage was still. A train passed every ten minutes or so, twenty-four hours a day, and when we arrived at the corner, my mother turned the carriage around and tilted it so that I could see the train in the full glory of its roar and speed, the tracks tremoring, sparks shooting down into the shadows. I goo-gooed and drooled and tried to sit up. A serious look came over my face as my eyes followed each window, each car. When the last one sped by, I was now looking at the immense azure sky and fell back and listened to the train slow down as it pulled into the Seventy-ninth Street station. Then I cried until I heard another train approaching. If the traffic on New Utrecht

Avenue was slight, say after a heavy snowfall, my mother burrowed the carriage through the snow and stopped in the middle
of the street to show me the train from directly underneath,
through the wooden slats. She allowed the sparks to rain down
on us, they diffused before reaching us, but for a few seconds up
there it was like a spray of star dust.

I also stopped crying on Saturday afternoons when my mother
and Elvira took me by the hand to the Hollywood Theater. I
watched with awe as they slipped twelve cents to the stationary
figure in the booth, then I was comforted as they spoke confi-
dentially to the Matron, a big woman with gray hair and thick
arms, wearing a white dress and holding a flashlight. "Please keep
an eye on him. He's alone." The main feature was a horror
movie, but I knew that every ten minutes a train would pass and
I looked up at the ceiling for consolation. While a train was
passing, I gripped the arms of my seat and pressed my feet against
the floor in order to feel the whole theater shaking. Before the
movie there were cartoons, one after another—what happiness
there was when you thought you had seen the last one and another
one came on! But I liked best the idea of the horse race. I was
given a ticket at the door with a number on it from one to thirteen.
If my horse came in, I could stay for another show. It was a real
horse race, run on a real track and with real horses and jockeys.
I jumped up and down rooting for my horse. I tried to keep an
eye on him around the far turns, but there were too many horses
and they were all bunched up. Sometimes the track was muddy
and so the lead horses kicked mud into the trailing jockeys' faces,
they looked so funny, and also into the flanks of the horses,
blotting out the numbers. And you didn't see the end of the race,
you didn't see the winning horse cross the finish line. Down the
homestretch the track suddenly disappeared and was replaced by
a number as big as the screen. I looked upon the result with
suspicion; the promotion people could project any old number,
one they hadn't given out at the door as much. I felt deprived
of the natural outcome of the race in all its excitement, but if my
horse won, I stayed for a second show.

From the West Fourth Street station to the Seventy-ninth Street platform in Brooklyn is about an hour's ride, and I arrived at the height of the rush hour. Night had fallen but the façade of the Hollywood Terrace was lit by spotlights. I positioned myself in front, Lee Iacocca's book in one hand, Mario Cuomo's in the other.

"Excuse me, sir—do you have moment? I'd like your opinion of Lee Iacocca?"

"That's one ginney who made the big time," then he kept walking.

A younger man now, svelte, with short-cropped hair and blue eyes. "Sir, do you have an opinion of Lee Iacocca?"

"Who?"

"Lee Iacocca, the president of Chrysler."

"I have no opinion at all of Lee Iacocca."

"May I ask you what you do?"

"I'm a dancer. My troupe just returned from engagements in Memphis and Paris. Do you live around here?"

"Uh, no. Thank you very much. Oh, madam, do you have a moment?"

"Yes..."

"I'm taking a survey of the people's opinion of Lee Iacocca's chances of becoming President of the United States."

"Lee Iacocca would make a wonderful President and I'll tell you why—managers have ruined this country because they don't have a heart, they don't know what they're doing. They're accountants, period, but Lee Iacocca has a heart and he loves cars. Do you know what the opposite of love is, young man?"

"Hate?"

"No—dogma. Just this past weekend I was reading the Bible where Christ tells His disciples that they know everything He knows so they're no longer disciples, they're friends and therefore should carry out His one desire, that of loving their neighbors."

"You think the Ten Commandments are dogma?"

"I'm surprised to hear you say that. Are you a Catholic?"

I removed my hat. "I went to Catholic school one semester."

"It doesn't matter—the point is that keeping the Commandments doesn't mean you're *doing* something. Lee Iacocca has *done* a lot! He turned Chrysler around after being fired by that awful man Ford. A lot of men fired after twenty years on one job kill themselves. Can I tell you a story, a very short one?"

"Sure."

"I had just gotten my driver's license, I must have been eighteen, and I was talking outside with my friends when my father rushed out. 'Hurry up, Viola,' he said, 'take the car and go down to the ferry—Benny was fired and he called and said he's going to throw himself into the river.' Well, I jumped into our brand-new car and in five minutes I was at the ferry. Uncle Benny had been the manager of a peanut plant for twenty-five years—we always had nuts in the house—then just like that he's fired. The ferry pulled in and I looked around for him. He was walking like a zombie along the water's edge. 'Uncle Benny! Uncle Benny!' I screamed. He turned slowly and I'll never forget his face, it was like he had seen a ghost, was walking in his sleep. He had been so happy-go-lucky, always cracking jokes—"

"A manic-depressive..."

"He finally climbed in and looked at me with a dead face. I tried to cheer him up. He needed shock treatments to snap out of it."

"How is Benny now?"

"Fine, fine. He accepted retirement and is happy watching his grandchildren grow."

"Well, ma'am, thank you very much. I must be moving along now."

"Where to?"

"Ted Pino's Photography Studio."

"Oh, Ted—what a lovely man he was! He took our wedding pictures. My husband died but I keep busy doing volunteer work. Come, I'll walk with you."

We walked the three blocks to Ted Pino's, then she went on her way. A boy passed by, about twelve, carrying a basketball under his arm. "Young fella?"

"My father told me never to talk to strangers."

"Your father is right, but I'm just asking people about Lee Iacocca—ever hear of him?"

"He a labor leader?"

"Kind of, yes..."

He looked at Mario Cuomo's book. "Can I ask you something, mister?"

"Sure."

"Why did Mario Cuomo quit baseball?"

"In his book he talks about looking beyond center field for something else."

"But I read in a magazine where he was beaned—that's why he quit."

"Oh, yes, Ken Auletta's fine series of articles in *The New Yorker*, I believe he says something about a beaning, but in his *Diaries* Mario Cuomo doesn't mention it. He talks about looking beyond center field."

"My dad says the same thing but I don't understand—when you play center field or any position, aren't you supposed to keep your eye on the ball? At least that's what I was taught."

"You were taught right. Here, take Mario Cuomo's book and get on home, you'll be late for supper."

"Sir?"—a big bruiser in a lumber jacket—"I'm gauging the people's feelings about Lee Iacocca."

"I read his book and I agree with Mario Puzo."

"Oh?"

"Didn't you read the newspaper article?"

"No, but if you tell me—"

"It was just a few lines at the end, where Iacocca met Mario Puzo at a party and Puzo said to him, 'You stay out of my racket and I'll stay out of the car business,' something like that. I agree one hundred percent." He looked me up and down. "What's your racket?"

"I'm between jobs right now."

"I see. Well, it's getting late and if I was you I wouldn't hang around here much longer, not the way you're dressed—what are you, Cloak and Dagger, with that black hat?"

"Yeah . . . I'm going now. Thanks."

I sat down on the curb and cried, not so much because I realized that Mario Puzo would probably write another book about the mafia, but because parts of his last one, *The Sicilian*, had the ring of truth. The way the Sicilian bandit Guiliano stole from the rich and gave to the poor, our Sicilian bandit Uncle Artie stole from his sister Rosie and kept everything himself. My father had little patience when the subject of Artie came up. "What manner of man is it," he used to say, "who takes money from his sister who goes out to work in all kinds of weather? He's sick!"

"There's something in it for Rosie, Pa," I'd say. "She loves her brother. Have you looked into Rosie's face recently? It's the face of a woman who loves and is loved. She makes Artie's bed, and once after he had gone out with another woman, he found his bed unmade. 'I'm your brother, not your lover!' he yelled at her, causing her to cry as she trundled through the snow toward her factory, her machine, where every stitch, every yard of fabric, evoked in her her love for her brother."

"Go on—Rosie never married because she had to support the bum! I'll never forget the time I got him the job at the dental lab. He came here himself and begged me to get him a job. That night I called Sammy Block. 'Sure, Doc,' Sammy said. 'Have him here tomorrow morning at nine.' The next morning I was in the office and Sammy called. 'He didn't come, Doc.' 'Maybe he got lost, Sammy. Go downstairs and look for him,' and the man walked up and down Jay Street, then up Fulton as far as DeKalb Avenue. I called Artie. Rosie answered. 'He doesn't feel well,' she said. Come on . . ."

Others of us tried to get Artie a job. Once we thought we had him a good one, maître d' in a supper club. Rosie went out and bought him a sharp tuxedo, bow tie, carnation. The night of the interview, a clear spring evening, Rosie put on a pretty dress and waited on the couch. Around eleven the door opened and Artie was standing there soaking wet from the fear. Rosie fetched a towel and slippers and helped him off with his tuxedo. He stood in his shorts while Rosie wrung out the clothes.

I took the West End line back to New York and when I reached Charles Street I saw Police Officer Mandel directing traffic away from my block.

"What's going on, Small World?" I called him Small World since the time we were standing in line for lottery tickets and the fellow behind me jostled me. The store was small, there was nowhere to go. "Take it easy, fella." We got to talking. He said he was a policeman attached to the Fifth Precinct. "I live next door," I said. "Small world," he said and then withdrew a small world from his pocket, a miniature globe spinning on its axis.

"A fire in your building," Small World said. "It's under control but we're looking for the tenant in number fifteen. He had four thousand books in his apartment and newspapers dating back ten years. He had been told they were a hazard. Do you know where he works, hangs out?"

"No. See ya, Small World."

As I walked up Charles Street I saw the usual cluster of patrol cars pulled up on my sidewalk but now their headlights shined on my door and policemen carrying walkie-talkies were walking in and out. Out in the street there was an ambulance and behind that an ASPCA wagon, and attendants in white coats holding long poles with nets were carrying out one cat after another. Behind the wagon was a fire truck. Firemen wearing rubber coats and black boots and the red hat that I loved were hauling in their hose. Smoke filled the hallway. Water ran down the stairs. I walked up, holding my mouth. My landlord, Mr. Trentacinque, Mr. Thirty-five, was on my landing and a medic was bandaging his arm. My door was open. My place was flooded and the firemen had laid their axes to my bathroom wall. Rubble, smoke, water everywhere. "What happened, Mr. Thirty-five?"

"What happened! I was almost mauled to death, that's what happened. I've left notes under Fifteen's door for years telling him to get rid of his books and papers, at least stack them on shelves, or I was going to evict him. Tonight the papers caught fire. Luckily the alky in number ten saw the smoke. I opened the door and twenty vicious cats jumped me. They tore my arms to shreds. Ever see the guy's place?"

"No."

"Go take a look."

I walked slowly up the corridor, then stopped at the threshold of my neighbor's apartment. Through the dark mist I soon made out the skyline of a city of smoldering books. Four thousand hardcover books and a decade of newspapers had been tossed haphazardly into a space thirty by ten feet, and so they naturally filled every inch and then built one upon the other until they rose close to the ceiling. I looked around for a bed, stove, refrigerator. I saw cat food and five-pound bags of litter. Then I heard it, more like a whale's siren than a human voice, and it came from the top of the staircase leading to the roof.

"Pst! Pst! Fourteen!"

I turned and saw the shimmering pole. Before it flashed out of view, I saw that it had sprouted a tiny, oval head, I could see the whites of the eyes, and the head did not sit directly atop its swanlike neck, there was considerable slack between, like the slack of a cord leading up to a kite. I walked up nonchalantly to give Mr. Thirty-five the impression that I was going up for a breath of fresh air. I waited at the roof door until my eyes grew accustomed to the darkness, to the landscape of aerials, chimneys, vents. In time the city around us, the Twin Towers, streetlamps, the stars and the moon provided enough light to see. Nothing moved. I walked out, stopped, and then a hand gripped my arm. The hand felt strong, warm. I couldn't see it. I turned and saw my neighbor. It looked like the way a child draws his first human body: circles for the head and torso, straight lines for the limbs. Its shoulders were exceedingly broad. Its voice was shrill and choked, reflecting pain, which at times I felt was so severe that it had caused its tiny almond eyes to bulge and its head to shrink. The whites of the eyes towered heads above me, and it trembled as it spoke.

"Before I go I would like to apologize for the fire—I was just getting around to reading the papers."

"Before you go? Fifty men down there are looking for you."

"I also want to thank you for the food. My cats loved it. And please thank your friend for the pies."

"You saw Elsa?"

"Yes, and I like her very much."

"Why didn't you come in?"

"I was afraid of the dagger."

"It's not a real dagger, I'm sorry…"

"If you can—you and your friends—please go to the ASPCA and reclaim my cats. Here are some photos and a list of names."

"Sure, sure. Listen, thanks for the books. Did you read all four thousand?"

"Bits and parts."

"Tell me a little about yourself."

"I come from Ohio but I'm working on changing it to Malibu. I have two younger brothers who I've moved up to older brothers."

"I see. Before you're arrested, I'd like to tell you something. If you're ever in a situation where you want to communicate love with a simple gesture, try to remember Mrs. Brandeis and her husband. Elsa has a friend named Flora who was once a companion lady to a Mrs. Mayer and then to Mrs. Brandeis. When Mrs. Brandeis and her husband started going out and then during their forty-year marriage and finally on his deathbed, they held hands and from time to time squeezed three times, which for them meant 'I-Love-You.'"

"I'll remember, Fourteen—bye now…" and then it released my arm, placed its feet together, arms at its sides, tucked in its tiny chin, and with a look of peace and with ostensibly nothing more than the will to fly, my neighbor lifted off the tar—slowly at first, at a forty-five-degree angle, but then about fifty feet above the roofs it accelerated, gaining altitude, shooting forth like an arrow in the direction of the Twin Towers. Momentarily I lost my balance and fell against the chimney. My neighbor in flight was blacker, denser than the lower levels of the night sky and so if I looked slightly to the side I was able to follow it quite a ways, until it became a speck, was consumed by the sky high above the river.

ACKNOWLEDGMENTS

For their much-needed help, support and patience I would like to thank my friends Irma, Rodney, Bart, Walter, and Larry; the television stations WNET and WCBS, for their programs on Tony Bennett, Mario Lanza and Christopher Columbus; and the following authors, translators and books: *History of Italian Literature*, Francesco De Sanctis, translated by Joan Redfern (Basic Books); *Sinatra*, Arnold Shaw (Holt, Rinehart and Winston); *Where have you gone, Joe DiMaggio?*, Maury Allen (Signet, NAL); *On Board the Emma*, Alexandre Dumas, translated by R. S. Garnett (D. Appleton and Co.); *Garibaldi*, Jasper Ridley (The Viking Press); *Garibaldi's Defense of the Roman Republic*, G. M. Trevelyan (Longmans, Green and Co.); *Garibaldi*, Peter de Polnay (Thomas Nelson & Sons); *The Roman Years of Margaret Fuller*, Joseph Jay Deiss (Thomas Y. Crowell Co.); *American Opinion on the Unification of Italy*, Howard R. Marraro (AMS Press); *The Selected Works of Cesare Pavese*, translated by R. W. Flint (Farrar, Straus, Giroux); *Hard Labor*, Cesare Pavese, translated by William Arrowsmith (Grossman Publishers, Div. of Viking Press); *An Absurd Vice*, Davide Lajolo (New Directions); *Valentino*, Irving Shulman (Trident Press); *Rudolph Valentino: The Man Behind the Myth*, Robert Oberfirst (The Citadel Press); *Valentino*, Brad Steiger and Chaw Mank (Macfadden-Bartell); *Rudolph Valentino*, Alexander Walker (Stein and Day); *The Intimate Life of Rudolph Valentino*, Jack Scagnetti (Jonathan David Publishers); *Leonardo da Vinci*, Bruno Santi (Becocci Editore); *Columbus: His Enterprise*, Hans Koning (Monthly Review Press); *Christopher Columbus, Mariner*, Samuel Eliot Morison (NAL); the Seamen's Church Institute; *Enrico Caruso*, Dorothy Caruso (Simon & Schuster); *Caruso*, Howard Greenfeld (Da Capo Press); *Masters of Italian Opera* (W. W. Norton & Co.); *La Bohème*, English-version libretto translated by Ruth and Thomas Martin (G. Schirmer, Inc.); "Mario Cuomo," Ken Auletta (*The New Yorker*); *Diaries of Mario Cuomo*, Mario M. Cuomo (Random House); *Iacocca: An Autobiography*, Lee Iacocca with William Novak (Bantam Books); *The Sicilian*, Mario Puzo (Linden Press/Simon & Schuster); *Caruso's Method of Voice Production*, P. Mario Marafioti (Dover Publications); *Johnny Torrio*, Jack McPhaul (Arlington House).